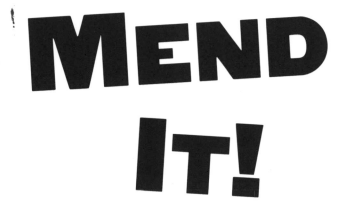

MEND IT!

400 EASY REPAIRS

for everyday items,
from kitchenware & jewellery
to furniture & textiles

SIÂN BERRY

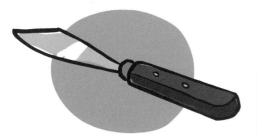

Dedicated to Walter Berry, who wasted nothing and could mend anything.

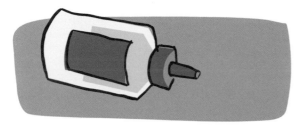

First published in Great Britain in 2009 by
Kyle Cathie Limited
122 Arlington Road
London, NW1 7HP
www.kylecathie.com

ISBN: 978 1 85626 881 3

A CIP catalogue record for this title is available from the British Library

10 9 8 7 6 5 4 3 2 1

NOTE TO READERS:
The author and publisher have taken great care to ensure the information in this book is accurate. However, the advice provided will not be suitable for every situation, and your own circumstances, materials, tools and repairs will vary. Your own judgment, an assessment of the work required, and an assessment of your skills are all vital. In different countries and territories, regulations governing work that can be carried out by non-qualified persons will also vary. If in any doubt, professional help and advice should always be sought. Neither the author nor the publisher of this work can assume any responsibility for loss, damage or injury incurred as a result of relying on the accuracy of the information given.

Design & Illustrations: Aaron Blecha
Photography: Sarah Cuttle, Jan Baldwin & Dominic Harris
Editor: Judith Hannam
Copy editor: Barbara Bonser
Production: Gemma John

Colour reproduction by Sang Choy in Singapore
Printed and bound in China by 1010 Printing International Ltd.

CONTENTS

CONTENTS CONTINUED ON NEXT PAGE

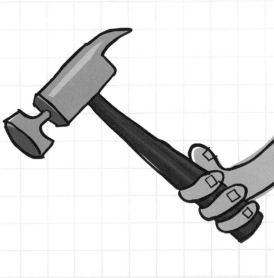

CONTENTS

INTRODUCTION

This book is a guide for anyone who wants to be able to solve simple household problems without paying for expensive help, or throwing much-loved items away. It's not about big DIY 'home improvement' projects, but about those simpler problems that are not time-consuming to fix, but are often ignored just because we don't have the confidence to get out our tools and mend things ourselves.

Evidence from around the world shows that people today are getting more and more clueless when it comes to practical work.

ONE QUARTER OF UNDER-40S DON'T EVEN KNOW HOW TO CHANGE A FUSE.

Fixing things to walls is enough to daunt one in five people of all ages. And we ladies, I'm afraid, are even worse, calling on our fathers to help when things go wrong.

NINE OUT OF TEN YOUNG WOMEN ADMIT THEY DON'T KNOW HOW TO COPE WITH SIMPLE HOUSEHOLD REPAIRS.

All over the world, children no longer learn manual skills at school. Woodwork classes have been replaced by 'design and technology', and 'Shop' classrooms in the USA are being ripped out in favour of computer labs. All very useful for a job in an office, but not so helpful when things go wrong around the home.

Portable home appliances are suffering, too. Toasters, irons and hairdryers are no longer mended but thrown away as soon as they go wrong. In the UK alone people throw away 200 million electrical items every year.

THE AVERAGE PERSON LIVING IN EUROPE TODAY WILL GENERATE MORE THAN THREE TONNES OF ELECTRONIC WASTE DURING THEIR LIFETIME.

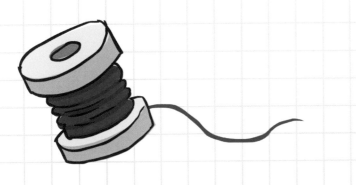

IN THE USA, THE VOLUME OF ELECTRONIC WASTE IS GROWING AT THREE TIMES THE RATE OF OTHER KINDS OF GARBAGE.

The tragedy is that most of these household items being sent to landfill dumps could have been used for much longer - if we had the ability to fix the simple problems that cause them to break down.

The benefits of mending things don't stop at saving cash and space in landfill sites. Putting in a few minutes to fix a sticking door handle or a wobbly table can save a lot of frustration, and taking time out to work with our hands can also be excellent way of relaxing our minds. So the ability to fix things can lead to a calmer life, as well as a richer one!

But if our mending skills are lacking, at least our attitudes are on the mend. Concern about waste is growing, and the need to save resources and money is getting more urgent all the time.

Recent surveys show that the number of people taking classes in traditional skills is rising, both as a result of wanting to save money and wanting to do more with their families at home. This is particularly true in Australia, where sewing, craft and DIY are all popular.

FOUR-FIFTHS OF AMERICANS NOW SAY THEY ARE PLANNING TO SPEND MORE TIME ON HOME PROJECTS.

These are all positive signs that we are keen to think again about how we look after our stuff. It's time to say 'Let's mend it!' instead of 'Let's throw it out!'

This book aims to help you gain the confidence to take on some of the most common household mending tasks. I won't try bamboozle you with big, complex jobs, but hope I can inspire you with just the right amount of simple, practical information to get things done, and show you some brilliant creative ideas that you'll be itching to try for yourself.

BEFORE YOU START

One of my aims with this book is to help give you the confidence to get stuck into fixing a range of different items around the home.

However, you won't get far without a few essential pieces of kit in your toolbox and, while I have no desire to put you off getting on with mending things, it's important that you are aware of a few simple safety precautions, too.

So, before you start, take a few minutes to read these short introductory chapters. They will help you choose the most versatile set of basic tools for your home, and help keep you safe and in one piece when you put them to work.

SAFETY NOTES & ADVICE

Most accidents happen at home – usually when doing something completely ordinary, such as getting out of bed or eating dinner. However, carrying out repairs and DIY work can bring extra hazards, especially if you are trying something for the first time.

Keeping safety in mind at all times – both for yourself and other people – is therefore very important. Please read this section carefully, as it covers a range of precautions to take when carrying out repairs.

SAFETY NOTE

Throughout the book, additional safety notes are provided to help you stay safe when carrying out specific jobs. Make sure you read (and heed) these, too.

READING WHAT IT SAYS ON THE TIN

All kinds of equipment and materials can be hazardous if used carelessly or incorrectly.

The tasks described in the chapters that follow give advice on using supplies and equipment, but this is no substitute for checking the specific instructions that come with the items you use to carry out repairs and refurbishments.

Not only will you be safer, but the information provided by manufacturers may also give extra hints and tips for getting a good result. So, always read and keep tins, packaging and advice leaflets that come with your tools and materials.

TAKING CARE

The basic safety advice for any repair is the same: think carefully and plan ahead.

Working carefully and not hastily will help keep you safe from potential dangers, and will save time in the end. Remember that taking precautions is always less time-consuming than clearing up after an accident has happened.

Get together all the materials and equipment you need before you start work, and take the time to think through your plans. If in doubt, sketch the work or make a list to ensure you have thought of everything you might use in the course of a repair. If you are unsure about any task, stop and look for more information or ask for advice.

A helper is often useful as they can provide a second opinion when you get stuck, and they can also help with heavy lifting and tricky jobs for which one pair of hands is not enough.

Take care of other people in the house, by letting them know when and where you will be working, and by putting up notices and warnings about hazards.

Children need to be warned clearly not to enter work areas. It may be possible to keep small children out of the way using a toddler gate, but ideally you should arrange additional childcare when doing major repairs – you don't want to be holding a hot soldering iron when a fight erupts!

While you work, place tools in a secure place, and never leave anything with a sharp edge lying on the floor, or on a surface where it can easily fall or be knocked off.

HEALTH AND SAFETY FOR SPECIFIC HAZARDS

WORKING IN HARD-TO-REACH AREAS

- Working above head level is very tiring, and you should make sure you have a strong, secure platform to work on whenever you need to repair fittings that are high up.

- For quick jobs, use a good stepladder, and ask a helper to keep an eye on you, and to pass up tools and materials.

- If you will be working on a high wall or ceiling for a long period, create a firm working platform by placing a length of scaffolding board between two sturdy step ladders, or rest one end on a flight of stairs.

- Always make sure ladders and platforms can't slip or get knocked over by people coming into a work area unexpectedly. Put up notices warning of the risk, or temporarily lock adjacent doors if necessary.

- Never lean excessively when working on a ladder. Move the ladder regularly instead, and only work within easy reaching distance.

- Working on outside walls or roofs can be very dangerous. Get professionals in for even the smallest jobs higher than 3 metres off the ground.

- In confined spaces, make sure you have enough light to work safely. A portable, battery-powered clip-on lamp can be a good investment.

- In small spaces in cellars and lofts, be careful of edges and corners that you might hit your head on. Wear an inexpensive hard hat for jobs that involve long periods working in these spaces. For a quick one-off job, reduce the risk by moving around very slowly and carefully, and by keeping one hand – palm upwards – on top of your head.

SAFETY NOTES & ADVICE

LIFTING AND CARRYING

• Incorrect lifting and carrying techniques can injure muscles, tendons and ligaments, and can also lead to serious long-term back or joint problems.

• Use the strongest parts of your body – your legs and hips – to take the weight of heavy lifting and carrying, and avoid putting strain on your arms, shoulders or spine.

• When lifting, keep your back as straight as possible, and use your leg muscles to provide the power.

• When picking things off the floor, always bend your knees not your back.

• Push heavy items that need to be moved. It's safer than pulling and enables you to use the weight of your body to provide extra force. Don't be afraid to ask for help if the item is too heavy for you.

• For a tall item, apply pressure below the centre of gravity of the item, so it doesn't tip.

• For very long or large items, get a helper to assist you.

PROTECTING YOURSELF

• Some repairs involve dealing with dust, toxic chemicals or sharp edges. Always check the advice given on packets and information sheets, and use any safety equipment these recommend.

• Wear gloves whenever possible when using sharp tools and strong chemicals. Rubber gloves will protect against liquids, and DIY or gardening gloves will give some protection from abrasions and cuts.

• Face protection to prevent inhalation is vital when your work produces dust. Open windows and doors, too, so that the air will clear quickly. Be particularly careful when sanding or removing old layers of paint, which may contain lead.

• Use spray paint outdoors whenever possible. The fumes aren't just toxic, they also carry tiny particles of paint, which will settle on your furniture and floors.

• Any process that produces lots of toxic fumes should be left to professionals, who will use proper, filtering face masks and safety equipment.

• Protect your eyes by wearing safety goggles when doing anything that might throw off particles or shards of material at high speed, including sawing, cutting glass, dealing with broken glass, and drilling into walls, wood or metal.

• Don't forget about the rest of your clothing. Never carry out DIY in a vest or singlet and shorts. Wear tough trousers, such as jeans, and tops with long sleeves that will protect your arms. Good strong shoes are also important to protect your feet from dropped tools and materials.

POISONS AND CHEMICALS

• Put lids on chemicals and paints when they are not in use – even if you are only leaving them for a few minutes. Store hazardous materials securely, and keep them out of the reach of children at all times.

• Keep everything in its original packaging whenever possible. If you need to decant a small amount of liquid into another container, label it properly with the correct name and copy any warning messages (such as 'toxic' or 'flammable') on to your label, too.

• Make sure you use non-toxic – ideally water-based – paints and finishes for all children's furniture and toys.

• Clean up any spills promptly. This also applies to non-toxic liquids, which can still present a slipping hazard.

• Don't dispose of paints, oils or solvents into drains or sinks. Contact your local waste officials to ask how to deal with these chemicals. They may collect them from your door, or ask you to take them to a recycling centre for disposal.

POWER TOOLS AND MACHINES

• Use a 'residual current detector' or 'circuit breaker' with power tools to protect you from faults, and to cut the power if you accidentally damage the power cable with your tool. Whenever possible, use a smaller battery operated device (see page 16).

• Tie back long hair, remove ties and avoid trailing or loose clothing when using power tools. All these items can get caught up in the mechanism and cause injuries.

WATER

• Always turn off the water supply to any pipe, tap or appliance before starting work on it.

• Mixing water and electricity can be fatal, so turn off the power to water-based appliances as well, and never use electric tools in wet or damp conditions. Empty or cover up any sinks, toilets or baths before using power tools nearby.

• Always check for hidden pipes when drilling or hammering into walls and floors (see page 16).

ELECTRICITY

• There are restrictions covering what electrical work can be carried out during DIY repairs, and these vary between countries and local areas. If in any doubt, consult your local government office or website to see if you can do a repair, or call in a qualified electrician to give advice.

• Always turn off the power supply to any circuit or appliance before starting electrical work. Then, double-check any wiring with a voltage testing screwdriver (see page 44). Check for cables before drilling or hammering into walls and floors (see page 16).

• If the worst happens, never touch anyone who is suffering an electric shock. Turn off the power at the fusebox instead, or push them free of the circuit using an electrically insulating item, such as a length of wood.

GAS

• Gas can be extremely dangerous if things go wrong. It is not just fires and explosions – a far more common danger is carbon monoxide, the 'silent killer' produced by inefficient burning in a faulty appliance such as a boiler. Carbon monoxide detectors are readily available in hardware shops.

• Apart from general cleaning of exterior fittings, any work on gas-fuelled appliances in the home must be carried out by a qualified, registered professional.

• Never try to fix broken gas appliances, and always call in a repair person as soon as you suspect anything might be wrong.

• If you smell gas, switch off your gas supply immediately, open doors and windows and call the emergency services.

FIRE SAFETY

• All naked flames and heating elements (such as soldering irons) should be used with care and not left unattended. Take great care to leave hot items to cool down completely in a safe place.

• Don't ever smoke while doing repairs, and be careful to clear dust and fumes thoroughly before lighting flames in areas where you have been working.

• Always use suitable non-flammable materials for repairs, and use fireproofing spray to protect card, paper and fabrics you use in furniture and fittings (see page 245).

• Follow the instructions and warnings that come with flammable liquids and sprays, such as paints, oils, lubricants, aerosols and solvents.

• General fire safety in the home means checking your smoke alarms regularly and putting in new batteries as soon as they are needed. If your alarms are wired into the mains, they should also have a battery back-up supply, so take the opportunity to test this whenever work means turning off the power to their circuits.

• It is also a good idea to invest in home fire extinguishers. Keep one on every floor of the house, making sure everyone knows where to find them. In the kitchen, keep a fire blanket instead, since cooking oil fires should not be treated with a water-based extinguisher.

A BASIC TOOLKIT

If you are a DIY beginner, and if you want to mend things in order to save money, you won't want to spend a lot of cash stocking up on a full tool shed, complete with work-benches, power tools for every job and a lot of equipment.

However, the right tool can make the difference between a frustrating, time-consuming bodge and a neat, quick repair. So, it helps to equip your home with a small number of good quality hand tools, some measuring equipment, glues and fixings and one or two versatile power tools. These won't cost a fortune and will ensure you can make timely repairs and save a lot more money in the long term.

Here's a short list of handy tools, which should see you through most home repairs without making the problem worse or giving yourself blisters in the process. Some of these are so useful you will need them for almost every repair in this book.

For particular jobs, such as glazing, plumbing, tiling, sewing and upholstery, special tools and materials will be needed and these are best bought when a job comes up. These extra items are described alongside specific repair jobs in each chapter.

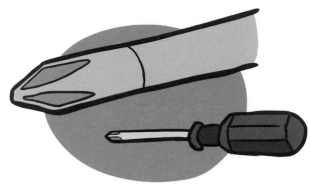

CROSSHEAD SCREWDRIVERS

A smaller screwdriver with an insulated handle is needed for electrical work (see page 44).

Choose screwdrivers with wide comfortable handles and magnetic tips and replace them if the tips get worn down.

SPANNERS AND WRENCHES
One adjustable spanner (or 'monkey wrench') can be used for a wide range of square and hexagonal nuts – although you may need an additional large wrench for plumbing work.

For really tough jobs, you can hold things more firmly with a set of 'mole grips' (also known as vice grips), which clamp around a fitting and hold in place. These can also be used as a vice to grip items being glued, or to hold materials steady when drilling or sawing.

HAND TOOLS

SCREWDRIVERS
You will need to have both flat and crosshead screwdrivers for repair work.

One medium-sized crosshead screwdriver will cover most jobs, but it's important that a flat screwdriver fits snugly into the slot on a screw, so you should get a set of these in a range of sizes.

ADJUSTABLE WRENCH

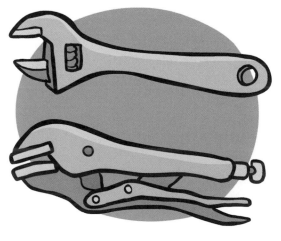

MOLE GRIPS

COMBINATION PLIERS

A blunt scraper (or 'stripping knife') does not have a cutting edge and can be used to remove wallpaper and paint layers from more delicate surfaces, such as wood or plaster. These are also handy for spreading filler over cracks and other jobs where you need to smooth something down.

PLIERS
Pliers give you extra grip and better accuracy when handling small or thin items. They are also useful for unscrewing wing-nuts that have become stiff and for unscrewing stuck lids. Get a set of 'combination' or 'engineer's' pliers, which have both flat and rounded gripping areas built in, and a cutting edge for wire.

SAWS
Saws can be bought as you need them, and three types will cover most jobs around the home.

A hacksaw can be fitted with different blades and can even cut metal – useful if you need to cut through a bolt or screw.

HAMMER
Choose a good, all-purpose hammer with a metal claw head, which is useful for pulling out nails. A medium weight hammer with a shock-absorbing handle will cover most jobs.

A tenon saw usually has fine teeth and a rectangular blade with a stiffened top edge, so it can cut neatly through wood, plastic and veneer without damaging the surface.

Neither of these saws will cut large sheets, as their solid upper edges will get in the way. For this, either invest in a power jigsaw or use a 'panel saw', which has a long, flat blade, for hand cutting.

CLAW HAMMER

HACKSAW

SCRAPERS AND CHISELS
A chisel is a very useful tool for cutting holes and recesses in wood and MDF (see page 88), for levering things like window frames and skirting apart, and for removing tiles. Used with a hammer, a chisel's sharp edge can make very accurate cuts and, used by hand, it can also scrape away paint and putty from glass.

KNIVES
An all-purpose trimming knife with replaceable blades (also called a 'craft knife' or 'Stanley knife') is a useful piece of kit for all kinds of DIY. It can neatly trim wallpaper, cut sheets of plastic, score wood, and remove packaging. Change the blade when it gets blunt as a dull knife can slip, marking surfaces and causing danger to your fingers.

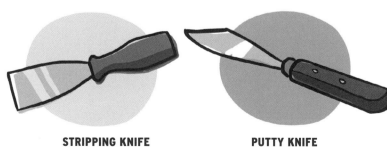

STRIPPING KNIFE   **PUTTY KNIFE**

CRAFT KNIFE

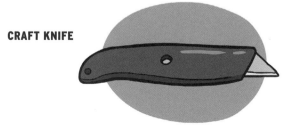

A BASIC TOOLKIT

MEASURING AND CHECKING

If in doubt, always measure up and sketch a repair rather than guessing – remember the maxim 'measure twice, cut once' to avoid costly mistakes.

STEEL RULER
This tool can be used for measuring short lengths, and is also useful as a straight edge for marking up and cutting.

TAPE MEASURE
A steel retractable tape measure helps make your repairs accurate.

TRY-SQUARE
Accurate lengths are important, but so are square corners. Get a medium-sized t-square (or 'try-square') to check inside and outside angles, and use it as a straight edge to ensure marking lines are perpendicular.

TRY-SQUARE

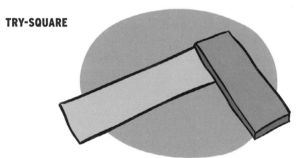

SPIRIT LEVEL
Use a spirit level frequently when doing repair jobs to make sure vertical and flat surfaces are properly level. Check table tops and shelves across the width as well as the length so that things placed on them won't roll off on to the floor.

See page 42 for how to use a spirit level to put up a perfectly level shelf.

SPIRIT LEVEL

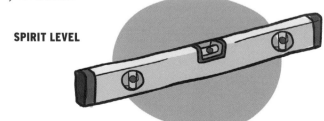

POWER TOOLS

DRILL
A portable drill is a valuable investment that will help with many of the repair jobs in this book. Used as a power screwdriver, it can also save plenty of wear and tear on your wrists. Choose one with variable speed and a reverse gear, and get a range of wood and masonry drill bits to use for different materials.

For extra safety, buy a cordless model with rechargeable batteries, which will eliminate risks from trailing wires. Drill bits come in different shapes and designs, suitable for drilling into different materials.

See the Common Home Repairs chapter on page 40 for more on using a drill and safety when drilling into walls. See the Furniture Repairs and Refurbishments chapter on page 82 for tips on drilling holes into wood.

CORDLESS DRILL

PALM SANDER

SANDER

Sanding is great exercise, but can be very laborious and time-consuming, making it tempting to give up before surfaces are properly smoothed. Avoid skimping by getting a power sander if you need to sand a floor, door or other large area.

An orbital sander has a flat plate which moves rapidly in small circles and can be used for both rough and fine sanding. Special 'palm' versions are available for smaller jobs, and larger machines can be hired for wide areas of flooring. Choose a sander with a built-in dust extractor to minimise health risks and irritation.

JIGSAW

If you develop a taste for woodwork, a jigsaw can vastly increase the creative possibilities. It's the most versatile power saw and, unlike a hand saw, makes curves, angles and complex shapes easy to cut out.

Jigsaw blades cut upwards, so mark your materials on the reverse side and work with the good surface facing downwards.

SOLDERING IRON

For electrical work, a soldering iron is a valuable, good-value investment. See page 54 for more about choosing a soldering iron and using it safely.

Solder can also be used to repair other light-weight metal objects, such as jewellery and lampshades. See the Personal and Household Accessories chapter, pages 238-44.

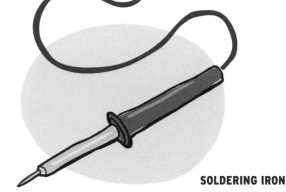

SOLDERING IRON

HIRING TOOLS

If you have a big task that you won't need to repeat, it can work out much cheaper to hire a suitable power tool than to buy one.

For a small amount of money, you'll get a professional quality machine that will do the job better than a budget model from a hardware shop. Tool hire companies mainly lend to tradespeople and will usually offer discount rates at weekends.

Hire shops also provide safety equipment and will give you guidance notes and health and safety information along with the machine.

JIGSAW

A BASIC TOOLKIT

STICKING AND FIXING

GAFFER TAPE

This wonderful product (also called 'household tape' and 'duct tape') can be used for a wide range of temporary repairs. It is a strong cloth tape with a plastic backing and very sticky adhesive, which will hold things together securely for long periods. Because of this stickiness, it will rip off paint finishes and leave a residue behind, but is very useful in emergencies.

GAFFER TAPE CAN FIX ALMOST ANYTHING

MASKING TAPE

This paper tape masks edges when painting or sealing. It peels away without leaving marks or glue behind, providing it is not left in place for long periods. Masking tape is also useful for holding delicate items together while glue dries and, as it can be written on, is excellent for labelling parts, wires and small components while making repairs. It can also be stuck on drill bits as a depth guide (see page 41).

ELECTRICAL TAPE

This plastic, coloured, flexible tape is also known as 'insulating tape' and is very useful for tidying up electrical work. Use it to hold wires and cables together, to stick trailing wires to surfaces inside appliances or to colour-code wires and components.

It can't be used to hold bare wires together or make electrical connections. Always use proper fixings and components for these jobs.

CABLE TIES

These single-use plastic ties are great for holding together bunches of cables, holding wires to pipes and many temporary fixes. Push the notched tape through the eye at the other end of the tape and it will lock in place to form a strong link. To remove a cable tie, simply cut through it with a craft knife or scissors.

WIRE

Having a supply of wire of different thicknesses can help with lots of emergency repairs, holding parts together on items from handbags to deckchairs, and – at smaller grades – for mending spectacles, jewellery and lampshades.

WIRE IS GREAT FOR FIDDLY REPAIRS

NUTS AND BOLTS

Nuts and bolts vary a lot in size and also in the way their screw threads are constructed. It is worth keeping any spares you come across in your tool box but, even so, finding a match for a missing nut can be difficult. You will usually need to take another nut from the same appliance to a hardware shop to find the right replacement.

NAILS

As well as being handy for hanging pictures, a nail in the right place can solve a range of problems, from a loose floorboard to a broken picture frame. They are very cheap so keep a supply of different sizes and thicknesses on hand. For specific jobs, such as glazing or upholstery, you may need to buy specialist types of nails (see pages 35 and 101).

SINGLE SLOT

CROSS-HEAD

SECURE CROSS-HEAD

SCREWS

Screws come in standard widths ('gauges') and various lengths, and you have a choice of single slot, simple cross-head ('Phillips') or secure cross-head ('Prodrive','Supadrive' or 'Pozidrive') head patterns.

An older 'Phillips' screwdriver may not grip modern secure cross-head screws, so invest in a new 'Pozi' or 'Pro' screwdriver to save on wrecked screw-heads and sore wrists. These drivers also work reasonably well on Phillips screws.

All types of crosshead screws give a better grip than single slots so, if you have the choice, use these for most jobs around the home.

Different screw tips and threads are designed to work better in different materials, and different metals can be used for screws in specific applications (e.g. rust-resistant brass screws for outdoor furniture). These properties are listed in the product descriptions for packs of screws in the shops, so look for 'wood screws' for carpentry and 'masonry screws' for plaster. If in doubt, staff in hardware shops can help recommend the right screw for the job you have in mind.

GLUES

Specific glues are available for many different repairs. See page 137 for more on the common types of adhesive you may need for jobs in this book.

EPOXY RESIN

This is probably the one glue that should be in every home toolbox. This two-part multi-purpose waterproof resin can fix almost any material, including plastic and metal.

STAPLE GUN

STAPLE GUN

Staple guns are brilliant for upholstery, where they make short work of fixing material on to wood in hidden places. They can also be handy in other situations where thin sheets need to be fixed in place, saving time when putting backing on chests of drawers for example.

Staples are sold in lengths up to 15mm, with special curved staples also available for fixing thin cables (such as telephone wires) to walls or skirting boards.

BRACKETS

Angled steel brackets can be used to hold broken wooden furniture together, either temporarily or as a permanent repair. So, it helps to have a few of these brackets in the toolbox for emergencies. See pages 76-7 for more options for furniture hardware and fixings.

MULTI-PURPOSE STEEL BRACKET

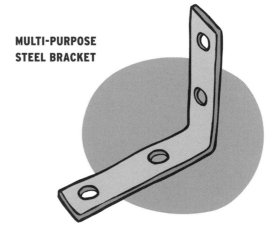

TWO-PART EPOXY RESIN

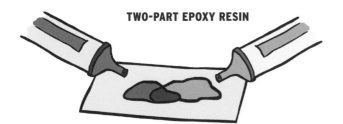

A BASIC TOOLKIT

PAINTS AND FINISHES

In general, you will want to choose the right paint or varnish for each repair job you need to complete. These don't keep forever and, once opened, will eventually become lumpy or dry out altogether. However, do keep any leftover paint from recent jobs, for minor touch-ups. Make sure you replace any lids firmly before storing them away in a cool, dry place out of reach of children.

BRUSHES

Very cheap brushes are a false economy as they won't give a good finish and will shed their bristles into your paintwork. Invest in good 2.5cm and 5cm brushes with nylon bristles, which will be suitable for most painting and varnishing jobs. Always clean brushes carefully immediately after use to keep them in good condition.

STEEL WOOL

Steel wool can also be used for smoothing paint finishes between coats and for fine smoothing of wood. Coarser grades are also good for cleaning rust and old paint from metalwork, and it is also handy for cleaning glass.

MAGIC ERASER

This special foam block is another good way to remove small stains and surface marks from solid surfaces, and is a useful addition to the cupboard. See page 62.

USE A SANDING BLOCK FOR NEAT EDGES AND CORNERS

SANDING BLOCK

For sanding by hand, a sanding block helps you avoid creating curved corners on sheets and blocks of wood, and makes the job much less tiring on your hands as well. Wrap a quarter sheet of paper around the block for each stint, and replace the paper when needed.

SANDING AND FINISHING PAPER

Glass paper is very cheap and widely available in a range of grades. It can be dusted off when it clogs but cannot be washed or used in wet conditions.

Finer silicon carbide paper can be used for smooth finishes on wood and for sanding paint and varnish between coats. It can be washed clean when it clogs up with dust and is also known as 'wet and dry' paper.

CORRECTION FLUID

This is a massive cheat, and not a permanent repair, but a bottle of brush-on correction fluid can be a very useful tool for touching up tiny but obvious defects on anything white.

Kitchen appliances, skirting boards, door frames, ceilings and walls will all suffer small marks and chips from time to time. A dab of correction fluid with its formula designed to cover ink in one coat, is a very quick and easy way to cover them up.

If the colour is too bright, rub over the area with a clean rag to dull the brightness after it dries.

SUNDRIES

LUBRICANTS
See page 26 for information on choosing lubricants for easing locks, hinges, windows and many other moving parts in the home.

WD40
When doing repairs, some of parts you need to move, such as nuts or taps, may have been in the same position for years and be very hard to shift. In these cases, a spray can of low-viscosity penetrating oil (the most common brand name is 'WD40') may seem like a miracle. Spray it on and wait for a few minutes while it works through rust and loosens the joint.

SOLVENTS
You should keep a small selection of common solvents in stock for use in cleaning and stain removal – see page 63.

White spirit is also useful to keep in the cupboard, as it is used to clean gloss paint and solvent-based varnish from brushes. Never start a painting job without checking you have enough white spirit in the cupboard, or you'll end up sacrificing a whole paintbrush to one repair.

RAGS
From applying solvents to stains to polishing wood, clean, lint-free rags are needed for plenty of different tasks. Save suitable clothing when it is beyond repair and cut it into strips or squares.

PENETRATING OIL IS A GREAT SUBSTITUTE FOR BRUTE FORCE ON STUCK TAPS AND NUTS

REALLY OLD CLOTHES CAN SERVE A FINAL PURPOSE AS RAGS

A BASIC TOOLKIT

A PLACE TO WORK

Finding a safe space to do your repair work is important. However, in the average house or apartment, you won't have room to set up a permanent workshop.

Don't worry if you end up working in your hallway or on the kitchen table, as long as there is space to work safely. However, do make sure you protect your home's fixtures and fittings while you work.

Here is some basic equipment that won't take up a lot of space, but can make things easier when doing DIY in temporary work areas.

A WORKBENCH

A folding, portable workbench is an excellent piece of kit for holding things steady while sawing and drilling without risking damage to your furniture. These are remarkably cheap and designed to be sturdy. The two parts of the worktop can be opened and closed to hold pieces of wood in place, and have integrated clamps, holes and guide marks.

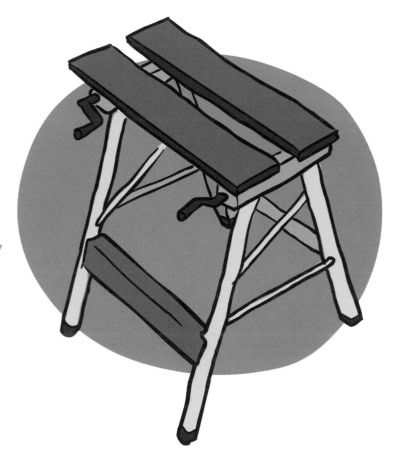

A FOLDING WORKBENCH IS A WISE INVESTMENT

VICE

A vice, which can be clamped to a workbench or table, is very useful for gripping small components while you saw, file, glue or solder them. Put a strip of wood or thick card between the clamps and your table or worktop to avoid leaving marks on the surface.

A VICE MAKES MANY JOBS EASIER

CLAMPS

A set of 'mole grips' (also called vice grips, see page 14) and a couple of G-clamps can be used to hold pieces of wood, tiles and glass steady. Remember to protect finishes on your materials from dents and clamp marks.

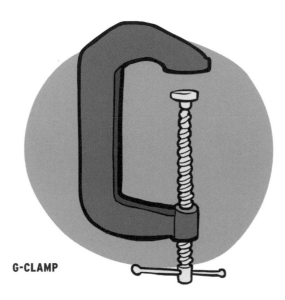

G-CLAMP

BOARDS

A large piece of scrap plywood or MDF is very handy to use as a work surface to protect floors or table tops when cutting with a craft knife or when painting or gluing small objects.

DUST SHEETS

Dust sheets are essential to protect floors and furniture when painting and varnishing large objects and walls. Invest in some cotton sheets which can be cleaned and re-used for years, rather than disposable plastic sheets.

COMMON HOME REPAIRS

The jobs in this chapter will be second nature to a DIY expert. However, since most of us don't know where to start when it comes to household maintenance, we'll begin with some basic tasks to see you through a range of common home repairs.

Later chapters will focus on specific rooms and on different kinds of furnishings and accessories around the home. But every room in a house will have a range of fixtures and fittings in common, including walls, windows, doors, light fittings and electrical equipment.

And, of course, every area of the home is vulnerable to stains and marks. These repairs will be needed in every home, so this chapter aims to give you a basic grounding in a range of tools and skills that will also come in handy for specific repairs later on.

DOOR DEFECTS

Doors get a lot of use, so it's not surprising they wear out over time and need mending.

Door handles, latches, locks and hinges all have moving parts that can break, and the small shifts in the foundations of a house can lead to doors that stick or won't close.

This chapter will show you some simple repair and maintenance jobs to solve the most common problems that crop up with doors and door fittings around the home.

SPRAY OIL IS EASY TO APPLY INSIDE LOCKS!

REALIGNING A LATCH KEEP

A misaligned 'keep' plate for an interior door can prevent it from staying shut - a very annoying problem!

The screw holes in a late will often provide enough leeway to realign the plate without removing it completely.

Loosen the screws by a couple of turns, then tap the plate gently in the required direction before tightening again. You can repeat this process several times until the door lines up perfectly.

After moving the plate to the correct position, you may find a gap between the plate and edge of its recess, which can be filled with wood filler before repainting.

For small gaps on a white frame, you can save time by touching up with correction fluid!

STIFF AND SQUEAKY HANDLES AND HINGES

A stiff or squeaking hinge, handle or lock needs nothing more than a touch of lubricant. Which one to choose depends on the location and ease of access to the moving parts.

WHICH LUBRICANT?

OIL
Light mineral oil (general household or bicycle oil) is suitable for interior doors, cupboards, locks and handles. Non-toxic silicone-based lubricant is also available for use where parts may come into contact with food.

GREASE
Thicker and more resistant to damp, freezing and evaporation than oil, grease is best used for exterior doors and gates, as well as folding metal garden furniture. The most common use for grease is for car parts, so you can get it from auto repair shops, as well as from general hardware stores.

WAX
Rub on beeswax (available in sticks) or candle wax to lubricate drawer and window runners. Beeswax or candle wax is also useful for easing a stiff bolt on a bathroom door.

POWDER
Powder made from graphite, talc or PTFE (non-stick coating material) is a better choice for locks, or where oil could stain fabrics, such as on curtain rails or hinged furniture.

SPRAY
Many oils and dry lubricants also come in spray cans, which makes them easier to apply to hard-to-reach parts, such as inside locks.

REPAIRING & REPLACING DOOR HANDLES

Handle and latch systems for interior doors are not complex and are easily mended using nothing more than a screwdriver. The basic construction is shown below.

A SQUARE SPINDLE ENGAGES WITH THE HANDLE AND THE LATCH MECHANISM

A common fault occurs when the spindle wears down and comes away from one of the handles.

Repair the mechanism by unscrewing a handle and replacing the spindle. These are easy to buy from hardware shops. Take the old one along to make sure you get the right size and type.

Replacing a broken door handle is just as simple. To find a matching handle for an older door, try searching at an architectural salvage merchant. New stockists also have 'antique' ranges that will give a close match.

If you can't find a similar replacement, take the opportunity to give your door a whole new look at very little cost by selecting and fitting a new set of handles.

To avoid scraped knuckles, only use round knob-type handles where the distance to the edge of the door is more than 80mm. Longer latch mechanisms are available to use with knob-type handles.

A DOOR THAT WOBBLES, OR DOESN'T FIT

Doors are designed to fit snugly into door frames. However, over the years, doors may shrink or expand, hinges may work loose or the frame may change its shape as foundations settle in your home.

Here are some minor repairs and adjustments to help them maintain a perfect fit.

FIRST, CHECK THE HINGES
A wobbly door, or one that catches on the frame, can often be caused by a hinge coming away from its fixings.

So, the first thing to check is whether all the hinges are tightly screwed in. Tightening these may be all you need to do to sort out the problem.

You may find that some of the hinge screws have pulled away from their holes completely, leaving nothing for the screws to grip.

In this case, you will need to refill the holes by glueing in short pieces of dowel or several matchsticks and then drilling holes for a new set of screws once the glue has set firmly.

Check that the wood in the frame is not rotten. If it is, a professional carpenter will need to be called in.

DOOR DEFECTS

An even simpler system has a roller latch that slots into an indented keep plate in the door frame. These are adjustable, so you can also use them to hold a door shut when a gap has developed between the edge of the door and the frame.

A Door that Scrapes or Jams

Doors that scrape their frames, or won't close at all, may not have loose hinges. They may be suffering instead from a small shift in the shape of their frame. If the change is small, re-shaping your door to fit better is a quick and easy job if you follow these steps.

1. IDENTIFY THE PROBLEM AREAS
Use a piece of paper with a transferrable colour to find out exactly which part of the door is causing the problem. Paint thin card or paper with a dark poster paint, or colour it in with chalk or wax crayon. Then, place the paper across the frame and shut the door repeatedly so that the colour rubs off on the problem areas.

2. GENTLY RESHAPE THE DOOR
Using the coloured areas as a guide, reshape the door with coarse sandpaper. Wrap the paper around a sanding block to ensure you remove material in a straight line. Without a block, you are likely to create a domed shape, and to round off the corners.

If more than 5mm of material needs to be removed, a plane or a coarse rasp speeds up the process. Or you could use the nutmeg side of a box shaped cheese-grater for this job - I tried it and it proved a perfect rough-sanding substitute!

Always finish with sandpaper, and take off slightly more than needed to allow for a new coat of paint. Finish off with fine grade paper and dust with a damp cloth before repainting.

If the door is scraping against the floor (a common problem after a new carpet is fitted), you should deal with this quickly before your flooring is permanently damaged.

Create a small amount of extra clearance at the foot of the door by placing sandpaper on a firm base on the floor and pulling the door back and forth across it.

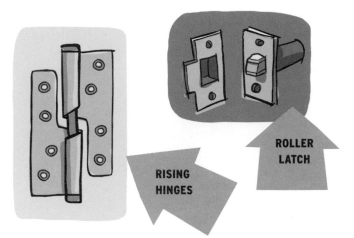

RISING HINGES

ROLLER LATCH

Alternatively, you can change the hinges to a type with a central spindle shaped like a spiral. These 'rising hinges' lift the door a few millimetres as the door opens.

REPAINTING PLAN
You may want to take this opportunity to give your whole door a new lick of paint. Wash and lightly sand the door first. Then, paint the sections of the door in the order shown, for best results.

Paint the frame last, and make sure the door stays open until the paint is completely dry.

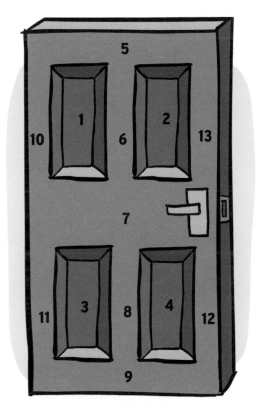

Window problems can be a real pain. Loose latches and locks can rattle in high winds, and draughty windows can waste lots of money in heating bills.

In summer, a working sash window can be used to cool down a room without using fans or air-conditioning – just open the sashes with an equal sized gap at the top and bottom and the air will circulate between the gaps, bringing in fresh air. However, this is hard to do if you have lost a weight due to a broken cord or if the runners are stiff and creaky.

This section will run through some essential window maintenance jobs you can do yourself, and show you how to mend a broken sash cord. It will also help you reduce draughts, whatever type of windows you have.

SMALL FIXES AND ESSENTIAL MAINTENANCE

Keeping your windows in good order is as important as knowing how to fix them when they go wrong.

LUBRICATE

Moving parts on windows, including hinges, pulleys and latches, need to be checked, cleaned and oiled regularly to prevent them from sticking.

Around once a year, clean metal parts with a stiff brush and spray with powder lubricant or light oil. You can also use this chance to tighten any screws or nuts that are working loose.

Sliding windows also need lubricating. Rub candle wax or beeswax along the wooden runners on your sash windows to keep them running smoothly.

MAINTAIN PAINTWORK

Timber framed windows often suffer from damp on the inside of the glass, which can run down and cause rotting or warping of the wood.

It is therefore important to keep the paintwork on a window frame in good condition. Repainting should be done every two years or so, and some retouching may also be needed in between.

To restore your window's paintwork, clean the area with detergent and water, let it dry, then lightly sand all around. Protect the glass with masking tape for this job, as it is easily scratched by sandpaper. Sand putty very gently so it doesn't wear away.

Don't place masking tape right up to the wood frame when you are repainting. Instead, overlap the paint very slightly on to the glass to protect the putty and wood from water.

Use a good, dedicated window brush or sash brush and this job isn't hard to do by hand, although you can mask a line at the right distance if you prefer. It's almost as easy just to aim for about 1mm of overlap all around and then tidy up any stray brush marks afterwards, using a cotton bud dampened with white spirit (also known as Shellite or Clear Gas).

SASH WINDOW REPAIRS

Sash windows (also known as 'double hung' windows) are a fantastic invention.

They are infinitely adjustable, with the option to have gaps of any size at the top or the bottom. The two panes are balanced with weights on either side, so they will stay securely in any position, and the mechanism can last for decades without repair.

But as sash windows get older, one of the cords holding a weight may weaken and break. When this happens, the sashes won't balance and will have to be propped open or locked shut.

REPLACING THE CORDS ON A SASH WINDOW

Replacing a broken cord is easier than you might think. Although the weights are hidden away in the frame, the window is designed to give you access to the cavity, and the weight and pulley system is extremely simple to repair.

The diagram below shows how a sash window is constructed.

You can carry out this whole job from inside the room. You will be taking the sashes out of their frames, so work with a helper if you can. However, it is possible to work alone, if you have a table or bench below the window to rest the sashes on while you detach them from the cords (or if you have three hands!).

SAFETY NOTE

Wear protective gloves for all but the most fiddly stages of this job, in case of splinters. The sashes are also heavy, so take extra care when handling them, and always make sure they are not likely to be kicked or trodden on when you put them down.

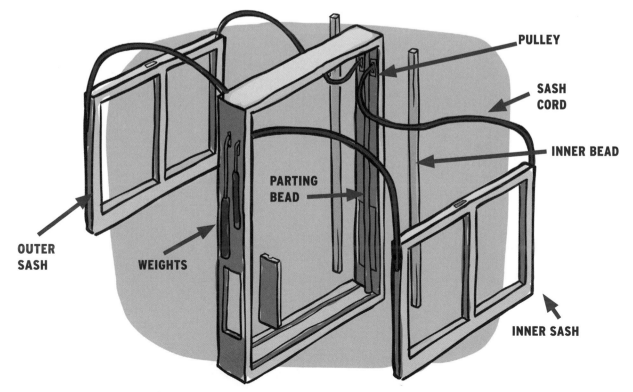

PULLEY

SASH CORD

INNER BEAD

PARTING BEAD

OUTER SASH

WEIGHTS

INNER SASH

TOOLS YOU WILL NEED

You'll need a good DIY knife, as well as a flat tool (such as a chisel or scraper) and a wooden mallet for prising away the wooden beading on the frame. You'll also need a supply of replacement sash cord, a ball of string, panel pins, sandpaper and paint for rebuilding and finishing off. A candle or block of beeswax is also useful for lubricating the runners, as is a few drops of oil for the pulleys.

1. GETTING IN

Start by prising off the inner strip of beading on each side of the frame.

First, run a knife blade along the join to loosen the layers of paint that may be holding it on. Then, starting in the middle, carefully prise it away from the frame using a chisel or scraper and a wooden mallet.

Remove any nails from the beading once it comes off. You will use new nails to replace it later.

2. REMOVE THE INNER SASH

You should now be able to lift the bottom sash and swing it into the room. If both cords are broken, you can take it right into the room. But, if either is still attached, you will need to rest the sash on a bench or table, placed under the window, while you cut the cord.

Hold on to the cord as you cut it and gently lower the weight into the bottom of the weight pocket. Now the sash can be taken into the room and placed carefully on the floor.

Mark the end position of the cord in the groove on the side of the sash, then pull out the nails that hold the cord in place and keep the pieces of cord, to help measure their replacements.

SASH WINDOW REPAIRS

3. OPEN UP THE WEIGHT POCKETS

To help you get into the inner-workings (the 'weight pockets') an opening is provided at the bottom of each side of the frame. The covers on these openings may be screwed on or just slotted in.

If you are only working on the inner sash, and there is a separate cover for each weight pocket, you can remove the pockets straight away.

However, sometimes there is just one cover for both slides and, if so, this is likely to be held in place by the central strip of wooden beading that divides the two sashes (the 'parting bead'). If this is the case, you should now remove the central beads with the chisel, in the same way as for the inner beads.

The pocket covers may be hard to see if they have had several coats of paint. Lightly sanding the runners should reveal their edges (and any screws holding them in place), and you can then use the chisel or a screwdriver to remove them and get at the weights.

4. REMOVE THE OUTER SASH

If you are replacing the cords on the outer sash, you can remove this now the parting bead has gone. Bring it into the room in the same way as for the inner sash, resting it on a bench while you cut the cords.

TIP!
Even if only one cord has broken, it is a good idea to replace all four cords at once. They are likely to be the same age and all coming to the end of their useful life. If another breaks in the near future, you will have to go through this whole process again. Therefore, you'll save work by doing all the replacements in one go.

5. BREAK FOR PAINTING

Now you will have an empty window frame and two sashes propped up inside the room.

This is a good time to pause the repair process and lightly sand the paintwork on the frame, in preparation for re-painting later.

It is also the ideal time to repaint the sashes themselves. You'll find it's much easier to work on them while they aren't attached to the windows, especially for parts that will be high up or facing outside.

6. INSTALL THE NEW CORDS

After removing the pocket covers, take out the weights and remove the old cords. Then, reassemble the old cord pieces for each window and use them to measure new lengths of replacement cord.

(This is also a good time to vacuum the dust out of the weight pocket!).

Next, take each new cord and tie a long length of string to one end and a short length of string with a heavy screw or nail attached to the other end.

Push the nails through the holes above the pulleys and let them fall to the bottom of the weight pocket. They will pull the cords over the pulleys.

Now remove the nails and attach the weights to the new cords. Use a secure 'figure of eight' knot to prevent the cord sliding through the hole (see diagram). Some weights will have a hole at the top and a slot or hole to hold the knot.

FIGURE OF EIGHT KNOT

Then, place them gently upright at the bottom of the weight pockets. You can now replace the covers on the weight pockets.

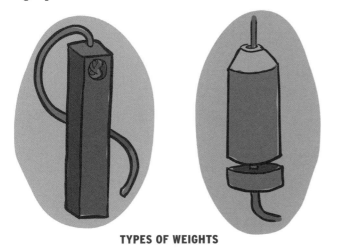

TYPES OF WEIGHTS

7. REPLACE THE SASHES

Re-install the sashes in the frame, attaching the new cords. This is one stage where having a helper to hold things while you work is probably essential.

Start with the outer sash. Rest it upright on the bench under the window and pull down the cords. Remove the guide strings, and place the ends of the cords in the slots on either side of the sash, in the same position as the old cord.

Nail each cord securely into place and then place the window in the rear track of the window frame.

The weights will help it to balance safely while you replace the parting bead to hold it in place. Hammer the beading into the groove on each side. You should not need to use any nails to keep it in place. Check that the sash moves freely in the frame.

If the runners need lubricating, wait to do this after re-painting. If you have been able to take the window apart very neatly (this is very unlikely!), you may not need to repaint, in which case you can run some candle wax along the runners now.

Repeat this process for the lower sash, attaching the cords and placing the sash in the runner, before re-attaching the two pieces of inner beading to the frame either side of the window, using panel pins.

Check the inner sash will run properly and your repair is done.

DRAUGHT-PROOFING WINDOWS

Windows with gaps and draughts can be very expensive in extra heating bills. Fitting good draught-proofing is therefore very cost-effective. In most homes, it will pay for itself in less than a year.

OUTWARD-OPENING WINDOWS

Windows that swing outwards when opened are known as 'casements' and can be very easily weather-proofed with self-adhesive strips.

These come in long rolls in a range of materials (see below) and are called 'compression seals' because they are compressed when the window is closed and make a tight seal between the two surfaces.

It is important to get weather-proofing that is not too thick, as this could make the window impossible to close. Weather-proofing is specified according to its 'maximum gap thickness' – given in mm. Rather than guess at the size of your gaps, a good tip is to measure them by slotting coins into the gaps when the window is closed.

When you find the thickest coin that will fit, measure the thickness of the coin across its edge with a ruler and get weather-proofing that will fill a gap of that size.

DIFFERENT OPTIONS FOR COMPRESSION SEALS

FOAM STRIP
This is very cheap and available in most DIY shops, but doesn't last long before becoming brittle, and can get easily damaged.

RUBBER STRIP
This is longer-lasting, more waterproof and tougher than foam, so is a good investment.

SAFETY NOTE

Good ventilation is needed in some rooms. Don't seal up windows in bathrooms and kitchens, or you will encourage mould. Gas fires and boilers need fresh air, so you may need to add an air brick if you draught-proof nearby windows - ask for professional advice about rooms containing these appliances.

TIP!

When applying self-adhesive weather-proofing, don't forget to make sure the surfaces are clean and free of grease before you start.

SPRING PROFILE STRIP
Sealant strips are available with a v-shaped profile that closes when put under compression. They are usually made of plastic or rubber and can be self adhesive, or come with a metal securing strip that is tacked on to the window frame.

SLIDING WINDOWS

Sliding windows, including timber sash windows, are harder to weather-proof. They have parts that slide over each other, which would quickly damage adhesive strips.

However, they are well worth sorting out, as they are often very draughty. The gaps around the average sash window can add up to the same area as a 10 cm circular hole – that's a lot of space letting cold air in!

At the top and bottom of sash windows, you can still use compression seals. But along the sliding edges use 'pile' strip instead. This sits inside a channel and has furry brushes that protect from draughts while allowing the sashes to slide.

PILE STRIP

Creating suitable channels in the frame of a sash window to hold the 'pile carrier' is very tricky. A good solution is simply to replace the beading with new piecea of wood that come ready-fitted with pile carrier.

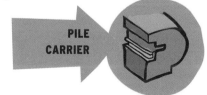

PILE CARRIER

These aren't very expensive, and can be fitted by following the steps described under steps 1 and 3 of 'Replacing the cords in a sash window' (see pages 30-3) to remove the old beads. Specialist merchants will even supply a DIY sash window draught-proofing kit, which contains all the parts you need, including the right amount of pile strip.

Working with glass can be dangerous so, if a large window pane breaks or cracks, it makes sense to get a professional glazier to fix it.

However, for smaller pieces of glass there is no reason to be afraid of replacing the glazing yourself. The work involved is not difficult and, if you don't need to cut the glass, you don't need any special tools.

Smaller panes of glass can be found in many places around the home – above interior doorways, in front doors and porches, or in bathrooms and kitchens.

These are also ideal locations to use the opportunity of a breakage to replace plain glass with something more decorative.

BUYING REPLACEMENT GLASS

Pieces of coloured or patterned glass can be bought from architectural salvage merchants, or you can specify something new from a local craftsperson or glass merchant.

Take the inner dimensions of your window frame to the shop. You want glass that is about 2mm smaller than the frame, and the glazier will cut glass to the correct size if you provide the exact details of the frame.

For a square or rectangular pane, measure the width and height, then check both diagonals. If they don't match, your pane isn't square and you should make a cardboard template instead. Use the same method for irregular and curved shapes.

SAFETY NOTE

When working with glass, safety precautions are crucial. Wear strong gloves and, if you're starting with a broken pane, wrap strips of cloth or bandage around your wrists to protect them. Protect your feet and legs from falling glass by wearing strong shoes or boots, and thick trousers, such as jeans. If you need to break off the old glass, always wear safety glasses, too.

HOW TO REPLACE A BROKEN PANE

TOOLS YOU WILL NEED
You don't need a lot of tools, although a special 'putty knife' is handy. A hammer, chisel and a pair of pliers will be needed to take out the old glass and glazing sprigs, and you should have a sanding block and brush handy for cleaning, too.

PUTTY KNIFE

You'll also need to get some putty (use the right kind for your window – there are different types for wood and metal) and some glazing sprigs (tiny nails that hold the glass in place).

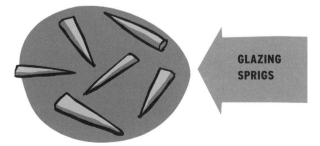

GLAZING SPRIGS

REPLACING PANES OF GLASS

1. SCRAPE AWAY THE OLD PUTTY
Use a chisel to scrape away the old putty from the outside and inside of the pane.

2. REMOVE THE OLD GLASS
The broken parts can then be pulled away – wear thick gloves for this job. Knock stubborn pieces out gently with the handle of a hammer, making sure to wear safety glasses.

3. CLEAR OUT AND PRIME THE REBATE
Remove the old glazing sprigs then use the chisel and a brush to scrape away any remaining putty and debris from the rebate. Never use your fingers for this, in case of splinters.

Lightly sand the area and paint with primer, if your window is made of timber. The primer will prevent the wood from drying out the putty, which should remain flexible in order to cushion the window and prevent it from rattling.

4. APPLY PUTTY
Knead the putty in your hands then work into a cylinder about 3mm in diameter. Push it into the rebate all around the frame.

5. FIT THE GLASS
Press the glass gently into the frame. Only press around the edges, never in the centre of the pane. The putty will then hold it in place while you fit the glazing sprigs.

6. PUT IN GLAZING SPRIGS
Knock in glazing sprigs every 8–10cm around the frame to hold the glass securely. Use the edge of your chisel, striking flush along the pane of glass.

7. APPLY A FINAL BEAD OF PUTTY
Work another 3mm bead of putty on to the inside of the pane to cover the glazing sprigs. Then scrape off excess putty on both the inside and outside of the pane using a blunt knife or the edge of the putty knife, aiming for a neat bevel shape. Gently brush with methylated spirit to smooth the putty's surface and remove marks from the glass.

8. LEAVE TO DRY BEFORE PAINTING
You should leave the putty for about two weeks before painting. This lets the putty dry out the correct amount – you want it to be strong but not so dry that it becomes brittle and no longer cushions the glass.

1

2

5

6

CAUTION !

If your leaded lights are very old, and the lead is deteriorated and weak, you can cause damage by trying to replace a pane yourself. If you are in any doubt, or if more than one or two panes need replacing, call on a professional leaded window expert for help.

CUTTING GLASS TO SIZE

For large panes, always get replacement glass cut to size by a professional. However, if you are fitting a small pane and want to use reclaimed glass, you may want to cut it yourself.

Cutting glass is relatively easy to get right, as long as you have a good quality glass-cutter. This is particularly important for the thicker panes of glass suitable for exterior windows.

A glass cutter has a small diamond cutting wheel at the base of an angled tool that has flat sides to help guide the tool against a straight edge.

TOOLS YOU WILL NEED

A glass cutting tool, some turpentine, a small paintbrush, fine sandpaper and a thick, square-edged wooden ruler or T-square.

LEADED WINDOW LIGHTS

Leaded windows have panels held in place with lead strips. These strips have an 'H'-shaped profile and are called 'calms' or 'cames'.

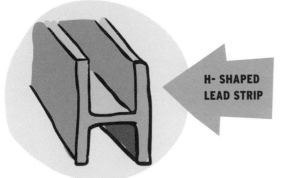

H- SHAPED LEAD STRIP

If you have a broken pane in a leaded window, you can replace it yourself by cutting the soft lead strips at the corners of the pane and raising the strips up with a chisel or knife to free the glass.

Insert a new piece of glass using putty suitable for metal windows or glue to hold it in place, and then fold the lead strip back over the pane.

REPLACING PANES OF GLASS

Always work with glass on a smooth, level surface without bumps. Any variations in the surface could cause the glass to crack when you apply pressure with the tools. You can help to cushion the glass on your work surface by placing a folded dust sheet or an old piece of carpet underneath it.

1. MEASURE AND MARK

To mark out your glass for cutting, measure the frame (in the same way as described above under 'Buying replacement glass' see page 35) and mark the correct shape on the glass with a fine permanent marker, taking about 1.5mm off the dimensions all around to allow for putty. Use as many of the existing edges of the piece of glass as you can, to reduce the number of cuts.

Before scoring, create measuring marks with the glass cutting tool at either end of your line. Place these about 2mm outside the line you drew. This is because these marks will be used to align your ruler, and you need to allow for the distance between the edge of the cutting tool and the diamond wheel.

2. LUBRICATE

Place the ruler against the marks, then use the paintbrush to run a small amount of turpentine along the surface of the glass the length of the ruler. This will help to lubricate the glass cutting tool and ensure a good score.

3. SCORE

Now score the surface with the tool, guiding it firmly along the edge of the ruler. This is the trickiest bit, so it can help to practise a few times on scrap pieces of glass, before working on the piece you are using for a project.

SCORING TIPS

- Keep up a constant pressure.
- Maintain a constant, steady speed, and do not rush.
- Do the whole score in one go, without stopping.
- Hold the tool at an angle of about 60 degrees, keeping the bottom edge of the tool parallel with the surface.

4. BREAK

Now break the glass along the score. For glass up to 3mm thick, gentle pressure from your fingers should be enough. Lift the glass very slightly off the surface and place your middle fingers under the score line at both ends. Then, use your other fingers to press gently down on either side. Your fingers will be in a similar position to when you hold a book open.

For thicker glass, place the ruler underneath, against the score line (make sure the ruler is on the 'good' side of the score, i.e. the piece you are going to use in your project). Then tap gently on the other side with the handle of the cutter.

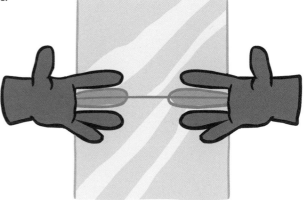

5. SMOOTH

Smooth off with fine sandpaper to remove any sharp edges.

OTHER TIPS

- If you want to cut mirror glass, score on the front, not the coated side.
- Textured glass should be cut on the smoothest side.

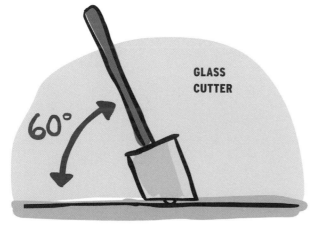

60°

GLASS CUTTER

It's easy to make a mess of filling a hole or crack in a plaster wall. Here's how to end up with a nice neat result instead.

SMALL DEFECTS

Holes up to about 12mm across can be filled using normal interior filler. Wider than this, and you should reinforce the break with special 'wallboard tape' which you can buy with its own adhesive, saving a lot of work.

For a small crack or hole, you'll need a fresh pot of filler and a filling knife.

Brush away any dust, then dampen the area slightly with a sponge so that the filler can stick to the surface properly. Then, use the knife to push filler right into the hole and spread more filler on the surface over and around the hole.

Most fillers shrink a small amount as they dry, so don't scrape the area completely flat while the filler is wet. Leave it to dry for 24 hours, then sand the area smooth using fine sandpaper and a sanding block.

LARGER HOLES

For a larger hole or crack, clean the area and fill the interior of the hole or crack as before. Wipe the surrounding surface dry then lay the sticky wallboard tape over the hole.

You can then cover the tape with another layer of filler. Again, leave the filler slightly proud of the surface to allow for shrinkage.

After 24 hours, sand smooth being careful not to catch the edges of the tape.

REPAINTING TIPS

It's very hard to retouch a paint job without the patches showing.

However, for a small repair, you can disguise the filler reasonably well by dabbing on a small amount of the original paint, using a damp sponge. A number of very thin coats applied in this way makes for a much better cover-up than one thick coat of paint.

For real invisible mending, take advantage of the need to fill cracks by repainting the whole wall – or even the whole room – at the same time.

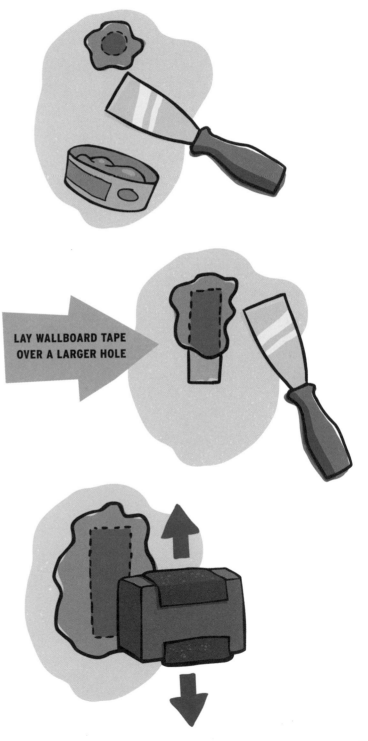

LAY WALLBOARD TAPE OVER A LARGER HOLE

FIXING THINGS TO WALLS

Many of the most common home DIY jobs involve fixing things to walls. From hanging a picture to putting up a set of shelves, being able to create secure wall-fixings is a useful skill for everyone.

HANDY TOOLS AND SAFETY ADVICE

A portable drill is essential kit for strong wall fixings. See the Before You Start chapter for tips on choosing a good, all-purpose drill that can be used for this and many other jobs.

You'll need a couple of different masonry and wood drill bits. Masonry bits have a hardened tip for breaking through brick and plaster.

Another useful purchase is a combined stud finder and metal detector. This clever device looks a few centimetres into your walls to help you find the wooden 'studs' that secure plasterboard walls. Finding the wall studs helps when putting up shelving and hanging heavy objects.

The metal detector also helps you find water pipes and electrical wires, which are important to avoid when drilling into walls.

LOW-TECH STUD DETECTION

If you don't have a stud finder, be a detective and use these clues to work out where your wall studs are.

Screws or nails that hold the skirting boards in place are usually fixed to the studs at equal intervals, so you can follow the studs up from these.

As a house ages, the nails holding the plasterboard to the studs can also pull away and cause small bumps in the wall (known as 'nail pop'). Shine a light sideways across the wall, and nail pops can be seen and marked, identifying the studs.

Use the 'audio' method: knock along the wall and listen for changes in the sound produced. The hollow gaps between the studs will produce a lower note than the wooden studs themselves.

Live electrical wires usually run vertically down from plug sockets into the floor space, or upwards from light switches, so it is best to avoid these areas when drilling. In new or rewired homes, live wires that run through a cavity are protected by a solid casing, and if you touch one of these while drilling it should be obvious.

It is also easy to tell when you have hit a metal pipe. However, it's impossible to over-emphasise how alert you should be to these issues when drilling into walls.

The rule to remember is: if you encounter any increase in resistance or change in the sound your drill makes, stop drilling and check the wall again.

FIXING LIGHT-WEIGHT OBJECTS TO WALLS

Small pictures and mirrors, hooks for keys and towels and other light-duty wall fixings can be placed on the hollow parts of the walls.

For very light-weight objects, a simple nail or panel pin, knocked in at an angle, is strong enough and the best (and quickest) solution. Another advantage is that this fixing can be removed without leaving a large hole behind if the object needs to be moved.

To hammer in a nail at an angle, start with the nail at 90 degrees to the wall and tap gently with the hammer to make a small dent. Then, shift the nail to a 45 degree angle and hammer with a few quick strokes to the right depth.

Other useful fixings include plastic picture hooks with integrated tiny nails, which are very reliable for light objects.

I would not recommend using any kind of adhesive hook on a plasterboard or plaster wall. These are cheap but not good value as I have never seen one last longer than a few months without coming off, sometimes taking a chunk of the wall with it. However, a plastic hook with a strong adhesive can be a very good solution for hanging something light on a tiled wall.

FIXING MEDIUM-WEIGHT OBJECTS

You can also hang medium-weight objects, such as heavier pictures (but not shelves) onto hollow plasterboard, as long as you use a suitable fixing.

The simplest option is an expanding plug. This has teeth which grip the side of a hole in the plasterboard when you add a screw.

For this system to hold well, it's important to combine the correct plug and screw sizes, and to drill the correct size of hole for the plug. Look on the packaging that comes with your plugs for the correct size drill bit to use.

FIXING THINGS TO WALLS

USING AN EXPANDING PLUG

1. DRILL A HOLE THE CORRECT WIDTH AND DEPTH FOR THE PLUG
To help you drill to the right depth, measure the plug against your drill bit and mark the bit with masking tape or electrical tape. You can then stop drilling when the tape reaches the wall.

Lightly mark the wall with a pencil cross in the place where you need the hole to be, then make a small dent with a nail to help anchor the drill.

A cross mark is better than a circle or dot. Smaller marks are obliterated as soon as you start to drill, whereas the points of the cross will still be visible as you work, helping you to make a more accurate hole.

2. TAP THE PLUG INTO THE HOLE
Use the tip of a hammer to push the plug into the hole. Tap gently until it lies slightly below the wall surface.

3. SCREW IN AND THE PLUG WILL EXPAND TO HOLD FIRMLY
For a more secure hold, use a fixing with a metal or plastic expanding clamp that grips the back of the panel. You push these right through a hole in the plasterboard, and they pull against the rear of the cavity as you tighten the screw.

SOLID WALL FIXINGS
When fixing things to brick or masonry walls, you should always use an expanding plug. If the material in the wall is very hard, using the 'hammer' action on your drill can make drilling the pilot holes easier.

TO HELP YOU DRILL TO THE RIGHT DEPTH, MEASURE THE PLUG AGAINST YOUR DRILL BIT AND MARK THE BIT WITH TAPE

FIXING THINGS TO WALLS

PUTTING UP A SHELF

This DIY task is a real rite of passage for the amateur handyperson. Getting it right, and putting up a secure, level shelf, brings a real sense of achievement and gives you a chance to learn some important skills in the process.

It's tempting to suggest you put up a new shelf in your home just to practise these skills and to have something to show off and say "I did that!"

Here, we'll work through the example of a simple, single shelf with brackets. These principles and steps apply just the same to putting up a 'shelving system' with long vertical brackets.

TOOLS YOU WILL NEED
For this job, you will need a drill, wood screws, a pencil, hammer and nail for marking up and a stud detector. You will also need a spirit level. This contains liquid with an air bubble to show when you have reached a true vertical or horizontal line. Get a level which works in both orientations and you can use it for a host of jobs around the house.

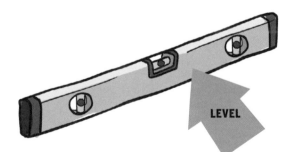

LEVEL

1. FIND THE STUDS
To put a shelf on a plasterboard internal wall, you'll need to find two studs to anchor your shelf brackets.

Use your stud detector to find them, and then lightly draw two vertical guides along the lines of the studs.

2. MARK HOLES FOR THE FIRST BRACKET
Take one of the shelf brackets and hold it up to one of the guide lines at the correct height. Use the spirit level to set it vertical and then mark through the holes with a pencil (or coat hanger wire if the bracket is too thick) to show where you need to make the holes.

Add a cross and nail dent to each mark, for more accurate drilling.

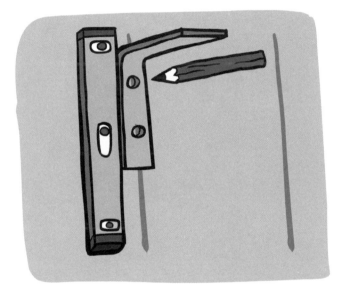

3. DRILL INTO THE WALL
Using a wood drill bit that is one size smaller than your screws, drill as far as the length of a screw (minus the depth of your bracket). Measure the screw and bracket against the drill bit first and mark the correct depth with tape.

Choose the right length of screw to properly anchor the shelf to the stud. This will be around 20mm more than the depth of plasterboard and bracket. Plasterboard can be anything from 9mm to 13mm, so you will probably need to choose screws upwards of 30mm in length.

4. SCREW IN BRACKET NO. 1

5. MARK HOLES FOR THE SECOND BRACKET

Take your shelf and balance it on the first bracket with your spirit level on top. Hold the shelf exactly level, then mark a short line along the underside of the shelf across the line you marked earlier for the second stud.

You'll now have intersecting lines on your wall, showing the correct spot for the top of the second bracket.

Put the shelf down and pick up the second bracket and spirit level. Place the bracket so it will support the shelf at the level of the horizontal mark, and repeat the method you used to mark the first bracket.

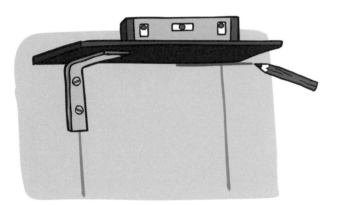

6. DRILL HOLES AND FIX THE SECOND BRACKET

Screw the second bracket securely into the stud, as before.

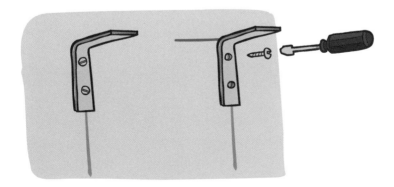

7. PUT SHELF IN PLACE, AND FIX WITH SCREWS IF NEEDED

Depending on your bracket design, the shelf may need to be fixed on to the bracket, or it may just balance on top.

8. CHECK THE LEVEL AGAIN (FOR SMUGNESS)

If you've worked carefully through the steps, your shelf should be perfectly level – good job!

NOTES ON SOLID WALLS

If you are fixing a shelf to a brick or masonry wall, you should follow the same steps as above.

However, you will need to use plastic wall plugs to make sure the screws are secure. Drill holes to the correct size and depth for the plugs, using a masonry bit instead of a wood bit.

ELECTRICAL REPAIRS

Many electrical problems around the home are simple to fix and don't require a qualified electrician on the premises. Fixtures and fittings, such as light switches, can also be replaced if you take care to get the wiring right.

However, there are limits to what is sensible for a keen DIYer to attempt. There are even legal limits on what you can change. So, while lights, plugs, sockets and switches may all be repairable at home (depending on your local regulations, which you should check), adding new sockets or making changes to the wiring within the walls of your home is strictly off limits. Call in an expert for anything that goes beyond these simple fixes.

TOOLS YOU WILL NEED

Your regular toolbox kit is adequate for most electrical repairs. As long as you have a set of insulated, rubber-handled pliers and a set of smallish screwdrivers, most jobs can be completed without any special equipment.

There are two extra tools to invest in: a voltage testing screwdriver and a soldering iron. Both are cheap and very useful for electrical work.

A voltage tester resembles a small screwdriver and contains a large resistor and a small lightbulb to help you check that no electricity is flowing through a fitting you want to repair.

You should always turn off the relevant circuit before working on electrical items. However, double checking is an essential safety measure you should carry out before taking any risks.

Touch the tip of the tester on to the wires you are working on, and press the button on the tip of the tool. Any current will be reduced to a very low level by the resistor and will pass through the light bulb before flowing through your finger to the earth (don't worry, it's a very small current and you won't feel it!) If the bulb lights up, your circuit is still live and you should check the fusebox again before starting work.

A soldering iron can be purchased for just a few pounds and is useful for other repairs too (see the Personal and Household Accessories chapter).

In electronics, solder provides both a mechanical and an electrical connection, using a low melting point metal alloy that melts and fills the gap between components.

Often a wire from the power cord will work free from its initial connection with an appliance, and this is very simple to reconnect. See the instructions at the end of this section for how to use a soldering iron for this repair.

Always buy a stand to go with your soldering iron (they are often sold without a stand). The tip of the iron gets extremely hot – hot enough to cause instant deep burns – and it should never be left anywhere it can roll around.

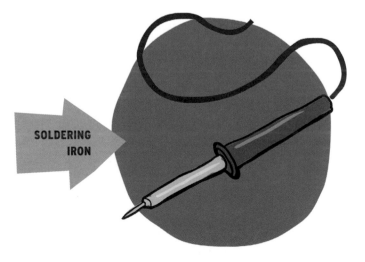

SOLDERING IRON

An appliance with a cracked plug casing or a damaged power cable, should not be used. You may be able to wire in a new plug to fix the problem. However, check your local rules and regulations to make sure this is a repair that householders are allowed to do themselves and, if not, get a professional.

WIRING A THREE-PIN PLUG

TOOLS NEEDED
Screwdrivers (cross-head and flat-head) and combination pliers.

THE DIFFERENT WIRES
Appliance cables will often have two or three colour-coded wires inside:
BLUE - NEUTRAL WIRE
BROWN - LIVE OR ACTIVE WIRE
YELLOW/GREEN - EARTH OR GROUND WIRE

Older cables may have a different combination of colours, such as:
BLACK - NEUTRAL WIRE
RED - LIVE OR ACTIVE WIRE
YELLOW/GREEN - EARTH OR GROUND WIRE

Some appliances may have cables with just two wires that are both the same colour. These can be connected to the live and neutral pins of your plug in either combination.

The plug should have a cartridge fuse in a cradle next to the live pin. Remove this to get to the wires, and replace it later. To remove the old plug, unscrew the removable screw heads or, if the posts have horizontal holes and integrated screws, unscrew these to open the holes.

Check the condition of the wires. If they are frayed or have a damaged plastic cover, it's best to cut the cable shorter so you can trim new, neat ends on the inner wires.

Cut the coloured wires so that they reach the relevant pins comfortably with no stretching and no kinks, using the snippers on a set of combination pliers.

You can then use the nose of the pliers or the cable stripping notch (if there is one) to remove the plastic covering from the end of each wire. Use the pliers again to twist the copper threads neatly before looping them around the posts at each pin, or securing them within the integral holes.

Tighten the screws firmly to secure the wires. Then ensure the main cable covering is gripped securely either with clips or a cable restraint. Replace the fuse, screw the plug cover back on and test the appliance.

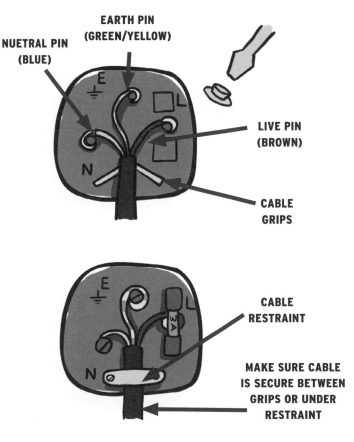

EARTH PIN (GREEN/YELLOW)
NUETRAL PIN (BLUE)
LIVE PIN (BROWN)
CABLE GRIPS

CABLE RESTRAINT
MAKE SURE CABLE IS SECURE BETWEEN GRIPS OR UNDER RESTRAINT

REMOVEABLE SCREWS & WASHERS

FUSE SLOTS INTO CRADLE

REPLACING PLUGS & FUSES

TWO-PIN PLUGS

Many areas of the world also use plugs with two pins, instead of three. These are used for appliances that have their own earths and safety features. Never replace a three-pin plug with a two-pin plug, as this could leave your appliance unearthed and unsafe.

There are a number of different standards for plugs, used in different countries around the world, but most countries now have plugs that are 'polarised', even if they have a two-pin standard. This means there are slight differences in the size or shape of the live and neutral posts and sockets, which ensures the plug cannot be inserted the wrong way around. When replacing a two-pin plug of this type, always make sure you connect the live and neutral wires to the correct pins.

Some countries in Europe have earthed plugs which have a hole in the plug casing that connects to an earth pin protruding from the wall socket. Inside the plug, these are wired up in the same way as a three-pin plug, with three connections.

TWO-PINS WITH EARTH

EARTH SOCKET

THREE-PIN PLUGS

TWO-PIN PLUGS

MOULDED PLUGS

Some power cables on new appliances come with a one-piece plug that is moulded directly onto the cable. These plugs cannot be removed from the cable so, if the plug or cable is damaged, you should replace the whole unit. Take the damaged cable and plug unit to an electrical shop and the staff should be able to help find the right replacement.

CHOOSING THE CORRECT FUSE FOR AN APPLIANCE

Replacement plugs often come with a 13 amp fuse included. However, this rating is too high for most appliances and will not provide proper protection from power surges or other electrical faults.

The electricity triangle shows how the power (in watts) is related to the voltage (in volts) and current (in amps) flowing through electrical goods. You can use the triangle to find out the right equation to use for calculating the correct fuse to use.

Simply cover up the value you need to find, and the arrangement of the other values will show the relevant equation. So, if you cover up the A (for current) the remaining items on the triangle show that to calculate which fuse you need, you should divide the power (W) by the voltage (V).

Most appliances have their maximum power stated on a label or plate, making the maximum amps (above which they should be protected by the fuse) easy to estimate.

ELECTRICITY EQUATION TRIANGLE

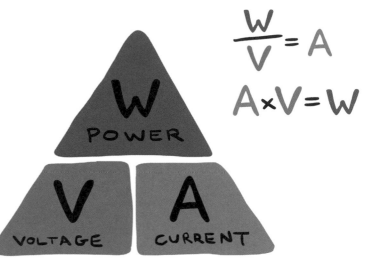

$$\frac{W}{V} = A$$

$$A \times V = W$$

CURRENT (AMPS) = POWER (WATTS) / VOLTAGE (VOLTS)

So, for a kettle with a maximum power rating of 3KW (3,000 watts), the fuse needed would be:

3,000 / 240 = 12.5 amps (13A fuse needed)

REPLACING PLUGS & FUSES

FOR A 1KW TOASTER, THE CALCULATION IS:

1,000 / 240 = 4.2 amps (5A fuse needed)

AND FOR A 100W LAMP:

100 / 240 = 0.4 amps (1A fuse needed – you won't find fuses lower than 1A, but this will still help to protect the bulb from damage in a power surge).

Note that some appliances need a higher rated fuse than their basic power figure would suggest. These include items with motors, such as vacuum cleaners. Consult the instructions for these appliances for the correct fuse rating.

THE MAIN FUSEBOX

The electrical wiring in your home will usually be controlled by a central fusebox, known as a 'consumer unit'. This fusebox is meant to be tended by you – the 'consumer' – so it is a good idea to get to know it before you experience any problems.

Your home electrics will be split into a range of independent circuits, each supplying electricity to different parts of the house – a simple example of how these might be arranged is shown below.

There will usually be separate circuits for lights and plug sockets in different areas. Some high-wattage appliances, such as the kitchen oven, will have their own individual circuits.

Each circuit will have its own fuse or circuit-breaker in your home's consumer unit and, every so often, something will happen to make one or more of these circuits 'trip'.

HOME WIRING

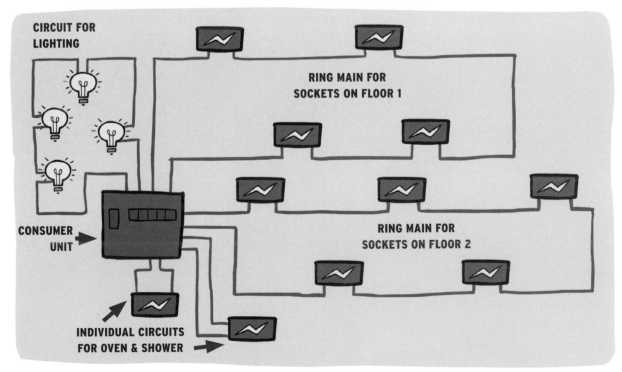

CIRCUIT FOR LIGHTING

RING MAIN FOR SOCKETS ON FLOOR 1

CONSUMER UNIT

RING MAIN FOR SOCKETS ON FLOOR 2

INDIVIDUAL CIRCUITS FOR OVEN & SHOWER

BEING PREPARED FOR A BLOWN FUSE

The most important piece of advice for looking after your fusebox is to be prepared. The time to become familiar with your circuit board is before things go wrong, not after you are plunged into darkness.

LABEL YOUR CIRCUITS
It is a good idea to label the circuit breakers with masking tape, to show which area is controlled by each switch. If you are lucky, this may have been done by the electrician who wired your home. To work out the labels yourself, a bit of detective work is required.

With lighting circuits, the best method is to turn on all your wall and ceiling lights and then switch off the circuits one by one and see which lamps are affected by each switch.

For plug sockets, move a portable lamp from room to room and turn off each circuit in turn until it goes out (or use a radio, which will save some walking back and forth as you can hear instantly when you have found the relevant circuit breaker). Bathroom and kitchen appliances are likely to have their own individual circuit-breakers.

DEALING WITH A TRIPPED CIRCUIT

Old-style fuses were simply made of wire stretched between two contacts on a plug of plastic bakelite, which slotted into the fusebox. These were fiddly to change and, when a fuse 'blew' it meant literally that – the wire would overheat and burn out, often with a bang.

New units are far more user-friendly, with the plugs replaced with self-contained circuit-breakers that detect high currents and switch off. To reset a circuit that has 'blown', you just need to flick the switch on the tripped circuit-breaker back to the 'on' position.

COMMON THINGS THAT MAY CAUSE A CIRCUIT TO TRIP

- a lightbulb burning out

- an appliance with a motor being turned off or on, or getting jammed (this can sometimes cause surges in the circuit)

- overloading (check that your overall power requirements for appliances on the circuit don't exceed the limit)

- appliances that have short-circuited (these will need professional repair)

MAXIMUM CIRCUIT LOADS

The electricity triangle can also be used to calculate the maximum load a circuit in your home can take.

The fuse in the main fusebox will be labelled with the maximum current in your circuit, and the total drawn by the appliances attached to the circuit should not exceed this.

As appliances are labelled with their power (in watts) rather than their current, you will need to calculate the maximum power the circuit will take instead.

So, for a circuit with a 32A fuse, the maximum power is:

32 amps x 240 volts = 7,680 watts or 7.7KW

Add up the total power of all the appliances and lights on this circuit (including those plugged into extension cables) and make sure they don't exceed this limit, or you will find the circuit is likely to trip often.

LIGHTING REPAIRS

Now you have a fully labelled fusebox, you can have the confidence to turn off individual circuits and carry out repairs on your electrical fittings.

Hardware such as light switches and plug sockets can stay in working order for decades, but should never be used when cracked, loose or otherwise damaged. Unless local regulations restrict electrical circuit work to registered professionals, you don't need to call in an electrician to make these replacements. The wiring is simple and this job is easy to do yourself with the right precautions.

You can also carry out these jobs to put in new, better looking fittings, or to add a dimmer switch – an ecologically sound move now that dimmable energy-saving lamps are on the market.

SWITCH REPLACEMENT

Most light switches are either 'one-way' or 'two-way'.

One-way switches have just two connections and simply turn a ceiling light (or set of lights on a wall) on and off. Two-way switches are used when a light is controlled by more than one switch, such as in a hallway, and have three connections.

All you have to remember when replacing any of these fittings is to reconnect the wires in the same way as on the original switch.

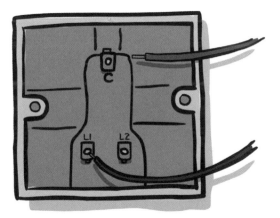

1. TURN OFF THE POWER TO THE CIRCUIT
At the fusebox, switch off the power to the relevant lighting circuit.

2. DOUBLE-CHECK THE POWER IS OFF
Unscrew the fitting to expose the wires and use your voltage testing screwdriver to check no power is flowing through them.

3. LABEL THE WIRES
There will be either two or three wires, attached to the light switch at points labelled L1/L2 and C or N. Before you detach them, make sure you know which wire goes to which connection. Small pieces of masking tape are ideal for this, as you can write on them and wrap them around the wires.

4. REMOVE THE OLD FITTING
Now you can unscrew the wires and remove the old fitting, leaving a set of labelled wires in a hole in your wall.

5. ATTACH THE NEW FITTING
This is the fiddly bit. Make sure you know where each wire needs to be attached before you start, as getting a good view of the back of the switch will become difficult once you have attached the first wire. Each wire needs to be attached firmly to the fixings in the new switch.

6. SCREW THE FITTING FIRMLY TO THE WALL
Once all the wires are attached, you can attach the new light switch to the mounting box in the wall, turn the power back on and test the switch.

**DIMMER UNIT
MORE BULKY**

FITTING A DIMMER SWITCH

A dimmer switch can be an extremely useful addition to a room where you want to control the lighting level, but can't accommodate lots of smaller lamps.

The connections on a dimmer switch are the same as in a normal switch, and they can be used to replace either one-way or two-way switches. However, never add two dimmer switches to a two-way circuit – they will make the lights flicker.

When installing a dimmer switch, you may also need to re-arrange the wires within the mounting box to create space for the bulkier unit behind the rotating button.

PROBLEMS WITH FLUORESCENT TUBE LIGHTS

Fluorescent tubes take a long time to wear out so, if you are having problems with a light that is failing to come on, the starter unit is most likely to be at fault.

These starter units provide the short pulse of high voltage needed to kick start the light when it first comes on. They are very cheap and simple to replace, and are often to be found simply sticking out of the side of your unit. In this case, buy a replacement starter and just slot it into place.

If the starter isn't visible, you will need to open up the main light fitting to find it. Turn off the relevant circuit, then remove the tube before opening up the unit, removing any screws if necessary.

Be very careful when handling fluorescent tubes. They are 'filled' with a near vacuum, so they implode dramatically if broken, creating thousands of small pieces of glass which take a long time to clear away.

TIP!

If you are working on a step-ladder and need to remove small components such as screws, take a large piece of Blu-tack up with you and stick it to the top of the ladder or the ceiling nearby. Then, you will have somewhere to keep the screws safe and handy while you work.

LIGHTING REPAIRS

CEILING LAMPS

There are several extra things to consider when working on lights attached to a ceiling.

Most important is to make sure you can work safely. Never stand on a chair to work on the ceiling. A secure step-ladder is best, but a sturdy dining-style table can be safe to stand on, if you are sure it will hold your weight without wobbling.

Ceiling lamp fittings will contain two sets of wires, rather than just one. One set comes in from the wiring in the wall and the other goes out down the cable to the lightbulb.

If you only want to replace the covering for the rose, you don't need to worry about the wiring (just remove the lamp holder from the bottom of the cable and slide up a new cover). However, if you are replacing the whole unit, it is vital to label the wires before detaching them, and making a sketch of the arrangement is also useful as an extra check.

It is also important that you use the correct flex. If you are replacing the lamp fitting that hangs at the bottom of the wire, and changing this from plastic to metal, you will have to change the flex from 'two-core' to 'three-core' as metal fittings must be earthed.

You should also be careful to train the wires over the hooks provided in the fitting before attaching them to the connections. Even the weight of a paper lampshade can put strain on wires without extra support.

Despite these precautions, you shouldn't be put off making changes to your ceiling fittings. As they sit above a hot lamp for years on end, they can become discoloured or brittle, so replacing them with new fittings can make a big difference to how a room looks.

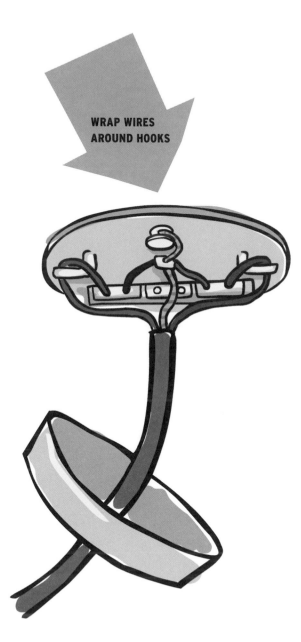

WRAP WIRES AROUND HOOKS

VERY SIMPLE ELECTRONICS

This book isn't intended to turn you into a trained electrician. But many household appliances are still very simple machines (despite the addition of microchips to almost everything!) and, therefore, tend to suffer from simple problems that can be repaired at home.

Portable appliances that are used a lot and have hand-held parts, such as hairdryers, kettles and telephones, often develop loose connections where the power cable comes in. It's not hard to spot the problem if this happens, and fixing it is not difficult either.

WHAT NOT TO FIX

There are only a few home appliances you should steer clear of opening up to investigate a problem.

These include new items that are still under guarantee – in these cases the manufacturer will be happy to repair or replace them for you.

As an amateur, you should also avoid trying to repair hi-fis and old-style televisions (which have components that can store a charge and cause a shock even when turned off). Luckily, it is still easy to find repair shops for both these categories of home appliances, and it is often cheaper to repair these than to buy a new machine.

GETTING INSIDE

I have been fiddling with broken appliances for years, and the main problem I have encountered – which is getting worse – is simply getting inside the things in the first place.

More and more manufacturers are making their machines with casings that clip together, rather than providing screw fixings that can be easily removed. I'm sure this saves lots of time in the factory, but it doesn't help when things go wrong!

Generally, I have found that brute force will get the back off most things in the end. But don't try this on new or precious items, and do watch out for the tiny but essential springs and catches that seem to fly out and hide in the corner when the casing eventually comes apart.

SORTING OUT A LOOSE CONNECTION

Diagnosing problems within the circuitry of an appliance is beyond those of us without a detailed knowledge of electronics. However, a common problem we can identify and fix is a broken connection in the main power wires.

These are very easy to spot. Look inside an appliance that stops working and you should be able to see the ends of any loose wires and the point where they were connected nearby.

Some loose wires can be reattached via clip connections or screw fixings, similar to those in a plug. But some wires will have come loose from a soldered joint and, for these, it's time to get out the soldering iron.

HOW TO USE A SOLDERING IRON

Solder is a low melting point alloy that is very useful for joining electrical components together.

Solder comes in soft wire coils and you only need a very tiny amount for an electrical joint. It melts almost instantly when it touches components heated with the iron, and will solidify rapidly when the heat is removed.

SOLDERING AN ELECTRICAL CONNECTION

TOOLS YOU WILL NEED
For this, you'll need your soldering iron and stand, and a couple of crocodile clips.

1. PUT THE IRON IN ITS STAND TO HEAT UP

2. PREPARE THE JOINT BY PUTTING THE WIRE IN THE CORRECT PLACE
Clamp the wire into place with a crocodile clip or paper clip, making sure it touches the connection.

3. PROTECT ANY VULNERABLE COMPONENTS NEARBY
Heat can damage components on circuit boards, so make a 'heat sink' by attaching a crocodile clip to something metal between the connection you are going to solder and the rest of the circuitry.

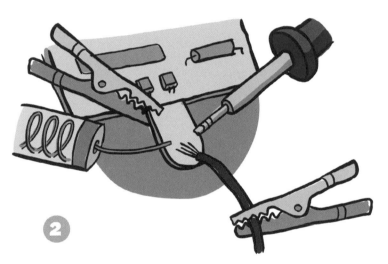

4. PREPARE THE SOLDER

Take the coil of solder wire and pull out a short straight piece a few centimetres long. Don't detach it from the coil or dispenser.

Note: these next two steps should take only about two seconds in total. Get ready with the iron in one hand and the solder in the other.

5. HEAT THE WIRE AND CONNECTION

Touch the tip of the soldering iron onto the circuit close to the wire connection.

6. APPLY THE SOLDER

After one second, touch the tip of the solder wire very gently onto the joint. It will melt and solder will flow into the spaces between the wires and over the connection. Remove the solder and iron immediately.

7. CHECK THE JOINT

The solder will solidify quickly, leaving behind a permanent joint, which should be shiny and not too large. The ideal shape is a domed pyramid rather than a ball.

If you have made a bad connection, it is possible to remove the solder with a special suction device (available cheaply in electronics shops or online) and start again. However, you should aim to get it right first time as reheating the joint repeatedly is not a good idea.

Soldering safety tips:
- Always place the iron in its stand when it's not in use – even if you only need to put it down for a few seconds.
- Never touch the tip of the soldering iron with your fingers.
- Be very careful not to touch the tip of the iron onto its cable.

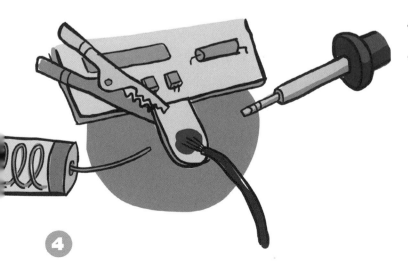

TELEPHONE REPAIRS

The telephone system runs off a very low voltage indeed – barely enough to feel it if you accidentally give yourself a shock. So, if a non-mains telephone unit stops working, you can really go to town fiddling around inside.

Telephones get a lot of abuse. Handsets get slammed down, cables get twisted, and they can even be thrown across the room in rage. So, it's not surprising telephones often develop problems with loose wires.

My 1980s vintage phone recently stopped working thanks to my boyfriend's habit of picking up the receiver and then walking away, dragging the unit off the table and on to the floor. Not surprisingly, something came loose and it stopped working, so I had to prise it open and put everything back into place.

Usually, you won't need a soldering iron to fix loose connections in the very thin wires that carry the signal – just twist the ends and slot them back into their fittings.

Sometimes the curly cable holding the handset will get snagged, crushed or frayed, which can cause crackling on the line. On newer telephones, you can replace this cable easily with a new one, as it is attached at either end with a socket. On older models you may need to take the receiver apart to attach the new cable inside the casing.

VERY SIMPLE ELECTRONICS

REWIRING A LAMP

Restoring a lamp is one of the best and easiest mending projects. There are no complex circuits, you don't need any special tools, and it's easy to find replacements for the parts you will need.

Here, I will show you how to replace all the electrics in an old lamp – a simple job that shouldn't take more than an hour from start to finish.

The basic components of a lamp are shown in the diagram. You have various options for replacing the different parts, depending on what your existing lamp uses, and the look you want.

These include choices between having:
- the switch on the cable or in the lampholder;
- a screw or bayonet lamp fitting
- a metal or plastic lampholder (don't use metal for lamps in damp areas, such as utility rooms, and always use three-core flex for metal fittings, as they must be earthed)
- white, brown or black cable.

You can even buy a special 'bottle kit' that will convert virtually anything to a lamp. This has a cork or plastic plug, and a cord that comes out of the side of the fitting, so you don't have to drill a hole in the bottom of your wine bottle.

All these components are cheap. So, for a very old or vintage lamp, it's a good idea to replace all the electrics at once when something needs fixing.

TOOLS YOU WILL NEED
All you should need for this job are a pair of combination pliers and two screwdrivers (cross and flat head), as well as replacement parts. You may also need some glue or tape to help with reassembling the lamp casing, if you need to take it apart.

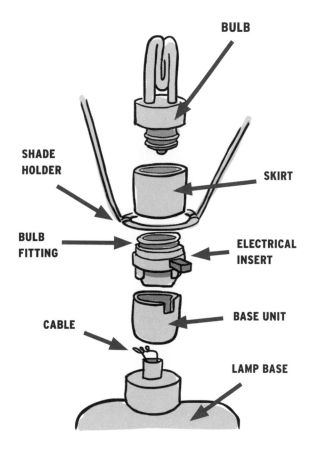

BULB

SHADE HOLDER

SKIRT

BULB FITTING

ELECTRICAL INSERT

CABLE

BASE UNIT

LAMP BASE

VERY SIMPLE ELECTRONICS

1. DISMANTLE THE LAMP
Start by taking the lamp apart. Unplug it from the mains, remove the shade, unscrew the skirt and lift up the electrical insert. There should be an electrical connection either side, which you can unscrew to release it from the wires.

Once the wires are free from the lampholder, you can pull the old wiring through the lamp from the base and discard it. You may need to take the lamp apart to free the cable from any clips or fittings that hold it in place within the lamp.

2. INSERT THE NEW CABLE
Take your new two- or three-core cable and feed it through the lamp before you prepare the end for connection with the lampholder. Used 'whole' it will pass much more easily through the lamp body as there will be no stray ends to get caught up inside.

Leave about 10cm of cable sticking out of the top of the lamp.

3. PREPARE THE WIRES
Pass the cable through the base unit of the lampholder and attach this securely to the lamp base. This is normally via a plastic or metal screw thread, but it may be held on with small screws or other fixings.

Then, strip the outer covering from the cable as far down inside the base unit as you can, making sure there is enough room to accommodate the electrical insert. Cut the individual wires to the right length so they will reach the connections on the insert comfortably, without leaving excess wire that could kink and break.

Strip about 8mm of insulation from the ends of the individual wires to expose the copper strands inside, then twist these neatly.

4. FIX THE WIRES TO THE CONNECTIONS
It is important to fix the wires neatly and firmly to the connections, without leaving stray copper strands that could touch the surrounding fittings. Make sure the insulation butts up closely to the connection – trim the copper ends shorter if necessary.

For metal lamp fittings, you should also attach the earth wire to the appropriate connection (which will be marked with the earth symbol).

EARTH SYMBOL

5. ASSEMBLE THE FITTING
You can now assemble the remaining parts of the lamp. Replace the electrical insert in the base unit and replace the shade before screwing on the upper 'skirt' which, on most lamps, holds the shade in place.

6. ADD A PLUG
Measure out sufficient cable to reach the plug socket, then trim the cable and fit a plug. Remember to add a fuse with the correct rating (most plugs come with a 13A fuse included, which is too high for a lamp, see page 47).

7. TEST THE LAMP
Add a bulb and test your fully rewired lamp to check everything is working.

VACUUM CLEANER TROUBLE-SHOOTING

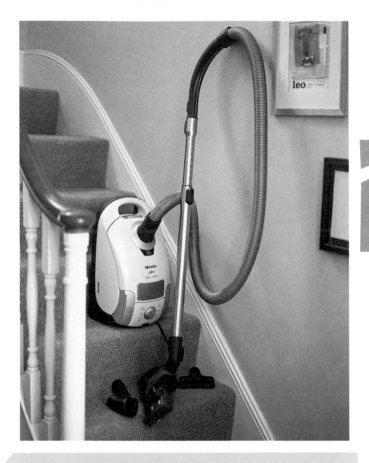

A vacuum cleaner is essential for every home and generally they are sturdy machines that can take a lot of wear and tear before they go wrong.

Almost every vacuum cleaner consists of a motor that produces suction (sometimes with a clever 'cyclone' action) to draw dust up a pipe and into a bag or chamber.

An upright machine also has a rotating brush in the nose of its base, which is driven by the same motor that produces suction, using an external drive belt.

There are a number of common problems that can reduce the efficiency of your vacuum. These can put the motor under strain, so act promptly and you'll increase the lifespan of your appliance.

COMMON VACUUM PROBLEMS AND SOLUTIONS

THE MOTOR IS WORKING BUT SUCTION IS REDUCED

MOST LIKELY CAUSE: A FULL BAG OR DUST CONTAINER
This is the first thing to check, and the solution is simply to empty the container or replace the bag.

TIP!

If you have a cleaner that uses disposable bags, purchase replacements several at a time so you always have a spare.

If you don't have a spare bag on hand, you can create some space to finish off the day's cleaning (which you will probably have made more urgent by opening up the machine and spilling more dust) by part-emptying the bag and replacing it.

To avoid a dust storm, place the bag fully inside a large bin liner. Then manipulate things through the plastic, shaking firmly until some of the contents have been removed. Ease the vacuum bag out very carefully, then tie up the bin liner immediately.

NEXT MOST LIKELY CAUSE: BLOCKAGE IN THE PIPE
Both upright and cylinder vacuum cleaners have plastic pipes that can become blocked with balls of dust and hair.

To remove a blockage, first remove the pipe from the cleaner. It may need to be unclipped, or you can often just twist and pull firmly to remove it. If the blockage is close to one end, it will be obvious and can be removed with your fingers.

If it's further down, you'll need a tool. A trusty wire coat-hanger is ideal for this (or a wire sink unblocker, if you have one). Straighten the coat-hanger and create a small hook at one end. Blunt the end of the hook with adhesive tape, so you don't pierce the pipe, and use it to push or pull the blockage out.

Replace the pipe and test the machine. If suction is still low, check for other causes.

NEXT MOST LIKELY CAUSE: BLOCKED FILTER

Most cleaners will have one or two filters – to prevent dust getting into the motor and to filter the air coming out of the machine. These can become clogged with dust or blocked with larger pieces of debris.

The filters will be in different places on different machines, but opening the cover and removing the bag should expose them.

The filter material will often be plastic or paper mesh, or made of spongy material. Replace the filter with the correct type for your model of cleaner. They can be ordered from electrical shops, but make sure you know the model name and number before you go shopping.

If you don't have a spare filter, you can temporarily clear the existing filters by removing them and shaking or tapping off excess dust. You can even try rinsing them out (and then drying them) if they are made of plastic.

THE BRUSH AT THE FRONT OF AN UPRIGHT MACHINE IS NOT TURNING

MOST LIKELY CAUSE: HAIRS OR THREADS IN THE MECHANISM

Tip up your machine and check for hairs and string that may be jamming the brushes.

The simplest way to clear this is to remove the brush. You will usually find a plate or cover on the base of the machine, which can be removed to release the brush. You are also likely to need to slide it out from under the rubber drive belt.

Remove all the debris wrapped around the cylinder, then replace it, screw the cover back on and test the machine.

NEXT MOST LIKELY CAUSE: DRIVE BELT IS LOOSE

If, once you clear the hairs, the brushes still won't turn, the drive belt may have stretched so that it doesn't grip the cylinder any longer.

In this case, you will need to replace the drive belt. These are made of rubber and come in standard sizes for each type of machine. You will be able to buy or order one from a good electrical shop. Again, make sure you take the correct name and number of your machine with.

**UNHOOK
DRIVE BELT
FROM MOTOR**

**REMOVE BELT
FROM CYLINDER**

STAINS AROUND THE HOME

Walls are usually painted or papered in light colours. This creates a wonderful sense of space in our homes, but also leaves them vulnerable to scrapes, stains and splashes, as well as everything our children can throw at them.

Floors are also in danger, with carpets and rugs just waiting to have food, drink, paint and other spills dropped on to them.

Unlike stains on clothing, we can't simply pop our wall and floor coverings into the washing machine, so we need new strategies to deal with these everyday marks.

STAINS ON WALLS

Painted walls are much easier to deal with than wallpaper, which can be very delicate, making stain removal a real challenge.

PAINTED FINISHES
Gloss and eggshell (low sheen) are easy to clean with normal household detergents. Don't let highly coloured substances, like curry or tomato sauce, sit on these finishes for long, or the stain may be absorbed into the paint, making it much harder to remove.

Matt wall paints are harder to deal with, but a simple detergent solution can usually be used to dab or wipe off a stain.

One tip to remember is to use a sparkling clean (ideally new) cloth or sponge on light-coloured painted walls. It also helps if you brush away any dust from the surrounding area before you start. This will help avoid horrible 'tide mark' effects at the edges of the area you have cleaned.

I keep a packet of disposable cleaning wipes handy for getting marks off my painted walls. These are a bit wasteful, so I save them for this job, but they start out perfectly clean and won't spread any new dirt on to the wall as the stain comes off.

WALLPAPER

Wallpaper can be very delicate, especially if it has a decorative finish, such as foil or fabric.

Some ideas for cleaning off stains are below but, whatever you try, remember to test the process on a hidden area of paper (such as behind the sofa) before using it on a stain in a prominent place.

TIPS FOR CLEANING WALLPAPER STAINS
- Brush away any surface dust before you start.
- Use a perfectly clean cloth or sponge.
- Use a mild detergent, without bleach, and squeeze almost all the liquid out (the last thing you need is drips running down the wall).
- Start at the bottom of the stain and dab gently upwards.
- Never rub the stain.
- Pat dry with a clean, lint-free cloth (not tissue paper).

GET A MAGIC ERASER
Several manufacturers produce a 'magic eraser' for removing stains from hard surfaces, and this is one cleaning product I highly recommend for occasional use.

All the products are basically the same and are made from melamine foam, which is dampened and then used to rub away stains.

The action is very gentle: the sponge has a fine foam structure, made of tiny, hard fibres, and these two properties combine to rub the stain away gently while absorbing it into the material. This means that, with care, you can use it on wallpaper as well as painted surfaces, but not on upholstery or carpets.

The block gradually disintegrates with use, and costs too much for everyday cleaning. But it is a great investment to keep in the house for stubborn stains on hard-to-clean materials.

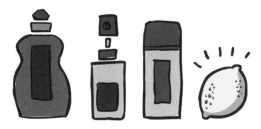

STAINS ON CARPETS AND UPHOLSTERY

Carpet and upholstery stains create a dilemma – you want to clean them effectively and quickly, but it's important to avoid getting the material wet.

The answer is to use very small amounts of the right solvent for the stain and to lift the stain off gently, using a dabbing action to avoiding soaking and spreading the stain.

WHICH SOLVENT?
Household stores and websites offer a whole host of specialist solvents and cleaners, each claiming to work on a very specific type of stain. These often work very well, but most are based on just a few different solvent chemicals.

Use these solvents in cheap, plain formulations and the only thing you'll be missing is the fragrances and foaming agents added to the commercial products. However, you'll save a lot of cupboard space by keeping many fewer potions in stock!

The basic solvents are described below, with a range of stains you can tackle with each one.

Remember, for curtains, carpets and upholstery, always follow these two golden rules:

- Don't wet the fabric – use a damp sponge or cloth to dab the stain away gently. For foaming cleaners, whip up a froth then dab on a small amount of the foam, without using the liquid underneath.
- Don't rub – this can ruin the finish of the fabric or carpet.

WASHING UP LIQUID
Dab a tiny amount of neat, non-coloured washing up liquid (eco-friendly brands are good) on greasy stains. After a few minutes, dab firmly, pressing down repeatedly with a clean, damp rag or sponge and the grease will lift off.

BIOLOGICAL DETERGENT
A strong solution of biological washing powder can be used to remove lots of 'natural' stains, including curry, beetroot, blood, coffee, tea and oil. Always test this on an unseen area first, especially on coloured fabrics.

STAINS AROUND THE HOME

METHYLATED SPIRIT
This doesn't smell very nice, but is the correct solvent to use for a range of stains, including ink, lipstick, shoe polish, wax crayon and coloured modelling clay. Fold an absorbent rag into a pad, dampen slightly then press it on to the stain repeatedly, to gradually lift it away.

BORAX
Borax is another name for the mineral sodium borate, and is normally used in the washing machine to boost the effect of detergent. Used on its own, it produces a mild bleaching action as it reacts with water to form small amounts of hydrogen peroxide. This will effectively remove many stains from upholstery and carpets.

Borax is usually sold as a powder of small crystals, which dissolve easily in water. You can make a brush-on paste of borax for light-coloured upholstery or carpet stains (vacuum up after half an hour), or dissolve a couple of tablespoons in half a litre of water to make a cleaning solution.

ACETONE (NAIL POLISH REMOVER)
Non-oily nail polish removers are almost pure acetone. This chemical can be used to dissolve glue stains and sticky tape residues. Never use on acrylic or polyester materials, as this solvent also dissolves some kinds of plastic.

BICARBONATE OF SODA
This is another cleaning agent for lifting off grease stains. Mix the powder with a small amount of water to make a paste, then spread on to the stain. Leave for less than an hour (don't allow it to dry completely) then brush away and dab the area with washing up liquid solution.

OXYGEN BLEACH
This is safer to use than chlorine bleach, as it doesn't affect colours. Make a weak solution and dab on to stains caused by substances like curry, blood and mould.

LEMON JUICE
A milder bleaching agent that can work well if dabbed neat on to some stains, such as rust spots and mildew.

WHITE SPIRIT (ALSO KNOWN AS SHELLITE OR CLEAR GAS)
Use for spills of paint or varnish. Don't allow these stains to dry, as they will be very hard to remove afterwards. Scrape off excess paint immediately, then dab with an absorbent pad dampened with white spirit.

STAINS AROUND THE HOME

SPECIFIC STAINS

WAX

Wax drips can be removed by absorbing them into a few sheets of kitchen paper using the heat from an iron.

Place the paper on the stain and iron gently using a warm setting (not hot). The solid wax will soften and be absorbed by the paper. To remove any remaining residues, dab gently with methylated spirit.

RED WINE

I have heard hundreds of different bits of folk wisdom telling me how to remove red wine stains. But, rather than hunting around for white wine, soda water or salt, I think the best advice is just to act very quickly to soak up the liquid before it gets a chance to stain anything.

If wine spills on the carpet, immediately place a whole newspaper over the spill and then press down hard for about 5 minutes.

Don't rub, just press as hard as you can, using all your weight by standing on it, if possible. If the wine starts to come through the paper, replace with a fresh dry newspaper and continue to press down.

This will take up virtually all the wine, leaving an almost dry carpet without stains.

You can use a similar method on upholstery. If the stain is on a cushion that can be moved, tip the excess wine on to the floor then use the newspaper method on both the carpet and the cushion.

If you can't move the upholstery, just press the newspaper on as hard as you can wherever the wine fell, sitting on it if necessary. For very light-coloured fabrics, you might want to use a folded towel or pile of clean tea towels instead, to prevent ink transfer. However, as the most important thing is speed (and a newspaper is likely to be closer at hand) don't delay by fetching a towel if the material is dark.

Afterwards, dab with detergent solution to finish the cleaning process, and then allow to dry.

BURNS

Burns and scorch marks are not really 'stains', as they represent permanent damage to the material.

The best way to disguise minor burns and scorches is to remove the damaged and darkened fibres gently. For this, you can use a razor to scrape off surface marks.

On carpets, a small burn can ruin the look of a whole room, but you can carry out the clever repair opposite to disguise the mark. See page 68 for how to deal with burns on wooden floors and furniture.

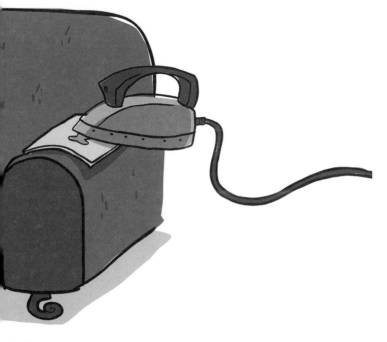

DISGUISING A CARPET BURN

Start by trimming away all the burned fibres. This will leave a hollow in the carpet, and may even expose the base fabric. Don't worry – you'll now cover this up.

Take some PVA wood glue and spread a layer over the base of the hollow you have created, being careful not to get any glue on the rest of the carpet. Let it dry for a few minutes while you carry out the next stage – you want the glue to be very sticky but not liquid when you put the new fibres in.

Now go to an inconspicuous edge area of the carpet with a pair of nail scissors and grip a bunch of fibres firmly between two fingers. Then, holding tight, snip them away as close to the bottom of the fibres as possible. Keep your grip exactly as it is and go back to the burned area.

Place the fibres directly into the hollow so that their bases are caught in the sticky glue. Don't fiddle with them at this stage, just push them in and return to the corner to collect another batch of fibres. Try not to get glue on your fingers during this process. If you do, wash it off before going to pick up more fibres.

Keep repeating this process until you have pushed fibres into place all over the area of the hollow. 'Over stuff' the hollow until no more fibres will go in. You'll find that some of them will stick up above the surface of the pile, and you'll tidy this up later.

Leave until the glue is properly dry, ideally overnight, protecting the area from foot traffic. Then, once the fibres are stuck firmly in place, take the nail scissors again and trim the ends so they match the surrounding carpet.

Finish off by taking a small paintbrush, screwdriver or other sharp implement and working it through the fibres around the edges of the hollow. This will help mix the new fibres in with the old, and disguise the edges of your repair.

This fix may not be completely invisible (especially to you, as you know it's there!) but will hardly be noticed by other people – and will be far less obvious than the burn mark it covered up.

Furniture Repairs & Refurbishments

Antique furniture is rightly prized, polished and kept for centuries. But modern fixtures and fittings tend to be treated less well, and are often dumped in favour of something new when they only need minor repairs.

Admittedly, a flat-pack coffee table isn't as valuable as a Chippendale chair, but it still represents many valuable resources and comes in useful when you need to put down your cup of tea. Replacing it takes money and shopping time, which you can save if you know how to fix it and keep it looking good.

And when a piece of furniture really does fall apart, or is no longer needed for its original purpose, why not use it to make something new – change a scratched chest of drawers into a stylish desk, or use the legs from a broken chair to make a side table?

In this section, I'll introduce you to some basic woodworking skills, show you how to deal with scratched and rusty metal furniture and go through some easy (and some more ambitious) upholstery projects that can put life back into tired soft furnishings to save them from the dump.

KEEPING WOODEN FURNITURE LOOKING GOOD

Wood is both a beautiful and durable. Looked after properly, it can last for decades but, too often, furniture is discarded because of surface defects that are easily sorted out. Burns, scratches and chipped paintwork can be fixed to professional standards if you use the right materials and tools.

These sections will show you how to repair damage to the surface of furniture made from wood, board and veneer. It will also show how to apply new finishes that will protect the wood beneath and look good for years.

REPAIRING SURFACE DAMAGE

FILLING CRACKS
Small cracks in a wooden or veneered surface can be filled with a substance called 'wood stopper' or 'wood filler'.

This is sold as a paste in tubes or pots. Designed specifically to fill wood, it dries hard but is more flexible than other fillers and comes in a range of colours to match different types of wood.

Use a filling knife to push filler into the crack. Leave it slightly proud of the surface then sand flat after it has set.

Larger cracks can be patched with spare slivers of matching wood. Cut the patch to the right width and length, then insert it into the crack and tap into place using a flat piece of wood to protect the surfac and a hammer. Then, push filler into the remaining gaps to hold it in place. Sand smooth and re-apply any finish after the filler has set.

NOTE
If a crack is actually a split in the wood, mend this with wood glue by clamping the two sides of the split back together again, see page 80.

RAISING A DENT
Dented wood has been compressed by a blow from a hard object (often a stray hammer blow). You can expand the fibres again using steam.

Place a damp rag over the dent and heat it by applying a soldering iron so that steam pours out of the rag and into the wood. Re-wet the rag if it starts to dry out or you will risk burning the rag and your wooden surface.

Once the wood has expanded to the same height as the surrounding surface, leave it to dry out before sanding it lightly to smooth it.

REMOVING BURNS
Floorboards, tables and sideboards can be burned and scorched by cigarettes, candles and hot cooking pots.

Depending on the depth of the burn you can polish it off or scrape away the burned surface and expand it to remove the resulting dent.

A very deep burn should be treated like a hole or crack and filled after scraping away the burned material.

MINOR SCORCHES
For really shallow burns you can polish off the thin blackened layer with a mild abrasive polish, such as metal polish. Rub it on gently with a clean rag. Once the burn has gone, re-polish or oil the bare patch of exposed wood.

LARGER BURNS
For more serious burns, use a sharp knife and sandpaper to scrape off the burned material until you reach the undamaged layer below. Then, use the steaming technique for dents to expand the wood in the area you have scraped away, so that the surface lies flat again. Sand to smooth it off then reapply the varnish or other finish.

The attractive natural patterns of wood grain look gorgeous when a finish such as oil, wax or varnish is applied to the surface. But, as the furniture is used, scuffs and scratches can mark the surface and remove the finish.

Sanding down the wood and re-applying a finish is a very satisfying job and will leave your wooden furniture looking beautiful again. Knowing how to do this properly also makes buying and renovating second-hand furniture a great, thrifty way to furnish your home.

SANDING

Old layers of chipped varnish or a battered and scratched wooden surface need to be sanded smooth before you apply a new finish.

For a small item, you can generally do the whole job by hand. For bigger jobs, a small power sander may be a good investment. If you want to renovate a large area of floor, hiring a special floor sanding machine is probably essential, or you will spend just as much money on therapy for a sore back! Make sure you follow health and safety precautions, working in a well ventilated area and protecting your lungs from wood dust.

Always sand in the direction of the grain and, at the ends of the grain, sand consistently in one direction.

Use the coarsest grade of sandpaper first and gradually move to finer grades, sanding off the scratches made by the previous grade before moving on to the next level. Finish off by raising the grain with a damp cloth and smoothing this down with fine wire wool or the finest grade of paper for a really smooth surface.

To sand irregular surfaces, edges and mouldings, wrap the sandpaper around a suitable piece of wood to ensure the surfaces are sanded evenly. And, for deep crevices, an emery board (usually used for filing fingernails) is an excellent substitute for sandpaper.

See the section on sanding down and oiling a wooden chopping board (see page 130) for more about sanding off scratches.

WRAP SANDPAPER AROUND APPROPRIATELY SHAPED OBJECTS TO SAND COMPLICATED MOULDINGS

MAINTAINING A NATURAL WOOD FINISH

CHOOSING A FINISH

Once you have a smooth, sanded surface, you can enhance and protect it with a suitable finish. The right finishing method depends on the use you will make of the item and the conditions it will need to withstand.

VARNISH
Varnish comes in a vast range of formulations, many designed for specific applications, but all use either oil and resin or polymers to protect the wood. Varnish will provide water resistance to a surface and, with several thin coats, can be very hard-wearing. Surface finishes vary from high gloss to a low-sheen 'eggshell'.

WAX
Wax is very quick and easy to apply, giving a gentle sheen to wood that gets light wear, such as in shelving or decorative pieces. As wax only penetrates the wood slightly, it is not as protective as oil. Mixtures of beeswax and plant waxes are available in tins, thinned with solvents for easy application.

OIL
Oil protects wood by penetrating deep into the pores of the grain, bringing out the pattern. With several coats, an oil finish can be buffed to a medium gloss. All traces of previous wax or varnish must be removed before applying oil, in order for it to sink properly into the wood.

Wood finishing oil is often sold under the name 'Danish oil'. Wooden items used around food can be protected with olive or vegetable oils.

APPLYING OIL

Apply oil liberally and rub it in with a soft cloth. Several coats should be applied, and the oil should be left to soak in thoroughly between coats.

After the final coat of oil has soaked in, the surface can be polished with a dry, soft cloth.

SAFETY NOTE

All oils are flammable, and rags soaked in wood oils can be a fire hazard while they dry. When you have finished applying oil, your rags should be laid out flat in a well-ventilated place or hung on a washing line, not left scrunched up, which can concentrate the vapours.

APPLYING WAX
Rub wax into your surface with a rag, and apply it to crevices and corners with a stiff paintbrush. Leave the wax to set and rub off any excess before applying a second coat. A third or even fourth coat can provide a more resilient finish. Once the final coat has hardened, polish with a cloth or a soft brush.

STAINING WOOD

If you want to change the colour of your wooden furniture, or if you need to colour a new part to match the rest of your piece, the best solution is to apply a penetrating stain. This will stain the wood permanently by sinking into the pores of the wood, and will help bring out the beauty of the grain. In contrast, coloured varnishes are difficult to use to get an even result and will cover up the grain patterns.

Both oil-based and water-based stains are available. Oil stains are easier to apply evenly and won't 'raise the grain' by wetting or expanding the wood and pushing fibres out on to the surface. Both types can be diluted with the appropriate solvent to reduce the density of the colour pigments. You can also mix different shades together to get a better colour match.

Stains give different results depending on the colour, smoothness and porosity of the wood. If possible, always test your stain on a spare piece of wood sanded to the same smoothness as the finished piece.

End grain will take up more stain than the rest of the piece, so you should use diluted stain on these surfaces, or protect them from absorbing too much stain with a product such as 'sanding sealer' available from hardware shops.

VARNISHING

The aim when applying varnish is to get a smooth finish without brushmarks. Acrylic varnish dries quickly, so you need to work rapidly in order to avoid brushing while the varnish is tacky.

Where you can, apply varnish to a surface that is lying flat, to reduce the risk of drips and runs. However, with most large pieces of furniture, this won't be practical and you will simply have to keep a close eye on the work and check that varnish isn't collecting in details and grooves. Bring the furniture into a well lit position to make this easier.

TOOLS AND MATERIALS YOU WILL NEED
Varnish (acrylic or oil-based), a good quality brush 2.5cm to 5cm wide (a smaller brush may also be needed for details), either water or white spirit to clean the brushes, and some fine steel wool to rub down the first coat. You will also need dustsheets or newspaper to protect your work area.

THE STEPS
1. Make sure the wood is clean, dry and dust-free before you start.

2. Load your brush with a reasonable amount of varnish, stroking the edges lightly against the sides of the tin to prevent drips.

3. Brush quickly and liberally on to the surface along the grain until it is completely coated. Brush with an even pressure, holding the brush at a 45 degree angle to the surface. On a vertical surface, apply this coat upwards at first and always brush outwards over the edges and corners to avoid drips. If your surface has mouldings or carved ridges, brush along these rather than across them. If your piece has complex carved shapes, dab the varnish into these firmly with the tip of your brush.

4. You now need to smooth out the first coat using a wet (but not loaded) brush to distribute the varnish evenly. Brush over the whole surface at least twice, first along the grain then across the grain, overlapping adjacent strokes very slightly to avoid leaving sharp edges.

5. Finish off with a set of very light strokes along the grain. Use the tips of the bristles very gently to hide the previous set of brush strokes and leave behind a near-perfect surface.

6. Then, leave this coat to dry in an area free of dust (don't sand anything nearby!)

7. Before applying a second coat, gently smooth down the first coat with steel wool and wipe off the dust. If you have used water-based varnish, this may have raised the grain fibres, and you should sand it with fine 'wet and dry' paper to smooth these off.

8. Apply a second coat in the same way as the first, and a third coat if you wish. Rub down each coat with steel wool, except the final coat.

BRUSH FIRST ALONG THE WOOD
GRAIN THEN ACROSS IT FOR AN EVEN
COAT OF VARNISH. FINISH OFF WITH
VERY LIGHT STROKES ALONG THE GRAIN

CARING FOR WOODEN GARDEN FURNITURE

Most wood used in garden furniture comes from hardwood trees, such as teak or oak. This is very durable, but should be protected with a coat of oil once a year to prevent the surface drying out and cracking.

Exterior grade varnish can provide a more waterproof protective coating for hardwood.

Softwood timber, such as pine or cedar, is sometimes used in the garden but is more susceptible to weather damage and rotting. It should be protected with a water-resistant coating of stain or varnish.

Once a year, check all your garden furniture for cracks, moss, lichen and rot. Scrub with steel wool or fine sandpaper to remove anything growing on the surface and fill any cracks or holes with stopper before applying a coat of water-resistant varnish or a combined stain and waterproofing treatment.

Don't forget the bottom surfaces of tables and chairs. Once the upper surfaces have been treated, turn over your furniture and apply the same treatment to the feet and other parts that will sit in contact with the ground.

Wipe petroleum jelly or lubricating grease on to any moving parts and apply a thin layer of varnish to nuts, bolts and screws to help protect them from rust. Don't forget to make repairs to garden furniture using rust-resistant galvanised steel or brass fittings – see page 96.

DON'T FORGET TO PROTECT UNDER THE FEET OF GARDEN FURNITURE

Painted wooden furniture can become chipped, stained or scratched. I would not recommend trying to strip paint from wood completely to return to a natural wood finish. This is possible, using either a heat gun and scraper or strong paint-stripping chemicals, but is a very laborious and dirty job, and it is very hard to get good results at home.

However, if you have solid wooden doors or a piece that you desperately want to return to its natural state, these can be sent to professional workshops for an industrial paint-stripping process known as 'dipping'. Your pieces will return completely bare, and you can then proceed to sand and finish them to suit your taste.

PAINTING WOOD

PAINTING OR REPAINTING WOODEN FURNITURE

Before you start, it's important to smooth and prepare the surface, as this will determine how good your finished paintwork will look.

Sand down the old paint thoroughly, and check the surface for any cracks and holes that you can fill using wood stopper, as described on page 68.

Knots in new wood can leak resin into the paint and cause ugly stains. Seal these knots by painting on a special 'knot sealing' compound, which is easy to find in hardware and DIY shops.

Once the surface is prepared, you can move on to applying your painted finish.

TOOLS AND MATERIALS YOU WILL NEED

Primer (if you are starting with bare wood), a suitable light or dark undercoat and your choice of paint for the final coat, some 'wet and dry' silicone carbide paper and fine steel wool.

Use good quality 2.5cm and 5cm paintbrushes, and a narrower brush for edges and mouldings. Make sure you have either water or white spirit ready to clean the brushes, and that you protect the surrounding area with dustsheets or newspaper.

CHOOSING PAINT

As with varnish, you have a choice between solvent- and water-based (acrylic) paints. Solvent-based gloss is more waterproof and has a shinier finish than water-based gloss. This makes it a better choice for areas where spillages are likely. For pieces that are less heavily used, either type of paint will give good results.

Gloss paint is also available in special 'one-coat' and 'non-drip' formulations. These can be easier to use for large areas, such as skirting boards and doors, and will give an even finish without being brushed over repeatedly.

1 SEAL KNOTS

2 APPLY PRIMER

THE STEPS

1. If you are planning to paint a new piece of wood, seal any knots by brushing on knot sealer, then prime the wood with a suitable oil- or water-based primer.

Brush on primer liberally with a normal 2.5cm or 5cm paintbrush, making sure it reaches all parts of the surface. It will soak in and doesn't need brushing over. After it dries, rub the surface down with fine 'wet and dry' sandpaper (see page 20).

2. Now apply two coats of a suitable dark or light coloured undercoat. Undercoat paint is cheaper than coloured gloss or matt paint and helps fill the grain and build up a smooth surface before applying the final colour.

Apply undercoat in two thin coats, brushing over using the same process as for varnish. Sand the undercoat smooth with fine 'wet and dry' paper before moving on to the final colour.

3. One or two coats of final colour may be needed, depending on the coverage given by the paint. Apply the final colour using the cross-brushing technique described for varnish, smoothing off finally with very light strokes with the tips of the bristles. Check the first coat in bright light for dust and specks and sand lightly with wet 'wet and dry' paper before applying the final coat.

For a flat surface you can eliminate brush marks completely by applying the final colour with a foam roller.

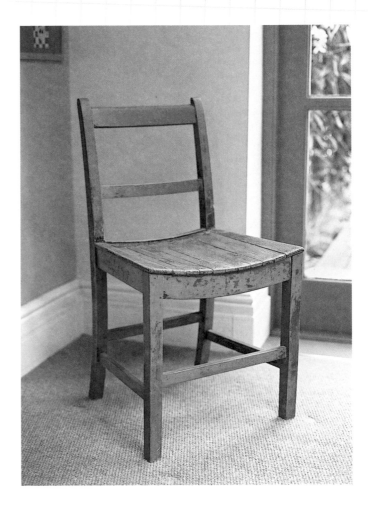

3 UNDERCOAT (SAND BETWEEN COATS)

4 PAINT

STRUCTURAL PROBLEMS

Furniture and fittings can develop a range of structural or mechanical problems, from a narrow split in the wood, to a wobbly leg, to a complete collapse.

The details of each repair will depend on the exact design of your furniture, but this section contains examples of the most common types of repairs that aim to give you the confidence to repair your furniture using similar techniques.

It will also show how to repair stairs and floorboards, how to give a coffee table a new veneered surface and how to transform pieces of furniture to fit new purposes.

REPAIRING BREAKS

Furniture can break in many different ways, needing a range of repair techniques and materials.

Commonly, an existing metal or plastic connector will come lose or snap, and fixing the problem is just a case of replacing the connector with another suitable fixing.

Wood can also shrink as it ages and dries out, which can mean traditional woodworking joints become loose. These can be repaired using nothing more than glue but, if they have to bear heavy loads, they may also need reinforcing with nails or screws.

WOODWORKING JOINTS AND CONNECTIONS

Craftspeople and professional carpenters create a variety of strong joints by shaping the pieces to be joined so that they fit together and lock the parts in place, often without needing glue.

The most common types of woodworking joints are shown opposite.

MITRE JOINT

The two surfaces to be joined are each cut at a 45 degree angle. Mitre joints can be reinforced with tenons and rebates, or with nails, dowels or biscuits.

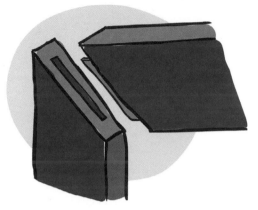

MORTISE AND TENON JOINT

The tenon is cut from the end of a rail or shelf, and fits closely into a mortise hole cut into the face of an upright rail or side panel. These joints are often used in the construction of tables and chairs.

TONGUE AND GROOVE JOINT

This joins boards together at their edges to create a larger panel.

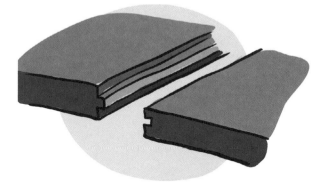

HOUSING JOINT

A shelf or panel fits into a groove in an upright component.

RALVING JOINT

Pieces of equal thickness are each cut down by half to form a neat joint that can be glued or nailed together.

DOVETAIL JOINT

Traditionally used to join the corners of a drawer, wedge-shaped 'dovetails' fit tightly between corresponding 'pins' to form a very strong joint.

DOVETAILS

PINS

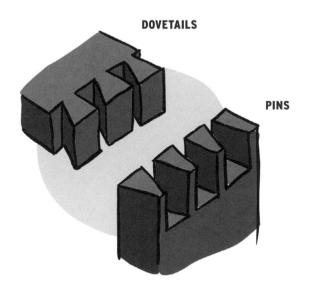

STRUCTURAL PROBLEMS

DOWEL JOINT

A simple joint, which can be created using only a drill. Short lengths of ridged dowel (which can be bought ready-made) are glued into holes drilled into both pieces.

BISCUIT JOINT

Similar to a dowel joint, manufactured wooden 'biscuits' are hammered or glued into slots cut into each component.

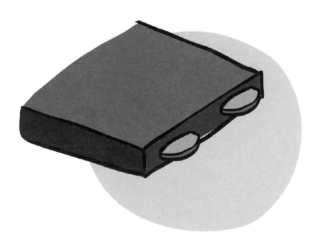

'KNOCK DOWN' JOINTS

Commercially made furniture, particularly 'flat pack' furniture for home assembly, often uses methods of connection that can be removed to take the furniture apart again. These are called 'knock down' connectors. If one of these fails, you can normally find a matching replacement in a hardware shop.

BLOCK JOINT

Metal or plastic blocks are attached to each component with screws. These can come in two parts which are then clamped together with a removable bolt.

BOLT AND BARREL
Two crossed channels must be carefully drilled to hold this fitting, but the final result can look very neat.

CAM FITTING
Similar to a bolt and barrel fitting, two connecting channels are drilled and the fitting is pulled tight when the cam bolt is turned.

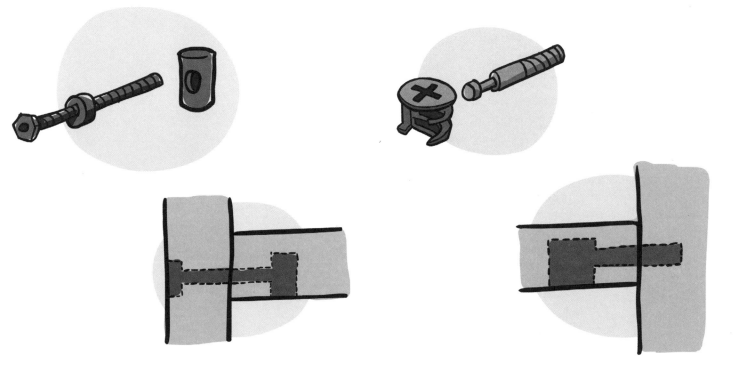

RECONNECTING BROKEN PARTS

GLUING WOOD

Many breakages can be repaired using wood glue. Surfaces to be glued should fit closely together and be clean and not dusty.

Apply a generous but not too thick layer of glue to both sides of the join. You only want a very small amount of excess glue to leak out of the space when the sides are pressed together.

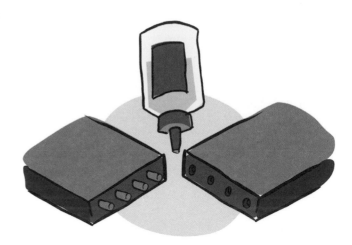

Wipe off any glue that oozes out of the joint before it dries, using a damp cloth. Clamp the pieces firmly until the glue has dried.

REPAIRING A SPLIT IN SOLID WOOD

Prise the split open slightly with a screwdriver or chisel and apply glue inside the split with a spatula or thin strip of wood.

Hold together firmly with a G-clamp, protecting the surface with strips of wood, until the glue is dry.

REPAIRING A WOODWORKING JOINT

If a woodworking joint comes apart, add glue to both parts of the joint and the surrounding surface.

Clamp a repair like this by wrapping two layers of thick cord around the pieces and twisting tight using a pencil, which will then rest against the piece to prevent it from twisting back.

REPAIRING A DOWEL JOINT

Replace any broken dowels and apply glue to the dowels, the holes and the surrounding surface.

NUTS AND BOLTS

Metal furniture is often constructed using nuts and bolts or rivets. A broken rivet can be pulled out of the holes in the metal sheets with pliers and replaced with a suitable bolt.

As nuts and bolts vary widely, it is best to remove a matching connection from elsewhere in your piece of furniture and take this to the shop to find a replacement for a lost fitting.

NAILS AND SCREWS

In furniture made from wood or board, parts may be joined with woodworking joints or with screws or nails. Non-loadbearing parts, such as side or back panels on a chest or wardrobe, are more usually attached with nails or tacks and these can be replaced if they come loose.

NAILING TIPS

Start off a nail by holding it perpendicular to the surface with your thumb and finger and tapping it in gently with a hammer, holding the hammer about half-way down the shaft for greater accuracy.

Then, switch to holding the hammer at its base for more power and strike the nail firmly 3 or 4 times until it lies flush with the surface. It should go in smoothly.

If you are using a thick nail, or are hammering close to the edge of a piece, prevent splitting by drilling a small pilot hole before hammering.

If the nail bends, remove it and start again. Your hammer head may be slipping on the head of the nail, so use sandpaper to roughen the surface of your hammer if this happens often.

Support a small nail or tack by pushing it through a folded piece of paper, rather than holding it in your fingers. Tap the nail part-way in then tear off the paper before hammering it flush.

Hold panels in place with nails perpendicular to the surface. Joints can be reinforced by placing nails at an angle.

REMOVING NAILS

Use the head of a claw hammer or a pair of pincers to remove old nails by levering them out. Make sure you protect the surface of your furniture with a strip of wood or board.

RECONNECTING BROKEN PARTS

USING SCREWS

Screws provide a more secure fixing than nails and can be a quick way of putting wooden furniture back together. Choose a screw of the right length to hold the loose component in place firmly. Screw through the thinner piece into the thicker piece – the screw should be at least three times as long as the thinner piece to hold it properly.

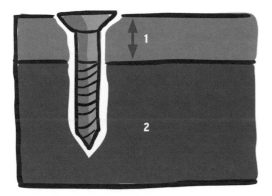

It is important not to risk splitting panels or boards when you add a screw. Screwing into the end grain of solid wood is also very difficult unless a pilot hole is drilled before inserting the screw. The hole should be slightly narrower than the width of the screw thread.

Adding a countersink to the hole will allow the head of the screw to sit flush with the surface. Use a large drill bit or a special countersink bit after you have drilled a pilot hole.

REMOVING SCREWS

A screw that is stuck can be loosened by heating it briefly with a soldering iron. The metal will expand and create more space in the material, which should help it to come out more smoothly.

DISGUISING SCREW HEADS

A number of different options for making the head of a screw less obvious are available.

CUPS

These framing rings are usually made from brass and will make a single-slot screw head look nicer without hiding it.

SCREW-ON DOME

These come with special screws that incorporate a threaded hole for the domed cap to fix on to. These are also known as 'mirror screws' and come in a small range of different metallic colours.

PLASTIC COVER FOR A CROSS-HEAD SCREW

These plastic caps simply push into the cross-head of a countersunk screw to cover it up.

SNAP-ON COVER

The bottom of this two-part cap is held in place with the screw head, and then the top cover snaps into place to hide the screw after fixing. You don't need to countersink the screw head when using this type of cover.

BRACKETS AND CORNER JOINTS

If a structural panel or shelf needs more strength than nails or screws can provide, you can fix it using steel brackets to hold the parts together.

These are fairly ugly and are only suitable for placing in hidden locations, such as inside a cupboard or under a shelf.

It is important to place the bracket so that it will pull and hold the pieces together firmly. Get a helper to hold the pieces in place while you mark the correct position for the screw holes.

Using a drill to create pilot holes may be difficult in a confined space. However, as long as you are not working within 1cm of the edge of a piece of wood or MDF, you can make a pilot hole by hammering a nail part-way into the surface.

A less conspicuous alternative to brackets can be a 'block joint' as shown on page 78.

Chairs come in a wide range of shapes, sizes and designs, held together with a combination of woodworking joints, screws and bolts, which may also be reinforced with stays or blocks.

If a chair becomes wobbly, check these joints and repair them before they fail completely.

If screw or bolt holes have become damaged or enlarged, fill them with pieces of dowel, stuck in place with glue, and drill new holes to the correct size before replacing the fixing. See page 27 for details of this repair, which is often needed to fix loose hinges on household doors, too.

Buy replacements for metal parts that become bent or twisted. Bending these back into shape will weaken the metal and make it more likely to break in future.

GETTING FURNITURE LEGS EVEN

If a chair, table or chest wobbles because its legs are not all the same length, use strips of wood to extend one leg.

Place cardboard under the shorter leg and check the surface with a spirit level. You may need to extend two legs to get the top surface of a table to lie horizontal.

If your furniture has wooden legs, find a piece of wood that is just smaller than the size of the foot and cut off several thin pieces using a tenon saw or fine-toothed hacksaw.

Then, ensuring the item is on a level surface, slip a number of these strips under the short leg until it is level and stable. Glue the pieces into place on the bottom of the leg, 'clamping' them while the glue sets using the weight of the furniture, or by placing a heavy object on the seat of a chair.

This extension to the leg should be virtually invisible while the piece is in use, but you may want to stain or varnish it to match the legs.

For a metal chair, glue a rubber or plastic 'foot' of the correct height to the bottom of the leg to extend it. There may be an existing plastic or rubber foot in place. If so, it may be better to remove this and replace it with a new fitting with more height.

The best glue to attach these different materials together is epoxy resin, which will set hard and be very durable.

TABLES

Wooden table legs can be attached in a number of different ways. Usually a frame that links the legs is attached with woodworking joints, which may be reinforced with a block or a metal bolt fitting.

Metal table legs are often attached in a similar way, with bolts replacing the woodworking joints. A tubular frame may simply be welded together.

If a table starts to wobble, you can often stabilise it by tightening any bolts or screws, or you may need to replace corner blocks, bolts or metal plates.

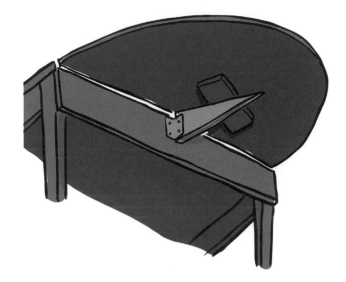

A SAGGING DROP-LEAF TABLE

Many dining tables have additional 'leaves' that can be folded up to extend the table top. Wear and tear, or shrinkage of wood components, can mean that the leaves sag and are no longer held completely flat by the folding supports.

It's very easy to fix this problem – simply glue a thin piece of wood under the table top to raise it up.

Another problem with drop-leaf tables may occur if the hinges are damaged and need replacing. See page xx for information about fixing furniture hinges.

DIFFERENT WAYS OF ATTACHING TABLE LEGS

ADDING A NEW VENEER SURFACE TO A COFFEE TABLE

Coffee tables suffer a lot, with frequent spills and hot cups damaging the finish, people using them to stand on or rest their feet, and children using them as craft tables.

They are also relatively small, and a single piece of natural veneer can often be large enough to cover them. The same technique can be used to put a new surface on many other small pieces of furniture.

CHOOSING VENEER AND EDGING

Natural wood veneers come in a very wide range of timbers and are sold in 'leaves' – strips that vary in width from a few centimetres to half a metre. The length of a leaf can be a metre or more. Veneer is very thin and delicate, but can make a very beautiful and durable surface once glued into place.

Veneer is sold mail order through websites dedicated to the craft of marquetry (making intricate veneer patterns) and is not very expensive.

Alternatively, you may prefer to add a laminate surface to your table. Laminates are stiff melamine sheets, which can have coloured or patterned surfaces, artificial wood patterns or a layer of real timber.

The advantage of laminate is that it comes in larger sheet sizes and the surface is pre-finished and hard-wearing. However, it is harder to cut with hand tools than natural veneer.

Veneer laminates are easy to find online and are sold by most timber merchants, who may also cut a piece to size for you.

When you have added the new surface, you will also need to add edging to your new table top. For both laminate and natural veneer surfaces, the best solution is usually iron-on edging strip, made from timber with a layer of heat-activated glue. Choose your veneer and edging strip carefully to get a close match – edging strip is only available in a limited number of timber types.

For non-timber melamine laminates, edging strips are also available to match a range of colours and patterns.

TOOLS YOU WILL NEED

A natural wood veneer is very thin, so you can cut out the rough shape using a craft knife. For laminate, you will need a hand saw or powered jigsaw if the supplier has not cut it to size.

You will also need sandpaper and a sanding block to prepare the surface, rags for cleaning, the appropriate adhesive and a wallpaper seam roller tool to press down the surface evenly.

TABLES

THE STEPS

1. First you will need to measure and cut out your veneer. For a small, flat table top, using the table itself, placing the table itself upside down on the veneer sheet is the best way to do this. Be careful to lift the table on and off the veneer without tearing it.

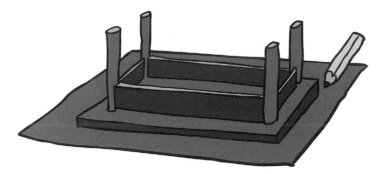

2. Once you have marked the reverse side of the veneer with a pencil, cut roughly around the shape a few millimetres outside the pencil line. If using laminate, cut the piece more accurately along the pencil lines to get a piece almost exactly the same size as the table top, which you can sand smooth later.

3. Now prepare the table top for glueing. Sand it flat with coarse sandpaper and a sanding block, then clean away any dust.

4. The right glue depends on the type of table top you have chosen. For laminates, a strong PVA wood glue is suitable. This is applied to both surfaces and then pressed down firmly while it dries. For veneer, contact adhesive gives a better bond. This is applied to both surfaces and sticks instantly when they are brought together.

5. If you are using PVA, you can adjust the position of the surface before the glue dries. But, if you are using contact adhesive, it's important to line things up properly before you let the veneer touch the table top. To help with this, spread glue over the table top and the veneer, then place a sheet of newspaper on the table, leaving just a centimetre of exposed glue at one end.

Then, take the veneer and line it up with the table top, keeping it clear of the glue. When you are happy with its position, stick it down at the exposed end then carefully pull out the newspaper.

8. Finally, lie the table on its side to apply the edging strip. Iron it in place, protecting the wood with a cloth. The overlapping edges of the strips can also be sanded off to create smooth corners.

Your table top is now complete. Finish the wood by sanding lightly and applying oil, wax or varnish. If the legs are made of a different type of wood, you may want to stain the legs or table top to get a closer match, or paint the legs in a complementary colour.

6. Use a wallpaper roller to smooth down the surface and push out any air bubbles. Prick any stubborn bubbles with the tip of a craft knife to release the air.

7. Use fine sandpaper to remove the overlapping edges of the veneer. It is so thin that a few gentle strokes with the paper along the edge will cut through it.

CHESTS & CUPBOARDS

The most common fixes needed for sideboards, cupboards and chests are re-attaching a door that has come away from its hinges and making repairs to drawers.

FIXING HINGES

When doors are pulled, twisted or have heavy loads placed on them, hinge screws can be pulled out and the hinges themselves can break.

It is unlikely that a screw will pull out so cleanly that a new one can simply be put back in its place, but creating a new, solid hole is a quick repair.

Use a thin piece of dowel or several matchsticks to plug the hole, gluing them into place with PVA wood glue. Leave the glue to harden for 24 hours then drill a new pilot hole for the screw.

If the door or frame is badly damaged, you may want to move the hinge to a new position.

Some types of hinges need to be set in a recess in the surface. Create this using a saw, hammer and chisel to mark out the edges of the recess and then carve out the wood.

USE A CHISEL TO CUT A RECESS FOR A NEW HINGE

REPLACEMENT HINGES

If the hinge itself breaks, you will need to replace it. If you can't find an exact match in the hardware shop, it helps to understand the different types of hinges available, so you can find one that will allow the door to open and close in the same way.

BUTT HINGE
For a door to sit flat against the cabinet, the two faces of this hinge should be set in recesses in the two faces.

FLUSH HINGE
In a flush hinge, one face folds inside the other. As the resulting plate is only one layer thick, it is not essential to set this hinge in a recess.

CONCEALED HINGE
These are very common in kitchen cabinets and allow adjacent doors to be fitted close together as they allow the door to open outwards, away from the cabinet.

The section attached to the door needs to sit in a hollow. If you need to replace one of these hinges, choose a model that will fit in your existing hollow, or you will have to extend it using a drill with a large 'spade bit'.

Concealed hinges are designed to be adjusted in order to line up a row of doors – see page 147.

180 DEGREE HINGES
Some doors and flaps need to fold back over the adjacent surface. Cylinder and counter hinges allow space for the two surfaces to fold over without impinging on each other.

MENDING DRAWERS

Most drawers have sides and backs made of unfinished MDF, plywood or thin solid wood boards, with a better quality solid wood or veneered front. Simple, glued wood-working joints – or more complex dovetail joints – are used to hold these panels together.

Each piece of the drawer has a groove near its bottom edge, which holds a hardboard or plywood base within the frame.

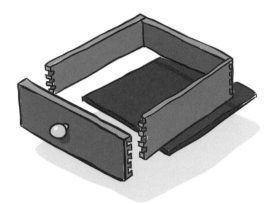

REPAIRING JOINTS

Drawer joints can be glued back together in the same way as other woodworking joints, and can be reinforced with panel pins if needed.

Glue is also the best way to secure a slot-in drawer bottom made of hardboard, if it starts to sag.

A broken drawer bottom is simple to replace. I recommend using hardboard as it is very easy to cut and shape. Remove the front panel of the drawer to slide the new base into place.

REPAIRING RUNNERS

Drawers may rest and slide on their bases, with a narrow shelf separating each drawer within the cabinet. Alternatively, they may run on strips fixed to the sides of the cabinet or metal fittings that are screwed on to the drawer and the cabinet.

If you need to remove a drawer that is held on metal runners, you will need to release the retaining screw holding the drawer on to the inner part of the sliding metal unit.

If a metal runner unit breaks, you can unscrew it and take it to a hardware or DIY store to find a replacement of the same size.

If a runner comes away from the cabinet, you can glue and screw it back into place. A broken runner can be replaced by a new one. Cut runners to the correct size and shape from plywood or solid hardwood, which will be durable and give a smooth surface for the drawer to slide against. You may be able to buy a plastic runner of the correct size, which is even easier to install.

Lubricate runners with candle wax to keep drawers running smoothly.

ADDING NEW HANDLES

Drawer handles may have integral screw threads that are driven into the drawer front, or they may be held in place with bolts and nuts tightened from inside the drawer.

Changing the handles on a chest can give it a whole new look. If you want to fit a different type of handle to your drawers, you can create new holes for bolts, or move handles to new positions by filling in and covering old holes with wood stopper or filler – see page xx.

CATCHES

A cupboard door that won't stay shut can be helped to stay in place by fitting a magnetic or ball and socket catch. These are very easy to find and fix in place.

STAIRS & FLOORBOARDS

Not strictly furniture, but I've included these items here as they require similar skills to mending other wooden items.

Stairs and floors squeak because adjacent pieces of wood are loose and rubbing against each other and there are many ways of fixing them back into place.

LOOSE FLOORBOARDS

A floorboard can be held down by hammering in new nails at an angle, or by adding a screw. Both these fixings must be attached to the floor joists beneath the boards.

You can see where the floor joists are by checking the pattern of other nails holding down the floorboards. However, you should also check for electrical cables and water pipes. Use a pipe and stud detector or lift the board up to check the space below.

If you are using a screw, drill a countersunk hole so that the screw head can sit below the level of the floor and then be hidden with filler (see page 82 for advice on drilling countersunk holes for screws).

CREAKY STAIRS

If you can get access to the space below the stairs, this will make repairs easier, especially if they are covered with carpet.

Any obvious problems with the blocks or wedges supporting the treads and risers that make up the staircase can be fixed from below. If the stairs seem secure, you will need a helper to walk up and down them so that you can identify which stairs are causing the creaks.

Screws placed upwards through the back of a tread into the riser above can help it to stay firm, or you can fix a new support block to secure it to the riser below (ask your helper to sit on the stair above while you fit the new block).

If you can't get access to the stairs from below, you will

STAIRS & FLOORBOARDS

have to fold back any carpet and screw down through the tread into the riser below.

Ensure you drill pilot holes for screws that you will insert into the edge of any solid wood boards, or they may split.

BANNISTERS AND HANDRAILS

Loose bannister rails and posts can be secured by driving long nails at an angle through the posts into the rail above or stair below.

Tap the nails beneath the surface after hammering and fill the hole with stopper or filler.

Separate hand rails need to be fixed securely to a wall using strong fixings. If they come loose, follow the advice on pages 40-1 to reattach them safely to the wall.

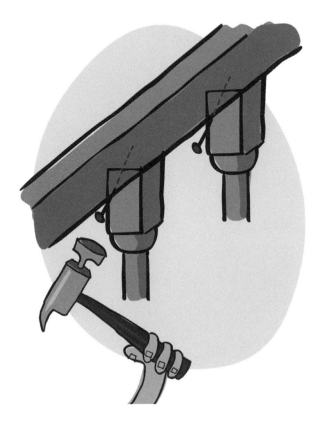

PICTURE & MIRROR FRAMES

Frames are usually built using mitre joints, with a rebate that holds the glass in place and a hardboard backing, secured to the frame with small panel pins or metal clips.

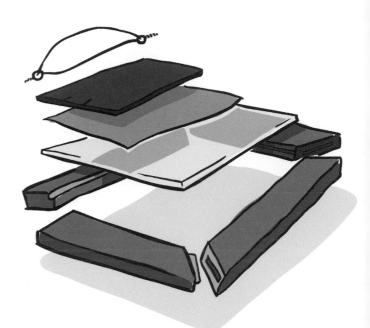

REPAIRING JOINTS

If the mitre joints come loose or break, you can fix them with glue, as shown on page 80.

'Clamp' the joints while the glue dries by wrapping strips of thick masking tape tightly around the frame in both directions.

If needed, strengthen the joints by hammering in a nail. Flat steel brackets can be used to brace broken joints on large, heavy frames.

REPLACING EYELETS

The simplest way to attach picture wire to your frame is to use threaded eyelets. Put these in place without the glass in the frame, to reduce the risk of breaking it with your knuckles while screwing them in. Make sure you leave enough space to reinsert the glass when choosing where to place the eyelets.

Eyelets can be difficult to screw into hardwood but, with the glass safely out of the way, you can grip them with pliers. Hammer a small pilot hole with a panel pin to help them go in more smoothly.

REPLACING GLASS

If you need to replace the glass in a frame or mirror, give measurements just smaller than the outside measurement of the rebate to the glass supplier, who will cut it to size. Tell them what the glass is for and they will supply a suitable thickness.

When measuring up, check the frame is square with a try-square, or by measuring both diagonals and checking they are the same length. If not, and the frame will shift slightly, square the frame using brackets to pull the joints into line or by using a nail to fix one of the corners.

If the frame is not quite square and can't be shifted, make a template from paper and take this to the glass supplier instead.

PICTURE & MIRROR FRAMES

REPAIRING A MOULDED FRAME

Part of a moulded or carved frame may become damaged, and you can patch this using epoxy filler.

Follow the advice on page 136 for mixing this two-part modelling material. First make a mould for the new part by pressing the filler over a part of the frame that isn't damaged.

Remove the mould carefully from the frame while still soft and let the epoxy mould harden overnight. Then, mix up a second batch of filler and press this into the mould. Pull it out before it hardens and leave it to set. Once it has set it can be cut and shaped to fit into the damaged section.

DECORATING FRAMES

Wooden frames can be finished with paint, varnish, oil, wax, stain and all the other wood finishes described in this section, but you can also use metallic paint or even gold leaf to make them look more spectacular.

Another excellent way to make the detail of mouldings stand out is to rub over a small amount of decorative gilt wax, which is available in craft shops. This can also be used to cover up scratches in a gilt frame.

Covering a frame in fabric or coating it in glitter are also good ways to achieve a decorative finish.

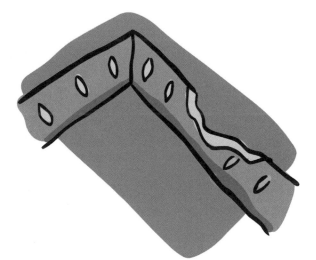

METAL FURNITURE

Garden furniture with metal parts and fittings is frequently wet and very susceptible to rust and corrosion.

Indoor furniture will not suffer from the same problems, but items in bathrooms and kitchens may need extra protection, and brass fittings may tarnish if they are not cleaned from time to time with metal polish. Make sure you protect the surrounding surfaces with masking tape while you use this abrasive substance.

DEALING WITH RUST

Rust forms when bare iron or steel is exposed to both water and air, so keeping metal parts dry and protective coatings in good condition is important.

A good way to protect shiny, plated metal is to add a thin layer of acrylic varnish. If it becomes chipped over time, it can be easily removed with a solvent and replaced.

It is also a good idea to paint a layer of varnish on to the bolts and nuts that hold garden furniture together.

Ironwork in the garden lasts longest when it is painted. Special types of enamel paint are designed specifically for this purpose and come in a range of smooth and 'hammered' finishes and colours.

Prepare the metal first by cleaning and scrubbing off any existing rust using coarse steel wool or a wire brush. Make sure the metal is completely dry before starting to paint.

Use a small, stiff brush to apply the paint to complex shapes and protect any paving from spills, which can lead to permanent stains.

REFURBISHING CHROME FURNITURE

Tubular chrome furniture was invented in the 1920s as part of a new utilitarian trend in furniture design, and was inspired by the tubing used to make bicycles. Since then it's been in and out of fashion and, in particular, was a huge phenomenon in the 1980s.

Not all of this tubing is chrome or silver in colour. Over the years, brass tubing has also been used to make some particularly garish furniture for bathrooms and bedrooms.

Much of this furniture is now reaching the stage of becoming old and being thrown away. However, even if other parts have worn out, the tubular parts of these pieces are ideal for reusing and recycling into new pieces.

I found an old metal-legged stool in a skip which I turned into a neat coffee table, and I have also painted an old metal lampstand in cream enamel to create a unique and stylish floorlamp.

The problem that most commonly affects plated tubing is rust on the surface. Scratches let moisture through to the steel below and soon the surface is marked with little brown spots. This is made much worse if things are left out in the rain, but even very rusty tubing can still be saved.

While you can't restore the original plating, you can add a new hardwearing and attractive surface by sanding it down and painting with tough enamel. This comes in a very wide range of colours and looks very modern when combined with natural or painted wood components.

A NEW TOP FOR A GLASS AND CHROME SIDE TABLE

Nested glass and chrome coffee tables were everywhere 20 years ago. The dark glass look is a bit dated now, but they are a great design and, with a lick of paint and a new table top, they can look very good again. Here's a very simple project to reclaim a classic for the twenty-first century.

TOOLS YOU WILL NEED
A suitable piece of plywood or MDF at the same thickness as the glass (usually around 6mm), a screwdriver, a suitable saw (hand hacksaw or a power jigsaw), sandpaper and enamel paint and brushes.

You may also need replacement supports for the table tops (see diagram) or replacement plastic inserts for the bottoms of the legs.

Choose the plywood or MDF to suit how you want the table to look. If you want a smooth, painted table, then plain MDF is great, or choose veneered MDF or a hardwood-faced plywood if you want a natural wood finish. Wood finishes are easier to keep going in the long term than painted finishes, although a painted gloss finish can last for years.

If you want to paint your table top, choose a colour to co-ordinate with the legs.

THE PLASTIC SUPPORTS MAY GET LOST. REPLACE THEM WITH DOWEL OR PLASTIC RODS FROM HARDWARE SHOPS.

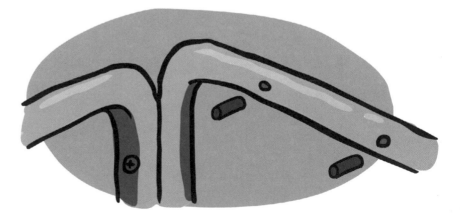

METAL FURNITURE

THE STEPS

1. Start by measuring up for your new table top. If the glass surface is intact, keep it and use it as a template. If it is missing, stand up the table legs, making sure they are square and measure carefully inside the frame. The best way to decide on the right curved angle for your corners is by trying out various circular objects from your home in the space, and then using the one that matches best to mark up your corners.

2. Once you have the dimensions you need, you can take the frame apart. The legs will be held together with screws or bolts, which you should keep for later.

3. Clean the separated table legs in warm soapy water and dry carefully before sanding them down with fine 'wet and dry' paper. This will remove the surface rust and get it ready for painting. You are not aiming to scrub away all the remaining plate, but to create a smooth 'keyed' surface texture.

4. Painting is the tricky part. One way to make it easier is by hanging up the legs using hooks made from coathanger wire.

5. Give the legs two thin coats of enamel paint in the finish you want, leaving the paint to dry completely between coats. This will give a much more durable finish than one thick coat, and will reduce the risk of drips and runs.

6. Once the legs are painted and dry, you can reassemble the legs with the original bolts or screws, insert new feet if necessary, and insert the supports that will hold up the table top.

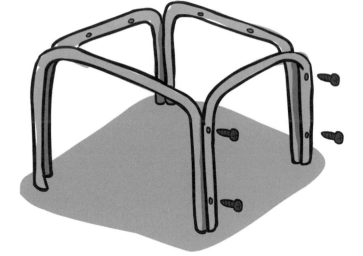

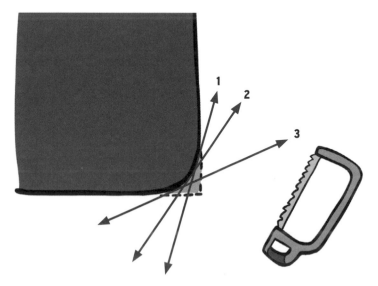

You may now also want to paint the heads of the screws with a thin coat of paint to match the legs. Do this carefully with a small paintbrush and avoid letting paint run into the joint, where it will dry and make the screw difficult to remove in the future.

7. Now (or meanwhile) make your new table top. Mark the shape on your MDF or plywood and cut it out using either a hacksaw or a jigsaw. A jigsaw can cut a smooth line right round the shape. If you are using a hacksaw, start by cutting out a square, then remove the corner material using a series of straight cuts and finally sand the corners to a smooth curve.

8. Smooth the edges and corners of the table top using glasspaper and a sanding block, or by clamping the piece and using a power sander.

9. If you are using veneered MDF or plywood, you may also want to iron on a strip of hardwood edging for a really neat finish, although this edge won't be easily visible on the final piece.

10. Finally, sand the surface of the table top and paint, oil or varnish it before dropping the new table top on to the supports. A great way to get a really smooth finish on a table top made of MDF or plywood is to apply primer then add several thin coats of gloss paint using a small foam roller. This will virtually eliminate brush marks and create a really long-lasting finish.

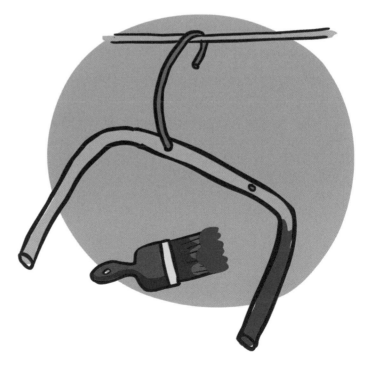

FURNISHING WITH FABRICS

It is often the soft parts of furnishings that wear out first. However, a burn, tear or permanent stain on upholstery doesn't have to mean throwing away the whole piece. Replacing fabric can be an excellent way to give your home a new look without splashing out on new furniture.

Upholstery is a skilled profession but, with some basic techniques and a careful eye, even an amateur can carry out a range of simple repairs that look as good as an expert job. If a project seems too much for you, don't despair – quotes from upholstery repair businesses may still work out cheaper than replacing furniture, and will save resources and support your local economy, too.

In this section, you can find out how to replace fabrics on more than just cushions. From deckchairs to desks, and from linen to leather, these ideas will inspire you to get to grips with soft furnishings all over your home.

Getting a smooth line and a comfortable finish on upholstered furniture depends on the foundations that underlie the final fabric covering. A simple foam cushion can be great for giving more bounce to a lumpy armchair base but, for upholstered parts of chairs, foam is not resilient or dense enough to create a long-lasting comfortable pad.

SAFETY NOTE

You should spray new covers and upholstery materials with fireproofing to help them resist flames and burns.

Household fireproofing spray is available from and hardware stores. Follow the instructions on the packaging to protect your fabrics, and reapply after washing, which will remove the protective coating provided by the spray.

Don't re-use old foam fillings, as these are unlikely to meet modern fireproofing standards.

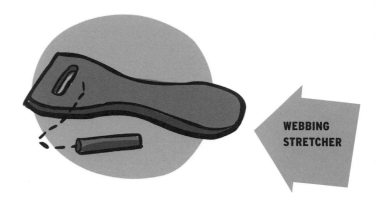

WEBBING STRETCHER

UPHOLSTERY TOOLS AND MATERIALS

Using the right tools helps make the job easier and neater. None of these tools or materials are expensive, but they can be difficult to find on the high street. Look for them in specialist craft and sewing shops, or get them mail-order from internet suppliers.

UPHOLSTERY NEEDLES
A special half-circle shaped needle makes an easy job of sewing a seam when you only have access to one side of the material.

UPHOLSTERY PINS
These are longer and stronger than ordinary dressmaking pins, with a looped end. You will need these only if you are covering large areas of cushion and fixing fabric at the edges and corners of a project, such as when re-covering an armchair.

WEBBING
Webbing gives support and 'bounce' to a hollow seat base. It must be stretched firmly over the frame and is nailed or clipped into place. It is easier to get the tension right on rubber webbing, as you can calculate the amount of 'stretch' you need to give it (usually ten per cent) and then pull it to the correct new length.

STRETCHER
If you need to use webbing, pulling it tight by hand can't achieve the right tension. This simple wooden tool grips the webbing and then levers against the edge of a frame to pull it tight.

HESSIAN
An inexpensive fabric that is used over webbing to help stop stuffing from escaping.

UPHOLSTERY TACKS

STUFFING

For thin pads, wadding (see below) can make up all the layers of stuffing. However, for thicker pads, a firmer result comes from using a layer of fibres to make up the bulk of the pad. Traditional stuffing was made with animal hair, but modern stuffing materials are made from synthetic black fibres or from plant fibres, such as coconut hair.

TWINE

This is thick, strong nylon or natural thread that is used to hold stuffing in place and help give shape to your pads and cushions.

CALICO

A plain cotton fabric that is used to contain and shape stuffing. A calico cover over the main stuffing layer helps create the final shape of the pad and is held in place with stitches, small upholstery nails or staples.

WADDING

Made from polyester, this fluffy material can be used as a filling in a thin pad, and is used as a final layer in thicker pads and over foam, to give a softer surface and fuller shape.

TOP FABRIC

This is the final, decorative layer, and is stitched or nailed in place. Finishing touches to hide seams and hold it in place can include domed decorative nails, or a row of trim, glued or sewn on.

UPHOLSTERY TACKS

These are wedge shaped with a very fine point which can be pushed into place by hand before tapping in with a hammer. They come in a range of sizes and weights, and which type to use depends on the material you're hammering them into and whether the head will show. Use the smallest tack that will do the job – you will use a lot of them, so each one doesn't have to hold a lot of weight.

HAMMER

An ordinary smallish household hammer is fine for most upholstery work. A very large hammer isn't easy to use accurately, and you will risk bashing and denting the surrounding wood.

DOMED UPHOLSTERY NAILS

These are an excellent way to finish off a pad on a solid base. They provide a decorative edge as well as holding the fabric securely. Tap in with a wooden mallet, rather than a metal hammer, to avoid damaging the finish.

STAPLE GUN

Not used by traditional upholsterers, but an excellent cheat's way to fix unseen fabric edges in place quickly. As staples are very thin, you risk tearing the fabric unless you place the staples very closely together to spread the load. You'll also need a claw-shaped staple remover, as you will often need to take out and replace staples to get a really neat finish.

DOMED UPHOLSTERY NAILS

ADVICE ON TOP FABRICS

There are a vast range of upholstery fabrics available in a variety of finishes, colours and patterns. Choose fabrics that match your style, but also bear in mind practical considerations such as wear and stain resistance.

For projects like re-covering an armchair, choose fabrics intended specifically for upholstery, with good fireproofing properties. These are also thicker and more hard-wearing, which is particularly important for fabrics covering corners and arm-rests.

Projects where the top fabric is easy to replace, such as re-covering a drop-in dining chair seat, have more flexibility. Look for good second-hand fabrics for these jobs, such as reclaimed curtains.

MAKING REPLACEMENT FOAM CUSHIONS

The foam cushions on sofas and armchairs can wear out in two ways. The fabric can be damaged or the foam itself may deteriorate, compress and lose its shape over time.

If only the fabric has failed, you can simply remove it and make a replacement cover following the steps below.

If the foam is worn out as well, you will need to get a replacement cushion. Luckily, foam is easy to find and very easy to shape.

CHOOSING FOAM

Foam comes in different materials, densities and levels of softness. The most common and least expensive types are made from polyurethane, but natural latex foam is also common. Make sure any foam you buy isn't made with ozone-damaging chlorofluorocarbons.

The more dense the foam, the more weight it can handle and the longer it will last. For seating, get foam with a 'density' of 35kg or more. Most suppliers will have foam products they recommend for seating cushions and will indicate these in their catalogues and websites.

SHAPING FOAM

Many stockists will cut foam to size and will create irregular shapes if you provide a template. If you need to make any adjustments, foam is easily cut with a craft knife (for thinner foam), with a hacksaw or even a serrated kitchen knife.

Foam will come with a squared-off edge, which will become slightly rounded once wrapped in wadding and stuffed into a cushion. If you want a more rounded profile, or a complex three-dimensional shape, stick layers together and fold over edges using contact adhesive or permanent spray adhesive (use this outside and not on a windy day!).

CREATE CURVED EDGES BY GLUING AND FOLDING LAYERS OF FOAM.

TOOLS AND MATERIALS YOU WILL NEED

A foam cushion (the old one, or a new one cut to size), wadding, calico to sew around the wadding, new top fabric material, a zip as long as the rear edge of the cushion, possibly some piping cord, a regular needle, an upholstery needle and lots of thread one shade darker than the main colour in your top fabric.

THE STEPS

1. Start by wrapping the foam in a layer of wadding and wrapping this, in turn, in a cover of calico. The calico can be very simply wrapped around the cushion, trimmed off and folded under. Sew seams in situ along the resulting edges with a running stitch, using a half-circular needle.

The calico will help stop the wadding or foam being caught in the zip. Sew it on relatively snugly, but not so tight that the foam is compressed.

2. Now measure up for the panels for your cover. Follow the pattern shown, with a two-part rear panel for the zip, and cut extra 3cm strips for piping along the relevant edges, if needed.

3. Pin and sew the straight side seams of the cushion up to 5cm from the front corners. Use a close running stitch and include piping in the top and bottom seams if necessary. Wrap the piping material around piping cord before including it in the seams.

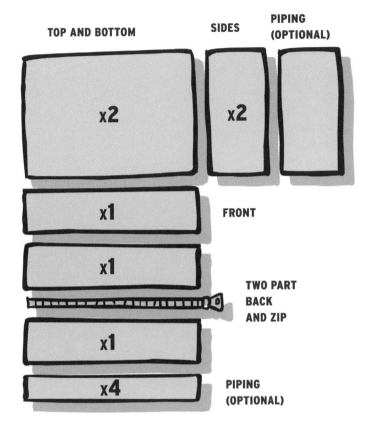

TOP AND BOTTOM   SIDES   PIPING (OPTIONAL)

x2   x2

x1   FRONT

x1

TWO PART BACK AND ZIP

x1

x4   PIPING (OPTIONAL)

MAKING REPLACEMENT FOAM CUSHIONS

PIN THE CORNER HEMS INSIDE OUT ON THE CUSHION

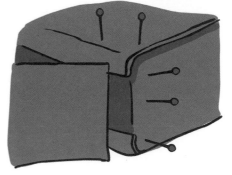

FINISH OFF THE BACK PANEL WITH THE GOOD SIDE OUTWARDS

4. To get the front corners right, it's best to pin these in place on the cushion itself. Place the half-sewn cover, inside out, around the cushion and adjust it to sit correctly at the corners. Now, use normal dressmakers' pins to pin the fabric (and piping) around the corner neatly, snipping the hem allowance if needed to get the fabric to lie flat.

Pin the hems right around the front edge, then remove the cover from the cushion, check the piping looks neat from the 'good' side, adjusting if necessary before sewing the pinned seams.

5. Now you need to fit the zip to the back panel. Sew the closed zip on to the two pieces of the back panel before attaching them to the rest of the cover. Leave about 2cm of space beyond the zip at each end and leave the two halves separate at the ends. Allow about 5cm of spare material each side of where the corners will lie.

6. Now pin and sew the back panel on to the cover, stopping about 5cm from the two corners.

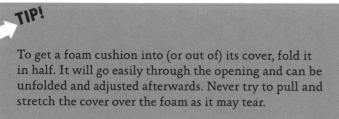

TIP!

To get a foam cushion into (or out of) its cover, fold it in half. It will go easily through the opening and can be unfolded and adjusted afterwards. Never try to pull and stretch the cover over the foam as it may tear.

USE SLIP STITCH WHEN SEWING FROM THE GOOD SIDE

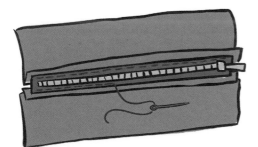

SEW THE ZIP INTO THE BACK PANEL BEFORE ATTACHING IT

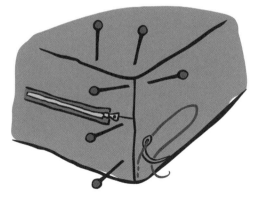

MAKING REPLACEMENT FOAM CUSHIONS

ATTACHING PIPING AROUND THE BACK CORNERS

Adding piping to the straight seams is relatively simpl but, when sewing up corners from the 'good' side of the chusion, including piping can be a fiddly process.

The best tactic is to use plenty of pins to hold the fabric and piping in place, thn use slip stitch to hold everything in place.

7. Finishing off the back corners is best done with the cover on the cushion – this time with the right side of the cover outwards. Start by folding the side panel material under the top cover and back panel, then fold under a hem allowance for the back panel and lie this on top of the side panel and under the top panel.

Pin this arrangement using upholstery pins or long dressmakers' pins, using them like skewers. Sew the top and side seams using slip stitch (see page 187) and a half-circular upholstery needle so that the seams line up with the physical corner of the cushion. Be careful not to sew the top fabric on to the calico.

Then, remove the pins, turn the cushion over and repeat this for the bottom corners.

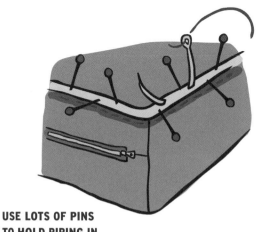

USE LOTS OF PINS TO HOLD PIPING IN PLACE BEFORE SEWING WITH SLIP STITCH

CHANGING A CANE SEAT FOR AN UPHOLSTERED PAD

Cane seats get frayed and dirty after a while. It's possible to weave a new cane seat – you can buy sea grass or other materials and thread this systematically through the holes according to the same pattern.

For a more individual look, and a longer-lasting and more comfortable replacement, why not follow these steps to replace the cane with a padded cushion instead? This project doesn't involve any sewing, and doesn't use a lot of fabric, so a small offcut can be used to revamp a whole set of chairs.

TOOLS AND MATERIALS YOU WILL NEED
Scissors, twine and a long, thick needle for repairing the cane (possibly webbing and a stretcher instead), staple gun and staples, hessian, calico, polyester wadding and top fabric, upholstery tacks and domed upholstery nails for the edging.

THE STEPS
1. First tidy up the cane to provide a support for your new pad. Depending on its condition, you can either reinforce it with twine (no need to do this very neatly) or remove it and add webbing instead.

Webbing should be stretched tightly over the seat, using a stretching tool, then held in place with tacks. Place the tacks near to the central hole, so you have space around the webbing to create your new pad. Rubber webbing should be stretched about ten per cent more than its natural length, which will give a firm, bouncy seat support.

STRENGHTEN THE CANE WITH TWINE

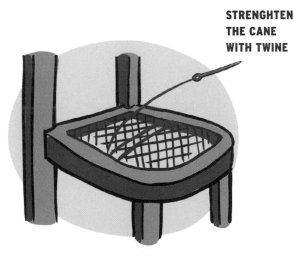

STAPLE ON A LAYER OF HESSIAN

2. Now cut a piece of hessian about 2cm larger than the hole, fold over its edges and staple it in place over the webbing or cane, placing the staples close to the inner edge. This will prevent the stuffing from coming through the holes in the webbing or cane.

3. Next, add the main layer of stuffing. For this project, a simple pad of pure wadding is fine. Pile up a few layers of wadding to around double the height of the final pad. Tease and taper the edges of the wadding so that it is almost flat at the edges of the seat.

ADD WADDING

COVER THE WADDING WITH CALICO

4. Now cover the wadding with a layer of calico. This is the stage that will determine the shape and neatness of your final pad and getting an even tension around the whole pad is important.

Start with two or three temporary (half tapped-in) tacks or staples at the back edge, pull the calico over to the front and attach it with two or three more tacks, then attach the centre of both sides. Check the tension and then work around the whole pad either stapling or tacking the calico every 2cm or so.

Be prepared to do this job carefully, removing and replacing staples or tacks until you get it right.

5. Finish the pad with a final thin layer of wadding and a top cover of fabric. Measure for the final cover across the the finished pad at its tallest point, allowing sufficient excess material all around for a 'hem' that will be held firmly by the finishing nails. Snip the hem allowance all around so that it will fold under without creating kinks.

Don't iron this hem, as you will be stretching the fabric into shape and it isn't possible, at this stage, to be sure exactly where the fold will need to be.

6. Small upholstery tacks should be used to attach the top cover at first. These are more easily hidden by the decorative nails than staples. Start tacking at opposite sides of the pad again, then work around at 2–3cm intervals to get a firm, even tension.

7. Once you are happy with the final shape of the pad and the top cover looks neat, finish off with a row of closely spaced domed upholstery nails all around the edge, very slightly overlapping the fabric edge and covering the tacks.

If you prefer, you can place the tacks more closely and then tack, glue or sew on a trim. You can get special tiny upholstery tacks for attaching trim. Trim on upholstery is also known as 'gimp', so these are called 'gimp pins' and come in a range of colours.

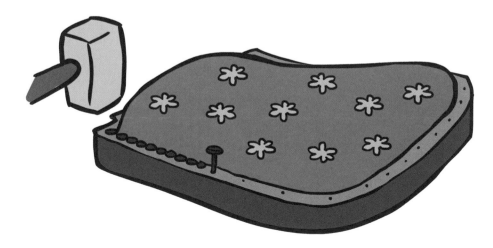

FINISH OFF WITH DOMED NAILS

RE-COVERING A DROP-IN SEAT ON A DINING CHAIR

Many dining chairs have a padded sheet of plywood or webbed frame that simply rests in a rebated hole in the chair to provide a seat cushion. Replacing the cover and stuffing on this 'drop-in seat' is a very easy job that can be done almost entirely with a staple gun, without needing special tools.

Bent wood 'café style' chairs usually either have cane seats or a wooden flat or moulded seat that sits in a similar rebate in the frame. Although these are often glued in place, you can also remove them to add an upholstered pad using these steps.

With a café seat, the space you have around the seat will be reduced by the padding, so you should sand down the edge of the panel by a few millimetres to ensure it will still fit once covered.

TOOLS AND MATERIALS YOU WILL NEED

Top fabric and calico, perhaps replacement hessian, twine, stuffing and wadding, a staple gun and a supply of staples.

THE STEPS

1. First remove the original top fabric. If it is tacked in place, use a small chisel to lever out the tacks. Check the condition of the existing pad. The stuffing inside may have been pushed out of shape by years of people sitting on it, and the edges may be very flat. If so, it's worth taking the pad apart and filling it again.

2. If you need to replace the padding, remove the calico cover and any wadding and take out the stuffing material. Keep the stuffing for re-use if the fibres are still in good condition.

3. You will now have a seat pad that has been reduced to bare plywood or a hessian cover on top of strips of webbing. Check the condition of these and see if they can be kept. Repair any webbing, if necessary, and staple on a new hessian layer.

4. Now you can add a layer of new stuffing. Make the layer thicker in the centre than at the edges, but don't leave the edges bare. The stuffing should slightly overlap them to protect the top fabric from fraying.

5. Now cover with calico, starting by stapling it on the reverse of the pad in the centre of one edge and stretching it over the stuffing to the other side. Then pull the sides over in the same way and check you have an even dome in the centre. Continue stapling towards the corners, leaving about 3cm unstapled at each corner.

6. Finish off the corners by pulling the calico firmly into a point and folding it under. Adjust the tension and replace any staples if needed.

7. Now finish off with wadding and top fabric. Check how the drop-in seat fits into the chair. If it's a tight fit, cut the wadding to finish at the edge of the seat. Measure the top fabric to give around 3cm of fabric under the seat.

8. Fix the top fabric using the same order of stapling as for the calico, taking care to get the tension even. Leave the corners until last, then pull the fabric firmly into a point before folding under the seat and stapling into place.

The drop-in seat should now have a smooth surface without creases and can be dropped into place.

RE-COVERING AN ARMCHAIR

Armchairs can become worn and tired and lumpy with years of use. The project earlier in the book showed how to replace the cushion but the fabric covering the rest of the chair may need to be replaced as well.

This is an ambitious project, but isn't as hard as it seems. With a half-circular upholstery needle and the ability to slip-stitch seams neatly, the job can be done effectively by a keen amateur.

I have covered both armchairs and sofas in the past, and love the process of fitting together pieces of fabric to cover a three-dimensional shape, and sewing up tidy corner seams.

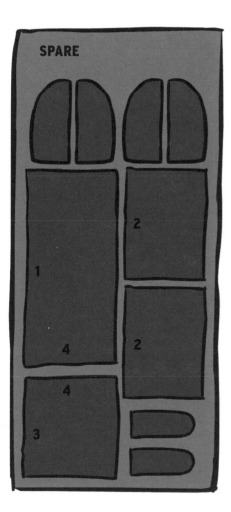

RE-COVERING AN ARMCHAIR

Before you start the project, plan the project carefully. Look at the way your armchair is made and where the fabric can be attached to the frame with staples and tacks, and where seams will need to be sewn.

Measure everything very carefully, and check your measurements twice before buying or cutting any fabric.

Measure up and sketch the pieces you will need for the top fabric on the original chair, allowing at least 2.5cm of excess fabric around every edge, partly to make up for the extra wadding, and so that you will be able to create a substantial 'hem'.

At the arms and back, allow extra length so that the top fabric can extend below the level of the seat by at least 10cm.

Sketch the pieces you will need on a shape that is the width of the fabric roll and then, depending on the pattern you have chosen, allow at least three pattern repeats of length to this to allow for matching the pattern when constructing the cover.

BUYING FABRIC

Plain fabrics and small patterns are the safest fabrics to choose. Large patterns can be very difficult to match up neatly, so save these for scatter cushions instead.

If this is one of your first upholstery projects, I don't recommend including piping in your plans, as it's very fiddly to fit neatly around all the corners. For neat results as a beginner, it's best to use a thick fabric with a simple textured or woven pattern and sew plain, neat seams around the edges.

TOOLS AND MATERIALS YOU WILL NEED

Wadding, top fabric, scissors, upholstery pins and tacks, hammer, staple gun and staples, straight needles, a half-circular upholstery needle and plenty of thread, one shade darker than the main colour of the top fabric.

THE STEPS

1. You shouldn't need to remove the current top cover of the armchair, but you may need to take off any trim. Check for areas where the padding is worn or lumpy. You can smooth this out with extra wadding later on. You will need to remove any bottom covering on the chair. Keep this to replace it later on top of the new top fabric. Check from below that the webbing on the chair is in good condition.

2. Now prepare a layer of wadding to cover the arms, wings and back of the chair. Where you can, staple this in place through the current cover on to the wooden parts of the chair. In difficult places with thick padding, such as the front of the arms, stitch the wadding into place instead with large loops of thread or twine.

With the wadding prepared, you can start fitting the new top fabric. It is important not to hurry this process, especially when finishing off the corners and edges. Seams should run along the natural edges of the shapes, and pinning each piece of material into place with skewer-like upholstery pins allows you to adjust tension and line up patterns before final sewing.

3. Start with the outside back of the chair. Lie the fabric over the chair and make sure it is straight before pinning along the bottom of the chair and turning it over to staple the fabric, with a hem, along the bottom of the frame. Place the staples close together and leave around 5cm unfixed at either side.

3. PIN AND STAPLE THE COVER FOR THE BACK

4. Put the chair upright again, remove the pins and drape the fabric over the top of the chair, tucking it down below the seat. Staple it to a wooden rail within the chair if possible, or sew it on to the original cover well below the level of the seat. At the sides, tuck the excess material gently into the wing folds – they will be nailed in place along with the wing coverings later.

If your chair has indented humped 'shoulder' behind the top edge of the back, you may want to fit the back cover in two pieces. If so, staple the first piece to the back rail under the shoulder, then arrange the second piece over the front of the chair and fold and pin a hem along the back to cover the row of staples. Sew this seam into place using a half-circular needle and an invisible slip stitch.

5. Now work on the sides and arms. Start by lying the material in place, matching the pattern to the back if necessary, making sure it is straight then pinning it along the outside of the bottom rail. Turn the chair over and staple the material under the bottom rail, again stopping 5cm from each end.

5. COVER THE INSIDES AND ARMS

RE-COVERING AN ARMCHAIR

6. Turn the chair upright and pull the fabric back over the arms, tucking it down below the seat and pulling it to the right tension, before stapling it to the frame below seat level. Repeat stages 5 and 6 for the other arm and side of the chair.

7. The next stage will cover the front of the seat. Put the material in place, matching the pattern as necessary, pin along the front of the chair, then turn over the chair and staple it, with a hem, under the front rail. Turn the chair upright and pull the material up over the front of the seat, making sure it is straight.

Tuck the excess down the sides of the seat. Don't attach this to the frame at the sides, or this will cause the fabric to split when someone sits on the chair. Then, making sure the tension is correct, fold a hem and pin the fabric to the existing seat cover before sewing it right across the seat with slip stitch, using a half-circular needle.

Now comes the fun bit: fitting the irregular pieces of fabric and sewing up the edges and corners. The rounded wings of the chair and the fronts of the arms need to be covered and joined together with seams that follow the edges of these shapes neatly. For this process, pinning all the pieces in each area together before sewing is essential, but the final result is very satisfying.

The methods and patterns you use in the following steps will depend a lot on the exact shape of your chair, and it might work out better to attach seams in a different order, or use more pieces of fabric to get a neater finish.

8. Depending on the shape of your wings, it may be best to cover them in two pieces of fabric. Pin the outside piece into place, letting it lie flat over the sides, then attach the second piece to the frame right inside the deep fold where the wing meets the back of the chair. You may need to use upholstery tacks for this, as the staple gun may not reach into the hollow.

7. SEW THE FRONT COVER TO THE EXISTING SEAT

8. YOU MAY NEED A HAMMER AND TACKS TO FIX THE FABRIC INSIDE THE WINGS

Once it is attached, pull the second piece over the wing to the right tension and fold it to form a hem before pinning it into place with lots of pins just inside the edge of the hem. Make neat folds if necessary, in order for the material to fit closely and firmly around the wing. Snip the hem allowance if needed to help the fit.

Where the wing meets the bottom of the arm and the sides of the back cover, follow the same process of pinning a folded hem over a piece lying flat over the wadding. Using long pins that pass right into the stuffing will help hold the tension.

Adjust the fit for as long as you need to get the cover looking tidy and taut, before sewing the seams with a half-circular needle and slip stitch.

9. At the front of the arms, follow the same process. Start by stapling the front panel to the bottom of the frame and then pull, fold and pin all the pieces of fabric that meet along the edges until the cover is taut but not strained and the edges are neat and straight. Then sew the seams with slip stitch.

9. USE SLIP STITCH TO SEW STRONG INVISIBLE SEAMS ALONG THE EDGES

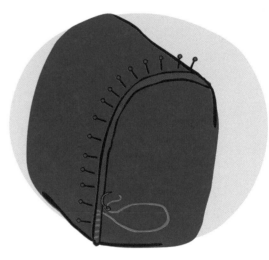

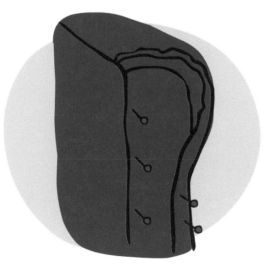

PIN AND SEW A NEAT SEAM AT THE BACK OF THE WINGS

ROLLER BLIND FABRIC REPLACEMENT

Roller blinds are very simple machines, with a top roller and a bottom rail attached to a roll of stiffened fabric. When a blind no longer matches your décor, or when it gets dirty, it can be hard to find a new one in anything other than plain colours, and it is a shame to throw away a working mechanism when only the fabric is at fault. So, why not make your own, individual blind, using the fabric of your choice?

You can also buy special roller-blind kits from craft stores, so this is also a good project if you don't have a broken roller blind, but would like to use your choice of fabric to create one.

This project need not involve any sewing, as iron-on webbing can be used to create all the necessary seams, although you can sew them if you prefer.

TOOLS AND MATERIALS YOU WILL NEED

Replacement fabric, pins, large sharp scissors, enough iron-on webbing to cover both side seams and the bottom seam, blind stiffener spray (available in craft shops or online) and ideally, a try-square for checking the blind is parallel.

1. Start by removing the blind from its brackets on the window unit and removing the old fabric. This may be clipped on to the top roller, held in place with double-sided tape or fixed with small nails or pins. Keep the fabric for measuring up its replacement.

2. Measure the new fabric against the fabric you have removed from the blind. Leave enough excess at each side for a 1cm hem and cut this very neatly, as the fold will show through the blind when it is hung at a window. At the bottom edge, add enough so that it can be folded over to make a pocket for the rail.

3. The new fabric needs to be hemmed and stiffened before attaching it to the blind. Hang your blind material up in a well ventilated place and spray on the reverse side with the blind stiffening spray, following the instructions provided by the manufacturer and any safety precautions they recommend.

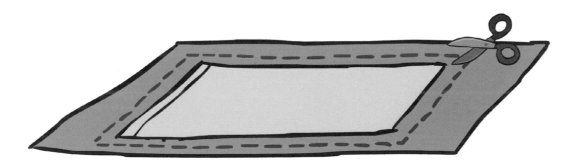

Then, fold the material over at the bottom of the fabric and place a line of pins parallel with the edge at the distance you have calculated, leaving about 1.5cm of spare material beyond the pins. Check with a try-square that the bottom edge and line of pins are exactly at right angles to the edge of the fabric. Then, place webbing under the hem beyond the line of pins and iron the seam to fix it.

4. Now hem the side seams. The material will now be quite stiff, so the easiest way to do this is with iron-on webbing. Fold over a straight, parallel seam and iron this flat carefully, placing a cloth between the fabric and the iron. Check the hem is straight and parallel before placing iron-on webbing into the hem and ironing again.

5. Now create the pocket for the bottom rail. Most rails are oblong, so measure its depth and height, add them together and add half a centimetre to the total you to get the correct depth of pocket. If the bottom rail is cylindrical, measure its diameter and multiply by 3.5.

6. You can now reconstruct your blind, inserting the bottom rail, and fixing the material to the top roller in the same way as it was attached before, making sure the edge of the fabric is at right angles to the roller. Roll the blind up around the top roller. If it bunches up to one side, it has not been fixed parallel to the top roller and you may need to make adjustments to the fixings to compensate for this.

7. Once the blind rolls up neatly, you can place it back in the brackets on the window and check it moves up and down smoothly.

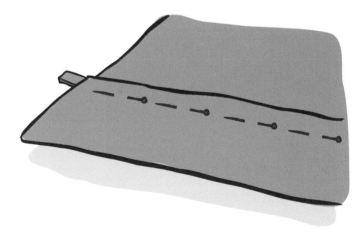

GARDEN CHAIRS

Garden furniture fabrics, such as the covers for foam cushions and the canvas seats of deckchairs, fade in the sunshine and can become mouldy if they aren't dried out thoroughly after rain.

Replacement foam cushions and covers can be made using the techniques used for indoor upholstery, and are an excellent way to make your garden furniture look like new again.

It is also simple to replace the fabric on deckchair and picnic chairs, as these projects will show.

REPLACING THE FABRIC ON A TRADITIONAL DECKCHAIR

Customising a deckchair is great fun and is also very easy.

The canvas needs to be replaced by equally strong material that won't stretch, and you can find a range of different patterns and colours. If you can't find exactly what you want, natural canvas can be dyed in the washing machine, or you can use fabric paint to add your own patterns and motifs.

TOOLS AND MATERIALS YOU WILL NEED
Pliers or pincers to remove the old nails or tacks, sandpaper and Danish oil or exterior varnish, rags or a paintbrush, replacement canvas, scissors, a hammer and large upholstery tacks or small flat-headed nails.

THE STEPS
1. Remove the old canvas from the chair, using pliers or a flat screwdriver to prise out the nails holding it in place. If it is sewn on, snip through the seams.

2. Take this opportunity to spruce up the wood of the deckchair. Sand it lightly all over, and treat with oil or varnish. Be careful varnish doesn't get into the joints of the chair and make it stick.

3. Use the old canvas to measure up a new piece of fabric. Cut it to size and either hem the edge or use iron-on webbing to stick down a hem.

4. Fold the chair and lie it on top of the sheet of canvas, with the front of the top of the chair facing down and away from you. Pull the canvas edge nearest you over the rail at the front of the seat section and tack the canvas along the rail, spacing the tacks about 2cm apart.

5. Now move to the other end of the chair and do the same with the top rail, temporarily tacking the fabric on to the rear side of the rail, placing just four or five tacks part-way into the fabric at first.

6. Unfold the chair and check that the canvas is in the right orientation, sits straight in the frame, and that it is at the right tension to provide a comfortable seat (don't sit in it – it won't hold any weight yet!). Estimate any change in tension that is needed.

7. Fold the chair down again, adjust the position of the canvas on the top rail if necessary and tack the canvas down firmly with tacks at 2cm intervals.

REPLACING THE FABRIC ON A TUBULAR METAL GARDEN CHAIR

Both the metal tubes and canvas on a folding metal picnic chair can be revamped to create a funky, retro piece of garden furniture. The steps to follow to replace the canvas are described here. Repaint the tubes with enamel following the same steps as for repainting the chrome table legs on pages 98-9.

They are likely to be quite rusty, and may already have been painted, so you may need to sand them thoroughly before repainting, and you should also use spray lubricant or grease to oil the joints. If the springs are rusty, scrub off the rust with household cream cleaner and a scouring pad then dry thoroughly before rubbing on a thin coat of petroleum jelly or grease to protect them in future.

TOOLS AND MATERIALS YOU WILL NEED

Adjustable spanner or hacksaw, replacement small screws with washers to fit the holes left by the rivets, screwdriver, replacement canvas, needle and thread.

THE STEPS

1. The fabric may be held on to the frame with rivets or bolts and be sprung against the back of the frame via a steel rod that passes through a pocket. Normally the rivets can be cut through with a small hacksaw and replaced with screws and washers later, and the springs can be unhooked from the rod.

2. Use the old fabric to measure a pattern for the new fabric, which should be strong canvas, as for the deckchair. Cut the fabric to the same shape, allowing excess for a hem and checking how the seams at the back of the seat are positioned.

3. Sew a hem right around the edge of the canvas and then sew the seam at the back of the seat, which also creates a large pocket for the metal rod. This should be sewn with strong nylon thread or twine, using a very strong stitch, such as backstitch.

4. Start to fit the canvas by attaching it to the front of the seat. Wrap it evenly around the tubing and replace the bolts, or use screws to attach it to the frame through the holes left by the rivets.

5. Second, attach the other end of the canvas to the tubing at the top of the back of the chair using the same method as in step 4. There will be no tension yet in the canvas, as the springs have not yet been attached to the back of the frame.

6. Next, thread the metal rod through the pocket behind the seat seam. Then, fold the chair and attach the springs to the frame at the back.

Finally, starting in the centre, hook the springs around the metal rod to pull the seat and back of the chair taught. If the tips of the spring hooks won't work between the fibres of the canvas, you may need to snip the material with sharp scissors to allow the springs to pass through the material and over the metal rod.

Unfold the chair and the springs should pull tight, creating a comfortable seat.

LEATHER IN FURNISHINGS

Leather looks great next to wood in pieces of furniture. If you like this traditional look, you can buy leather hide by the square foot from fabric and upholstery suppliers to revamp your furniture.

It is more expensive than fabric and I would not recommend, as a beginner, that you try to use it for projects that involve sewing. However, both the seat pad and the drop-in seat projects described in this book involve securing the top fabric only with tacks or staples, so there is no reason why you should not use leather for these projects if you prefer.

Alternatively, if you want to be thrifty, you can buy some very convincing artificial hides nowadays, including soft faux suede and breathable fake leather. These aren't as durable as leather, but are easy to work with and look and feel almost as good as the real thing.

REPLACING A LEATHER DESK-TOP

One common use of leather is as a durable, soft writing surface on the top of a desk or table. If you are renovating a desk with a leather inlay, you can replace this at the same time as revamping the wooden surfaces.

Strong glues are not necessary and the new leather can be stuck down with simple wallpaper paste.

Hide suppliers frequently have to supply these desk-tops and they will sometimes offer a service where they will cut the inlay to size for you and add impressed or gilt decorations around the edge for an extra fee. When ordering plain leather, measure the inlay and add a few millimetres to each measurement to allow for an overlap. For a decorated piece of hide, you will need to give the supplier the exact measurements and they will add an overlap and place the decorations in a suitable position.

It is usually best to replace the leather after renovating the wooden parts of a desk. If you need to sand or treat the wood around the recess after fitting the leather, remember to protect it from being scratched or marked with oils and stains.

TOOLS AND MATERIALS YOU WILL NEED
Replacement hide, stripping knife, sandpaper and sanding block, possibly wood filler, a duster or soft cloth, wallpaper paste, a steel ruler and very sharp craft knife.

THE STEPS
1. Remove the old leather from the desk. It should have been stuck down with glue that can be removed with soap and water, and you can help preserve some of the leather for future, smaller projects by peeling it away carefully and dabbing at the join with a sponge and solution of washing-up liquid. Once the leather has been removed, clean the recess with the scraper, a scouring pad and soapy water to remove any residue of glue.

2. The surface must be completely flat and smooth, as any bumps or defects will show through the leather. Sand the surface using a sanding block, fill any cracks with wood filler, and scrape the edge of a steel ruler across it to identify any bumps or dents. Fill in dents with wood filler and sand flat once it has hardened.

3. When the surface is ready, place the hide in the recess to check the orientation and fit, then keep it ready and apply a layer of wallpaper paste to the recess. Then, lie the hide in place, pulling it out to each corner and adjusting its position if necessary.

4. Next, smooth and press the leather into place, using a soft cloth rolled into a ball. Start from the centre and smooth it gently but firmly towards each edge, pushing out any air bubbles and being careful not to crease the leather. Keep smoothing and pressing for as long as you think is needed, pressing it right down into the corners as the paste starts to become stickier, using the edge of the steel ruler padded with a few layers of the cloth.

5. Leave the glue to dry for a few hours, then use the ruler and craft knife to cut neatly around the leather at the edge of the recess. Press the edges down again using the ruler and cloth, using tiny dabs of extra glue if needed.

The techniques and ideas in this section can be used to mend broken items, but they are also useful for using old furniture in more exciting projects as well.

For example, you can take an unwanted chest of drawers, add a table top and legs and turn it in to a useful desk...

SOLID WOODEN LEGS AND A NEW FRAME HAVE BEEN ADDED TO A CHEST OF DRAWERS TO SUPPORT A NEW DESK TOP

... take the legs from an old chair and add a new surface to create a side table.

THIS COFFEE TABLE HAS BEEN CUT DOWN TO MAKE A HANDY FOOTSTOOL

... or cut down the legs of a coffee table and add an upholstered pad to create a footrest.

These are just some of the ways you can take unwanted pieces of furniture and turn them into something more useful. The techniques and principles used here can be employed in many other similar projects, only limited by the items you have and your own imagination!

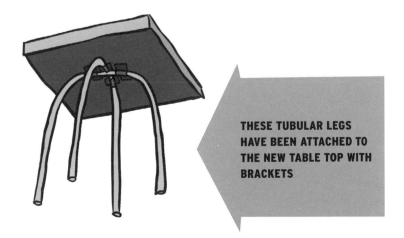

THESE TUBULAR LEGS HAVE BEEN ATTACHED TO THE NEW TABLE TOP WITH BRACKETS

KEEPING THINGS GOING IN THE KITCHEN

The kitchen is at the heart of every home and is packed full of activity and appliances. Nearly half of the electrical items in the average household are found in this one room, and more than half the energy we use is consumed in the process of cooking and storing our food and washing our clothes and dishes.

Keeping the kitchen in good working order is therefore crucial in keeping down household running costs, not just in preventing things from breaking down.

Items in the kitchen are frequently splashed with water, and come into contact with food, waste and a wide range of spills and messes, which means things get washed almost every time they are used. Kitchens need plenty of maintenance to ward off problems caused by so much liquid sloshing around.

And, of course, however well you care for your kitchen, the heavy use we make of it inevitably leads to things going wrong. So, here are some useful and simple tips for keeping your kitchen ship-shape, as well as advice on dealing with the most common breakages and breakdowns.

FIGHTING THE SCALE

Hard, white deposits of limescale can cause a lot of problems in the bathroom and in the kitchen, and if you live in a hard water area you will certainly know it!

Limescale is formed when minerals in 'hard' water come out of solution. The most common mineral in limescale deposits is calcium carbonate (dissolved from limestone or chalk in the area where the water originated).

Limescale is a particular problem in appliances where water is heated. At warm temperatures, some of the calcium bicarbonate in hard water can change to less soluble calcium carbonate, which is then left behind inside your boiler, shower or kettle, threatening to block them up.

Cold water can also leave behind limescale when it dries, and a dripping cold tap will quickly build up a stalactite in exactly the same way that beautiful cave formations build up underground.

In the home, of course, limescale isn't beautiful and you'll want to keep it at bay. Here's how.

PREVENTING SCALE

The best way of keeping washing machines and dishwashers free of scale is to use water softening salts along with your detergent. These softeners react with the calcium minerals, replacing them with more soluble sodium salts that don't form scale, even at high temperatures.

Using a softener won't just prolong the life of your machines, it will also improve the effectiveness of your detergent and leave your pots and glasses sparkling. You can generally use about 25 per cent less detergent than you would normally need in a hard water area if you use a small amount of water softener alongside it.

A build-up of limescale on heating elements prevents the efficient transfer of heat to the water, so you can also save energy by cutting down on scale.

REMOVING SCALE

It's possible to scrub off limescale deposits. However, the minerals involved are very hard, so abrasives that will effectively scrape them off are also likely to damage the finish of the material underneath.

Luckily, calcium carbonate is easily dissolved in a range of mild acids. You can buy brand-name limescale removers, but many common household substances will also do the trick.

Two of the most effective are lemon juice and ordinary vinegar. Lemon juice is usually the most effective (and will also leave a lovely smell behind). Stronger pickling vinegar and lime juice are both even more acidic and can be used for really stubborn deposits.

The problem with removing limescale is not usually finding an appropriate acid around the home, but making sure the acid stays in contact with the surface for long enough to do its job. Limescale is not so easy to remove that you can simply wipe it off with a cloth soaked in juice. Instead, you need to leave it soaking for an hour or more to really do the trick.

Try these different methods to remove scale from all appliances around the home.

KETTLE/COFFEE MAKER
Your kettle is a ready-made liquid container, so the descaling process is pretty simple.

Start by quarter-filling the kettle with vinegar or lemon juice and leave for an hour.

Then, leaving in the acid, top up the kettle with water and boil it. Pour away the boiled water before it cools, then rinse out the kettle with several changes of cold water to remove any traces of vinegar or lemon juice (not a good taste with coffee!).

This method can also be used to descale coffee makers. Add the acid to the water compartment as before, then top up with water and run the coffee-making process with this solution and no coffee. Repeat this twice more with plain water to rinse.

DISHWASHER
To shift a build-up of limescale in your dishwasher, run an empty load with a large cup of vinegar or lemon juice in place of the detergent.

This has the added benefit of freshening up your machine and removing any musty smells.

TAPS – VINEGAR METHOD
Taps are tricky to keep in contact with your descaling liquid. The best method I have come across is to take a small cup of vinegar and wrap a tea-towel around the tap head to hold the cup in place.

Use a plastic cup (a yoghurt pot is ideal), not china or glass, as there's a risk you'll drop the cup into the bath or sink and break it.

For limescale build-up around the posts and other parts of a tap, soak a pad of cotton wool in your descaling liquid and wrap this firmly around the relevant parts. Leave it there for an hour or two, giving it a squeeze now and again to make sure the acid gets into all the corners and grooves.

After this time, all parts of your taps should be able to be wiped clean, though you may need to scrub with a plastic scourer to loosen the more stubborn bits of scale.

TAPS – LEMON METHOD
A couple of real-live lemons are what you'll need for this clever descaling trick.

Cut the lemons in half then squeeze them gently into a bowl to gather some juice. Don't use a lemon squeezer, as you want to make sure the fleshy parts remain intact for the next stage.

Then, take a lemon half and shove it on to the spout of your tap, twisting gently until it stays in place. The fibres and chambers inside the lemon should catch on the edge of the spout, preventing the lemon falling off. Now you can simply leave it to do its descaling job. (If the lemon won't stay in place, you can use the tea-towel trick from the vinegar method to hold it up).

Meanwhile, use the juice you collected to create a cotton wool 'dressing' for the rest of the tap, as before.

Wait an hour then rinse and scrub your tap clean. If any scale remains, simply replace the lemon for longer and scrub again.

TILES AND OTHER SURFACES
Limescale deposits on flat surfaces are much easier to get rid of. In most cases, simply wiping or scrubbing gently with vinegar or lemon juice will get them sparkling again.

DISHWASHERS & WASHING MACHINES

These two machines are found in almost every home these days and most of us take them for granted – right up to the day when they go wrong.

Fate dictates that this will always happen at exactly the wrong moment, such as during the Christmas holidays or before an important meal. However, by carrying out a few regular maintenance jobs, we can all help prevent problems (and avoid lectures from repair people!).

MAINTENANCE

Here are a few tasks to schedule on a regular basis in order to keep your appliances working well.

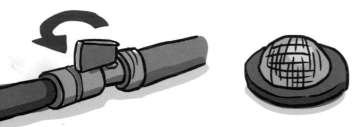

CLEAN INLET FILTERS

The pipes bringing water into your machines will have mesh filters (usually built into a washer) at the point they enter the appliance. These prevent debris getting into your machine but can become clogged and should be checked every year.

Depending on your machine, there may be two inlet hoses, one for cold and one for hot water. They will probably be colour-coded and attached to pipes coming from your plumbing system.

Before removing a hose inlet from your machine, ensure the water supply to it is switched off. The connection between the hose and your water pipes may have inbuilt taps to make this easy, or you may need to turn off a stopcock under a nearby sink.

Once the water is off, place a towel on the floor to catch any remaining drips and unscrew the pipe connector on your machine. Remove the filter and clean it before replacing everything securely.

CLEAN WASTE FILTERS

Washing machines also have an outlet filter. This can become clogged with fibres and eventually prevent the machine from draining.

The location and design of this filter will vary between machines, but it will usually be found behind a panel at the front of the machine. You may need to unscrew the filter to remove it, or use a coin to release a plastic bolt.

Important:
Don't remove this filter while the machine is full of water or it will run out all over the floor! See the section on how to drain a machine manually for how to get the water out when you have a filter blockage.

Your dishwasher also has filters that do the same job, and these are found in the base of the washing chamber. Your manual will contain instructions on how to release and clean these filters, which may be held on with clips, screws or other fixings.

FRESHENING

Your dishwasher or washing machine may occasionally develop a musty smell, but a regular freshening wash will keep this problem away.

Both vinegar and lemon juice will do a great job of freshening up your machine's innards, and will help to remove any limescale deposits at the same time. Use a large cup of either liquid in place of your usual detergent and run a normal washing cycle (without clothes or dishes). In a dishwasher, pour the liquid into the base of the machine rather than the detergent dispenser.

For dishwashers, you should regularly remove and clean the interior fittings, including the spray arms, whose small holes can become blocked with grease or tiny particles.

You don't need to climb inside your machine to do this! The spray arms will be removable and you should be able to find instructions in your owner manual.

CHECK DOOR SEALS

The final thing to keep an eye on is the condition of the rubber door seals on your machines, which may become damaged over time.

Check them once or twice a year and call in a professional if they need to be replaced. It is much better to get this repair done in plenty of time, before the seals develop a leak and cause a flood.

WHEN THINGS GO WRONG

There are various reasons why a washing machine or dishwasher may stop working. A fuse may blow, a power cut may interrupt the program, or the electronics may 'crash' (yes everything's run by computers these days, so turning it off and on again may well do the trick). Blockages can also prevent water from draining, causing the machine to halt and remain locked shut, full of your wet washing.

If the machine stops, you will want to remove your washing and get the machine repaired. But, with the machine full of water, you can't.

Here's how to drain the machine by hand. You won't need any special tools, just a bucket and a towel.

THE STEPS

1. Turn off the machine at the plug.

2. The outlet hoses from your washing machine and dishwasher will empty into an upright pipe that feeds into your normal waste water system, often under the nearest sink. Move the machine aside and pull the outlet hose out of the pipe, keeping it upright.

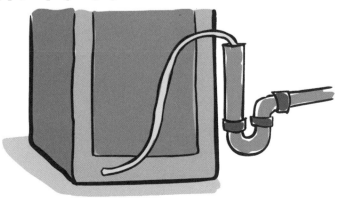

3. Lower the end of the hose into the bucket and, thanks to gravity, water should flow out. You can stop the flow at any time by raising the hose above the level of the machine.

4. If the problem is a blocked filter, the flow may be very slow. If nothing comes out at all, you may have to replace the hose in the waste pipe and clear the filter using the slightly messy 'quick change' method described below.

'QUICK CHANGE' FILTER UNBLOCKING

Clearing the filter with the machine full of water is always a bit messy. If the water in the machine is still hot, wait until it has cooled before you start, then place towels around the floor, and work with a helper if possible.

Put a large bowl (such as a washing up bowl) below the filter outlet to catch any water. Then get ready with a damp towel, which you will use to plug the filter hole.

Then release the filter and pull it out of the machine. It may pull the blockage with it, in which case water will start to flow out. If so, immediately place the towel plug into the hole and press hard to stop the flow.

Your helper can now remove the fluff and debris from the filter. Once this is done, remove the towel and reinsert the filter as quickly as possible. Now you can finish draining the machine using the outlet hose and the bucket, as before.

Don't forget to clean the filter more thoroughly after the machine is empty.

OVENS & MICROWAVES

Cooking food can be a messy business. Pans and casseroles can bubble, splash and boil over, leaving behind nasty burned-on food stains that are difficult to clean off. This section will provide some tips on making this job easier and less toxic.

Because gas, microwave radiation and high voltages are used in these appliances, you shouldn't try to repair them unless you are a qualified professional. However, there are a few regular maintenance jobs you can carry out safely to keep your cooking appliances running more smoothly.

OVEN CLEANING WITHOUT AMMONIA

With modern appliances, you should never need to resort to using harsh chemical oven cleaners.

The inner surfaces of most ovens now have a 'self-cleaning' coating, which means you can burn off grease and stains by running a special cleaning cycle (check your oven's manual for how to activate this) or by heating the oven to its highest temperature for an hour or two.

Once the oven has cooled, you can simply wipe away the ashy remains of grease and stains using normal washing up liquid or household cleaner.

Before running the oven at a high temperature, remove as much of any large deposits as possible, as these will produce a lot of smoke as they burn off. It's a good idea to open a window while you run a cleaning cycle anyway, as the cleaning process will always produce a small amount of smoke.

The glass door and the metal fittings inside your oven will not self-clean, and you should remove the wire shelves for separate cleaning before turning up your oven.

CLEANING STOVE TOPS

A wide range of different stove top cookers are now available, and each comes with different advice for cleaning. However, all stoves benefit from cleaning up spills quickly, rather than letting them burn on and become hard to clean.

Keep and follow the cleaning instructions that come with your appliance. Ceramic stoves, in particular, need to be looked after carefully and often have specialist cleaning guidelines. For example, sugary spills should be cleaned off ceramic stoves while the surface is still warm.

These appliances are also often supplied with a special razor tool for scraping off burned food – this preserves the surface much better than scrubbing with a scourer.

The control knobs on all kinds of stoves can usually be prised off, making them easy to clean – scrub around the posts with household detergent or cream cleaner (being careful not to scrub off temperature markings) and simply wash the knobs in soapy water.

MICROWAVE MAINTENANCE

Microwave ovens are incredibly easy to care for. During microwave cooking, food can bubble and spit, so it is a good idea to wipe the walls after each use. This will prevent more major cleaning jobs being necessary later.

You should never pour liquid into your microwave or use a very wet cleaning cloth. A damp sponge should be all you need to clean the inside and outside of your oven.

Sometimes, cooking something with a strong smell (such as fish) in your microwave will leave behind a persistent odour. Among its many other uses, lemon juice will also do an excellent job of freshening up your microwave.

Just place a bowl containing half water and half lemon juice in the machine and 'cook' it for a few minutes. Afterwards, wipe away the condensation that forms on the inside of the oven. This process is also useful for loosening dried-on stains.

MICROWAVE SAFETY

Most microwave ovens have numerous safety features to prevent electromagnetic waves from leaking out, and these will normally stop the machine from working if a problem develops.

However, if the casing or door of your machine gets damaged, even if it still seems to work, it is important to have it checked by a specialist.

Never take the back cover off a microwave yourself – the components inside can give you an electric shock even when the machine is unplugged.

GAS STOVES

A gas stove can become dangerous if it is allowed to get dirty. As well as regular surface cleaning, you should dismantle and clean the parts thoroughly every few months using a scourer and normal household cleaner (cream cleaner works well). For stubborn burned-on deposits, a paste of bicarbonate of soda is a good way to loosen them.

The burners have tiny holes all around the edges, and keeping these clear is important for safety. If you ever notice the flames from a burner are yellow, or that areas around the jet aren't burning, clean these holes out immediately or inefficient burning may create poisonous carbon monoxide gas.

Clean the holes in the burners with a brush or a wooden toothpick. Don't use metal implements as these can damage the holes. And be careful not to leave wooden splinters or bristles in the holes after cleaning.

The fittings on a gas stove are made of plain steel (not stainless steel) so make sure you dry them thoroughly after cleaning to prevent rust. Turning on the burners for a minute after you replace the parts will drive off any dampness, and is a useful check that everything is working properly.

FRIDGES & FREEZERS

Neglecting your cold kitchen appliances is not a good idea. A frosted-up freezer will cost you in higher energy bills, and will not preserve your food in good condition either.

Regular cleaning will prevent bad smells and dangerous bacteria being harboured in your fridge or freezer. And checking essential parts, such as the door seals, will help prevent serious problems springing up without warning.

DEFROSTING A FREEZER

Ice will form in most freezers fairly slowly, so you should only need to defrost about once a year. If you notice that ice is growing back quickly, you may have a problem (such as a faulty thermostat or a broken door seal) or you may be letting the temperature rise too high by leaving the door open when retrieving food, or by placing cooked food in your freezer before it has fully cooled.

If you suspect a technical problem, get it checked out quickly. It probably means your appliance is using up a lot of energy and money, not just creating a lot of ice.

An annual defrost is not a big or scary job. If you follow these steps and tips, it should only take a few hours, at most.

Schedule a defrost for when the stocks in your fridge or freezer are low. It's a good idea to deliberately use up stored food to reduce the amount you have to keep cool while the appliance is out of action.

TOOLS YOU WILL NEED
Newspaper and plastic bags or 'cool bag' picnic hampers, towels, some bowls, a wooden spoon or cooking spatula, bicarbonate of soda, and a cleaning cloth or sponge.

THE STEPS
1. Empty the appliance and place the frozen food in a cool bag or wrap it in newspaper and store it in plastic bags in a cool place. Remove any internal racks or fittings and wash them in hot soapy water.

2. Turn off the machine at the plug, open it and place a folded towel on the base of the compartment. Place another towel on the floor outside if your appliance is a front-opening model.

3. In theory, all you have to do now is wait until the ice melts, squeezing out the towels and replacing them as they soak up the resulting water. However, you can speed up the process considerably by placing bowls of just-boiled water in the compartments. The steam will spread through the space and help the ice to melt. Refill the bowls with fresh hot water as it cools.

4. Remove any large pieces of ice that break free from the walls and roof of the appliance and leave them in a sink or bath to melt. If necessary, prod and loosen them gently with a wooden spoon or spatula.

5. When all the ice has melted and been removed, clean the inside of the appliance thoroughly, and wipe the internal surfaces with a solution of bicarbonate of soda to keep it smelling fresh.

DEFROSTING DOS AND DON'TS

DO

Take out pieces of ice and leave them to melt in a sink or bath. With the power switched off, you will find they come loose from the walls of the appliance quite quickly.

DON'T

Chip away at the ice with metal tools. It is very easy to puncture the walls of the appliance, and this can release toxic (and ozone- or climate-damaging) gases, as well as breaking the appliance beyond repair.

DON'T

Use electrical heating appliances inside or near a defrosting fridge or freezer. Electricity and water don't mix, so don't listen to people who say blast the ice with a hairdryer. Turn on a heater elsewhere in the room if you want to raise the temperature without risking your life.

CLEANING

Although a fridge or freezer slows down the growth of bacteria and mould, low temperatures don't completely prevent nasties from breeding, so it's important to keep your fridge clean.

Immediately wipe up any spills that occur inside your appliance, and every so often, empty it and clean the walls and floor with bicarbonate of soda, which will also keep everything smelling fresh.

CHECKING DOOR SEALS

Well-fitting door seals are crucial to keeping a fridge or freezer working properly. They should be checked regularly to make sure they are forming a proper seal and enabling the appliance to stay cold without using up lots of energy.

Testing a seal is simple – all you need is a sheet of A4 paper. Trap the paper in the door and check that it will hold the paper firmly enough to resist a gentle tug. If so, your seals are in good condition.

If you find any problems, first clean around the seals and door frame thoroughly. Dirt and debris can prevent a proper seal forming.

CHECK FRIDGE DOOR SEALS

If you find a seal is split or damaged, you will need to have it replaced. You cando this yourself.

On most appliances they are fixed in place with screws hidden underneath the plastic flaps, and they can be removed and refitted in a few minutes.

However, it is very important that you order the right new parts from the manufacturer, and that you double check the new seals are correct before removing the old ones.

Finally, don't forget to clean the ridges and pads of your door seals when cleaning your appliance. They are perfectly designed to harbour dirt and create smells, so a rinse with bicarbonate of soda will also help to keep them fresh.

REVAMPING A WOODEN CHOPPING BOARD

Lately, plastic chopping boards impregnated with antibacterial compounds have been promoted as a more hygienic alternative to the traditional wooden chopping board.

However, while plastic boards may be a sensible option in a commercial kitchen (where they can be cleaned at high temperatures), there's actually very little scientific evidence to prove one way or the other which kind of board is better for everyday hygiene.

It seems that natural oils, and the ability of wood to expand and close up cuts, help prevent a wooden board from harbouring bacteria.

However, chopping boards can become badly scratched and battered with age, and the oils can be stripped away from their surfaces with frequent washing. So, keep your wooden board hygenic and in good condition by revamping them every so often, sanding away defects and replenishing their oils.

TOOLS YOU WILL NEED

For this simple project, you'll need a sanding block, a range of different sandpaper grades, from coarse to very fine, a bottle of ordinary olive oil (extra virgin is not necessary!) and a few soft rags. A damp sponge is also needed to help raise the grain in the final stages of sanding.

THE STEPS

1. SAND OFF THE SCRATCHES

First give your board a good scrub with a scouring sponge and hot water to get off any surface dirt.

To keep the board from sliding around while you are sanding, rest it on a towel on a solid surface, such as the floor or a heavy table.

Starting with the coarsest grade of sandpaper, use the sanding block to smooth the surfaces of your board. Sand parallel to the direction of the grain on each side and avoid sanding in curved arcs or circular motions, as scratches across the grain are very hard to remove. For sides with the end of the grain visible, sand in the direction that feels smoothest.

Keep going until you can no longer see any of the scratches. This may take several sheets of sandpaper – using a quarter of a sheet each time – but must be done thoroughly. Think of it as great exercise for your upper arms. If you have a power sander, you can get this stage done much more quickly, but it won't be as good for you!

2. FINER SANDING

Now use the finer grades of paper to get the surface really smooth. Keep sanding with each grade until the scratches made by the coarser paper have disappeared. Brush off the dust between sanding stints to see how you are getting on.

3. RAISE THE GRAIN

For a really smooth long-lasting surface, your final sanding should be done after you have 'raised the grain'. This involves dusting all the surfaces then wiping your chopping board all over with a very slightly damp sponge.

Water will be absorbed into the wood and this will cause the wood between the fibrous grain lines to expand and push out tiny fibres. If you look carefully across the wood as the dampness soaks in, you'll see it becomes slightly dull looking and furry.

Sand the wood a final time with finest grade paper or steel wool to remove these fibres and leave a very smooth finish.

4. OIL YOUR BOARD

You now need to replenish the protective oils in your wood. Use plain olive oil, rather than synthetic woodworking products, which are not suitable for use with food.

Start by pouring a small pool of oil into the centre of the board, then rub this in with a soft, lint-free rag. The wood will soak up the oil quite rapidly, and you may need to add more. Rub the oil in evenly until the surface is shiny, then do the same with the other sides.

Leave this coat to soak in further for an hour, then apply another coat in the same way. Two or three coats should be enough.

5. POLISH

Once the final coat has soaked in, take a new, dry rag and use this to rub off any surface oil and polish your board to an attractive sheen.

LOOKING AFTER YOUR BOARD IN THE FUTURE

Your newly sanded and oiled chopping board will be resistant to stains and water but shouldn't be subjected to harsh cleaning methods.

To clean it, simply scrub away food residues with a nylon scourer or brush, using hot water and small amount of detergent. Don't submerge it in water and never put it in the dishwasher.

Repeat the sanding and oiling process about once a year to keep your chopping board in great condition for years to come.

REPAIRING CHINA & GLASS

China and glass are two of the oldest man-made materials with some excellent qualities that make them ideal around the kitchen. They are waterproof, hard, strong, heat-resistant, long-lasting and easy to make into a wide range of shapes and sizes.

Unfortunately, they are also brittle materials, which means they constantly run the risk of getting broken in use. Here I'll show you how to deal with cracks, chips and other breakages in your crockery and glassware.

Remember, home mending is not suitable for valuable pieces – always take your real heirlooms for professional care.

PREVENTION FIRST

OK, so accidents will always happen, but here are some top tips to reduce the frequency with which your prized possessions get damaged.

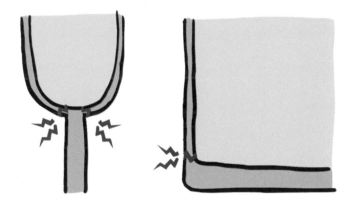

REMEMBER THAT GLASSWARE HATES CHANGES IN TEMPERATURE
Glass is much less heat-resistant than china or earthenware. It will heat up and cool down quickly, and the expansion and contraction caused by these changes in temperature can lead to fractures.

The danger points on any piece are where a thin part meets a thicker part, such as where the stem of a wine glass meets the bowl or, on a tumbler, where a thin side meets a thick base.

NEVER RINSE A HOT GLASS UNDER A COLD TAP

When the piece experiences a sudden change in temperature, the thin part will heat up or cool down much more quickly than the thicker part and this can create enough stress to cause cracks where the two parts meet.

So, never pour hot or boiling water into non-heat-resistant glassware, and avoid plunging glasses into very hot washing up water. Similarly, don't take glasses out of hot soapy water and place them under a cold tap to rinse – this could be disastrous.

Dishwasher cycles reach high temperatures, but will raise the temperature at a much slower rate, reducing the chance of heat shocks.

KNOW WHAT CAN SCRATCH
Avoid getting scratches on china and glass (including mirrors and windows) by never using harder materials to clean, rub or scrape them. See the 'hardness hierarchy' for what materials to avoid.

HARDNESS HIERARCHY

HARDNESS HIERARCHY

The hardness hierarchy is a handy guide to which combinations of materials to avoid. Materials with a higher hardness rating can make scratches on materials further down, while materials lower down the scale can safely be used to scrub and clean harder materials. So, use metal wool, not sandpaper, to scrub paint marks from glass and you will avoid causing permanent damage.

Wood is a composite material and its hardness depends on the type of tree it comes from and which part of the structure you look at. Paper will generally not scratch household materials, particularly when wet, as this softens the fibres even more.

DON'T LET A CRACK IN CHINA SPREAD

A crack in china will tend to spread through the piece slowly over time, but this process speeds up a lot if water is allowed to get into the crevice. If a favourite piece develops a small crack, avoid leaving it in water for any length of time.

Regular washing up will also make the problem worse, so it's a good idea to stop using anything precious for day-to-day eating and drinking as soon as a small crack appears.

Instead, why not reuse a favourite cup or bowl for trinkets on your dressing table, soap in the bathroom or pens in your study? That way you can continue to enjoy it, and not risk causing it to break completely.

REPAIRING CHINA & GLASS

REPAIRING SCRATCHES ON GLASS

Nothing will effectively hide a deep scratch, but shallow surface scratches on glassware, windows and mirrors can be polished away.

This job takes quite a lot of time and elbow grease. You can only use very gentle abrasives, as anything rough will just make the problem worse.

• A dry chamois leather is suitable for gently polishing away the tiniest scratches.

• For more persistent marks, use a small amount of brass cleaning fluid, which contains tiny abrasive particles but won't dull the surface.

• Newspaper, due to the hard fibres of wood in the paper, can also work to polish off mild scratching on windows and mirrors. Newspaper is better than plain paper as the printing ink will help lubricate the polishing process. Use it dry, since water would soften the fibres – and would make it disintegrate in the process.

PATCHING THE SILVER ON A MIRROR

Old mirrors can be beautiful, but the silvering on the back of the glass can deteriorate with age, creating blackened patches and spots.

A precious mirror should be taken to a professional repair shop to be re-silvered. However, you can patch small areas yourself with nothing more than ordinary kitchen foil and get remarkably good results.

You may need to remove the glass from its frame to do this. Be careful to keep safe any fixings you remove.

TOOLS YOU WILL NEED
For this repair you'll need some all-purpose clear glue, a razor blade or craft knife and a patch of fresh, uncreased kitchen foil.

THE STEPS
1. Place the glass face down on a folded towel. This protects it from invisible bumps in a hard surface, which could cause it to break if you put pressure on it while mending.

2. Use a razor blade or craft knife to scrape away the silvering from the blackened patch. When scraping, try to 'feather' the edges of the area slightly, so you don't end up with sharp edges on your patch, which may show on the other side. Polish the glass that shows through the hole with a soft cloth.

3. Now cut out a patch of kitchen foil slightly larger than the hole. The foil will be placed shiny side down on the back of the mirror, so bear this in mind when marking the shape.

4. Apply a thin layer of clear all-purpose glue to the glass, then lay the foil down carefully. Use a soft cloth to press it down perfectly flat on to the glass without rubbing.

When the glue has dried, the mirror can be replaced in its frame and the repair should be barely visible.

REPAIRING CHINA & GLASS

COVERING UP CHIPS ON CHINA

A chip in the rim or base of a china ornament can ruin it and, if you don't have the broken piece, gluing it back in place is not an option.

Antiques should be taken to a professional, as home repairs can reduce their value. However, for vases and ornaments with only sentimental value, this hidden repair can do a good job of hiding a chip or replacing a missing part.

TOOLS YOU WILL NEED
For this job, you'll need a small amount of two-part epoxy filler and tiny pots of enamel paint to match the colours of the glaze on your china. Both are available from craft and hobby shops. A blunt knife or spatula, as well as some cotton wool and cold water to help shape and smooth the filler are also useful.

THE STEPS
1. Clean and dry your china piece. Brush the broken surface with a paintbrush after drying to remove dust and help ensure a good bond is made with the filler.

2. Mix a small amount of filler compound from the two parts supplied in the pack. The filler is self-hardening and sets using a chemical reaction between the two substances (a similar process to epoxy resin glue). For the resin to set hard, it's important that the two parts are properly mixed, so knead the compound in your hands for at least 5 minutes.

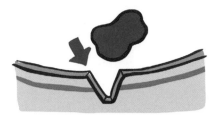

3. With your fingers, mould the filler into a suitable shape and push it into the gap in your piece of china, making your initial moulding slightly larger or fatter than the missing piece. Leave it for a short time to harden slightly.

4. Over the next hour, the texture of the filler will become stiffer and more resilient. During this period, you can use the knife or spatula (and your fingers) to scrape and mould it into a more exact shape. When you are happy with the shape, smooth the surface with damp cotton wool to remove finger prints and other bumps.

5. Clean any filler from your tools immediately you are finished, or it will become rock hard and impossible to remove.

6. Leave the filler to set hard overnight. After this, you can paint it with enamel paint to match the surrounding glaze and make your repair almost invisible.

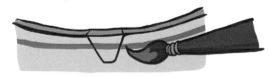

This is a fairly solid repair but, for large chips, remember that the filler is not as strong as the ceramic, so avoid knocking it or picking up the piece by holding the repaired part. The filler is also not suitable for food and drink products or cooking, so use the mended piece only for display purposes, such as holding houseplants.

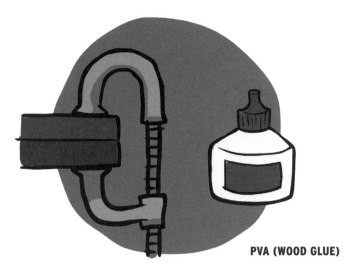

PVA (WOOD GLUE)

MENDING BREAKS

Some breakages cause more damage than a simple chip in the edge. Dropping a plate, bowl or cup can cause it to break into several pieces, but this doesn't necessarily mean it has to go in the bin.

While you can't restore these breaks so the pieces can hold water again, you can use glue to repair them neatly enough so they can be enjoyed as containers for solid or dry items – or, of course, just to look at.

GLUE GUIDE

This is a good place to look at the range of glues in more detail. Here's a handy guide to the most common adhesives – not just for repairing china.

The right glue for the job depends on three factors:
• the materials to be stuck
(their composition and flexibility)
• the shape and size of the area to be joined
• the conditions under which the final object will be used

In addition to the basic types described below, there are also many specialist glues for specific situations, such as mending glass or the soles of shoes. These can be very useful since the packages will contain detailed instructions.

PVA (WOOD GLUE)

This is the same white glue that is used for art and craft in schools. It is water soluble until it dries to form a flexible plastic bond. PVA very strong when used to join two flat surfaces, especially if the surfaces are slightly porous (such as wood, paper, thick cloth, leather). The two sides should be pressed or clamped together firmly until the glue dries.

REPAIRING CHINA & GLASS

CLEAR ALL-PURPOSE GLUE

These glues are available in most general stores, and are very flexible when dry. This makes them good for sticking fabrics and paper. When dry they are clear and colourless, so are recommended for the mirror repair in this book. Spillages can be peeled off when dry, or wiped away with acetone (nail varnish remover).

SUPERGLUE

These glues are all based on the chemical cyanoacrylate and will form a strong bond immediately. Superglues can be used on almost amy material where the two surfaces fit closely together. However, they have several disadvantages. They are often thin and runny, so won't fill gaps, and they are not very water resistant. If you get superglue on your skin, it will therefore wash off (eventually) with soap and water.

EPOXY RESIN

This glue sets because of a chemical reaction between the two separate chemicals, in contrast to most adhesives, which dry as a solvent evaporates. The two parts must be mixed very thoroughly for the glue to set hard. Your mixing and spreading tools will end up covered with hard resin, so mix your glue on cardboard and use scraps of waste wood or plastic to apply and mix the glue. Spillages can be cleaned off with either acetone or white spirit.

CONTACT ADHESIVE

This is an excellent glue for sticking sheets or plates to flat surfaces. You apply the glue to both surfaces and then wait until it is tacky and almost dry. The two surfaces stick when pressed together and the final bond is very strong.

PLASTIC CEMENT

This is the classic glue used to put together model airplane kits. It dries quickly and is ideal for mending toys and other solid plastic items.

HOT GLUE

Hot glue guns are an enormous amount of fun to use. Glue sticks are melted in an electrically heated gun and applied through a nozzle. The glue is strong and sticks rapidly as it cools. This is another good way of sticking flat items and most materials are suitable for sticking. However, as the glue softens when hot, it can't be used where heat resistance is needed.

REPAIRING CHINA & GLASS

GLUING CHINA AND CERAMICS

If you break a piece of china, mend it as quickly as possible. If you leave it – or worse, use and wash it repeatedly with a piece missing – the surfaces will wear down and you will never be able to match them back together precisely.

Choosing the right glue is important – most crockery items will need to stand up to heat and water occasionally, so use an epoxy resin rather than 'superglue' for a longer-lasting fix. Resin is also much better for getting a join to match exactly, as it doesn't set immediately.

TOOLS YOU WILL NEED
You will need epoxy resin glue (a quick-setting brand is ideal), a toothpick, and some acetone (nail varnish remover) for wiping away any glue that oozes from the join. Masking tape is also useful to hold the pieces in place while the glue dries.

THE STEPS
1. Before mending, make sure the two surfaces are clean and dry. After drying, dust them with a paintbrush to remove any specks of dirt that would get in the way of matching up the two surfaces.

2. Using resin glue means you'll need to support your item while it sets, and the best way of doing this is usually with modelling clay. Large pieces of clay are excellent for holding the flat pieces of a plate together on a surface. Alternatively, use masking tape or, for a handle repair on a cup or mug, fill a bowl with rice and bury the piece with the broken faces upwards.

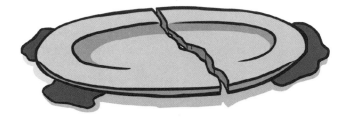

USE MODELLING CLAY TO SUPPORT REPAIRS WHILE GLUE DRIES

3. Mix the two parts of your resin glue together then, using a toothpick, apply the glue to the surface of the supported piece.

4. Carefully bring the other piece into place, looking all around the join to make sure it lines up perfectly. Use masking tape to secure the pieces (a good insurance against people accidentally knocking into the piece while the glue dries – it may take up to 15 minutes for the glue to hold it properly).

5. Before the resin sets, wipe away any glue that has escaped from the join or got on to the surface of your piece, using a cloth dampened with acetone or white spirit (don't over-wet it or the solvent may run into the join).

6. Leave for about an hour to set fully. If necessary, touch up any remaining surface defects using enamel paint or nail varnish that matches the original glaze.

FILL A BOWL WITH RICE TO HOLD A CUP WHILE REPAIRING THE HANDLE

REPAIRING CHINA & GLASS

GLASS REPAIRS

Small chips in the edges of quality glassware can be 're-paired' by grinding the pieces down to below the level of the chip. This is only to be tried by professionals, but many artisans and antique experts are available to help if your good crystal is damaged.

Home mending of breakages is also possible for glassware. Epoxy resin glue will hold glass together perfectly well. However, it dries to a cloudy white colour which yellows with age, and this will make the break obvious.

It's better to use special light-activated clear glue, which will make your repair much less visible. Always follow the instructions that come with this glue, as the formulation will vary between brands.

Light-activated glue won't work very well on coloured glass so, for these items, you should use epoxy resin and follow the same methods as for china above.

The glue won't set until it is placed in sunlight, so apply it and reassemble your piece under a lightbulb, using masking tape to hold the pieces together firmly.

Then, place on a sunny windowsill and the glue will set firmly in a few hours – exactly how long depends on how bright the light is, so will vary depending on the season.

If, after hardening, any glue has oozed out of the join, scrape this away with a metal blade – don't use sandpaper, which will scratch the glass.

LIGHT-ACTIVATED GLUE SETS IN SUNLIGHT

SAFETY NOTE

Be very careful when handling broken glass. Wear gloves that protect your hands and wrists.

KNIVES, FORKS, SPOONS & MORE

We do like to abuse our cutlery drawer, often by treating it as an impromptu toolbox. Who hasn't used a spoon to open a tin of paint, or made a butter knife stand in for a screwdriver?

We also leave our knives and forks sitting around in water for hours and put them through hot dishwasher cycles, so no wonder we have problems with handles falling off.

Sharp knives also lose their edge over time, and we're often more willing to put up with a blunt knife than find out how to sharpen it properly and make chopping vegetables easy again.

In this section I'll show you how to keep your cutlery drawer in good order, by sharpening, straightening and mending your kitchen tools.

SHARPENING KNIVES

Chopping, carving and slicing food with a blunt knife isn't only messy and frustrating; it's also quite dangerous. With a blunt knife, you need to use more pressure to force the blade through, and this means your knife is more likely to slip off a surface or bounce off a bone and cause an accident.

There are two separate cook's skills you should learn in order to keep your kitchen knives in condition: steeling and sharpening.

STEELING

You should use a 'steel' to straighten the edge each time you use a sharp knife, after washing and drying it.

A steel is a rounded, usually metal, rod with a handle. It will often have either fine grooves carved along it or a diamond coating. You may have seen chefs wielding these on TV. The sight of an expert flashing a blade up and down a steel with a whooshing sound is very impressive but this is, in fact, not a difficult skill to learn if you follow these tips.

It is important to remember that, by using a steel you aren't 'sharpening' your knife, but 'honing' it by straightening up the edge.

Think about the thin metal point along the edge of a really sharp knife. When you use it, the blade will knock against your chopping board and the very thin edge of the blade can become folded and bent. Using a steel simply whips this edge back into line, ready for the next time you need to use it.

HOW TO STEEL A KNIFE

1. Hold the steel firmly in your non-primary hand, slightly away from your body. It should be at a comfortable upwards angle, and your elbow should be bent.

2. With the knife in your other hand, hold the base of the blade on top of the tip of the steel at an angle of about 20 degrees, with the sharp edge of the blade facing you.

3. Holding the knife steadily at the same angle to the steel, move your hand downwards and towards you, drawing the edge of the blade along the steel. You want the tip of the knife to end up sliding off the steel at its base. This movement can be done very quickly and smoothly with practice, but don't worry if you are rather slow to begin with.

4. Repeat this three or four times with the blade on top of the steel. You don't need to put a lot of pressure on while steeling. Remember that you are realigning a very thin strip of metal, and this doesn't need a lot of force.

5. To steel the other side of the blade, repeat the process, this time with the blade tilted upwards under the steel, also at an angle of 20 degrees. Press slightly downwards with the steel onto the blade (rather than upwards with the knife). Apart from the change in angle of the blade against the steel, all the movements are identical to the previous step.

SHARPENING

Needless to say, steeling won't help sharpen a knife that has no edge at all. If steeling doesn't make your knife more effective, look along its edge towards a window to inspect it. A really sharp edge will hardly reflect any light, but a blunt or rounded edge will be very noticeable.

HOW TO SHARPEN A KNIFE

For this job, you'll need a whetstone. As its name suggests, this is a flat abrasive piece of stone, often attached to a block of wood or plastic that supports it.

To sharpen an edge, wet the stone, place it on a firm surface, then stroke the knife along it in long, steady strokes, working one side at a time.

For a good edge, it's important to ensure you keep the knife at a constant angle, both within a stroke and between strokes. An angle of around 20 degrees is usually suitable.

There are several ways to hold the knife that will keep the angle accurate and steady. Pressing the rear edge of the knife into your fingers or thumb (depending on how you grip it) is a good method, as it will leave an impression on your skin, which you can use as a guide to place the edge in the same location when you turn over the blade.

You could also rest the edge of the knife on a small item of the right height, such as a block of wood. Whatever you choose must be able to slide smoothly across your work surface while supporting the blade.

Swap sides after each half a dozen strokes to grind a symmetrical edge. Each side of the knife blade may need ten, twenty, thirty or more strokes across the stone to grind a really sharp edge, depending on the hardness of the steel on the edge of the blade.

After you have ground your new edge, make sure it is straight with a few strokes of your steel, before finishing.

A NOD TO THE PROFESSIONALS

While this is a home repair that can achieve very satisfying results, remember that knife sharpening is a genuine skill, and that a professional knife grinder will always do a better and more long-lasting job.

KNIVES, FORKS, SPOONS & MORE

CARE FOR YOUR KNIVES

Good kitchen knives should be kept out of the dishwasher. High temperatures can soften the steel blades and they can easily receive knocks and bumps from other items during the washing cycle.

For more long-lasting knives, wash them gently by hand after use, dry immediately with a tea-towel (to prevent rust) and then steel them lightly before putting them away.

STRAIGHTENING CUTLERY

Cutlery gets bent out of shape for a range of reasons – often when we use it as a substitute for a proper tool. If your cutlery drawer is starting to look like you've had a visit from a wild-eyed mystic, here's how to get things back in line.

Most cutlery is made from stainless steel. This is a virtually rust-proof alloy made with high concentrations of chromium and nickel. Unlike silver cutlery, which is soft and easily bent, stainless steel is very strong, which makes it difficult to bend back into shape.

To make it easier, and to reduce the risk of snapping, work on your cutlery while the metal is warm. Soaking in hot water is the best way to heat your knife, fork or spoon evenly, and won't risk it getting too hot to handle (which could easily happen if you placed it in the oven, for example).

Don't grab your cutlery directly with pliers or a clamp, as the metal grips on these tools will leave marks behind. Instead, wrap the piece in a cloth to protect the surface.

TIPS FOR DIFFERENT PIECES

BENT SPOON HANDLE
Grip the handle of the spoon firmly in a clamp (or improvise by placing it between books in a tightly packed bookcase). Ensure the bend sits exactly at the point where the handle emerges from your clamp.

Hold the bowl of the spoon in two hands, using a cloth or towel to get a firm grip without digging into your hands.

Bend firmly but slowly until you feel the metal give. Don't bend too enthusiastically: it's better to straighten it in two or three stages than to go too far and end up having to bend it back again. This will weaken the metal and make it more likely to break.

BEND IN THE TIP OF A KNIFE
This can be straightened out roughly by clamping the handle and using pliers to bend back the tip (make sure you wrap a cloth around it). However, you will get more accurate results by hammering out the kink instead.

Place a warmed knife blade flat on a wooden chopping board with a cloth laid on top. Then, hammer the end using many firm (but not violent) blows with a metal hammer. You may need to re-warm the thin tip of the knife several times during this process to ensure the metal stays slightly softened. Keeping a cup of hot water nearby can help make this easier.

KNIVES, FORKS, SPOONS & MORE

FORK TINES BENT OUTWARDS

If the prongs of a fork (or 'tines', to give them their proper name) have splayed outwards, you can squeeze them back together while warm by wrapping the fork in a cloth and squeezing with pliers. If pliers won't fit around the fork, lay it on its side and hammer the tines gently with a hammer, switching sides from time to time to squeeze them together evenly.

FORK TINES MISALIGNED OR BENT INWARDS

A wooden ruler is the best tool for realigning the tines if they bend inwards or are out of line.

Place the ruler between the tines and use it as a lever to bend the tines back into a flat row.

A good technique is to 'nudge' the tines using several small movements, rather than trying to force them into the right place in one large movement. This risks going too far the other way, and moving them back may lead to 'work-hardening' and weakness, which may cause a tine to break off.

REPLACING CUTLERY HANDLES

With frequent use, the glue inside the handle of plastic- or bone-handled cutlery can perish, making the handle wobble or break off. This kind of cutlery shouldn't be washed in a dishwasher or left to soak in water, as this will speed up the deterioration of the glue and make problems more likely.

If a handle does work loose, it is easily repaired in a few minutes with glue and few simple tools. Since your knives and forks will need to be washed regularly, you should choose a water-resistant glue for this job, such as two-part epoxy resin.

THE STEPS

1. If necessary, remove the loose handle. You may need to pull it out with pliers – if so, wrap the metal parts in a cloth to prevent marking.

2. Clean any glue deposits from the metal post that is inserted into the handle (the 'tang').

3. Clean the old glue out of the hole in the handle using a thin scraping tool suchas a nailfile or thin woodworking file. It is a good idea to wash out the handle after scraping, so that any dust is removed and doesn't prevent the glue from making a firm bond.

4. Mix up a suitable quantity of glue. Then, wrap the handle in masking tape to protect it from smears and then put glue into the hole in the handle, using a toothpick or wooden skewer to push it right inside. You want to end up with the hole about two-thirds full with glue.

5. Push the tang back into the hole and wipe away any glue that is pushed out of the hole, using a rag and a small amount of acetone or white spirit.

Once the glue has set, you can remove the masking tape and your cutlery will be as good as new for several more years.

Cupboard doors in fitted kitchens normally start out perfectly aligned. But, after a while, knocks, bumps and heavy use (including being used as a swing by your children!) will mean they get out of line – sometimes to the extent that neighbouring doors bang together.

You have probably noticed that the special hinges on these doors have an array of screws holding them in place, and have probably also thought that adjusting these might help with the wonkiness. However, working out which screws to adjust can be a barrier to getting out the screwdriver and sorting out this simple problem.

In order to help, here's the definitive guide to adjusting your cupboard doors.

This isn't only useful in the kitchen, of course. Many cupboards and sideboards elsewhere in the home use the same type of hinges and can also be fixed with this method.

ADJUSTING CONCEALED HINGES

The concealed hinge has a very clever design, which allows the door to swing open without needing extra space to the side of the cupboard. It achieves this by allowing the part of the hinge attached to the door to extend, moving the door outwards as it swings open.

CONCEALED HINGE SCREWS

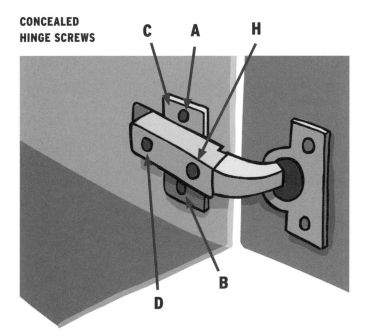

THESE HINGES CAN BE ADJUSTED IN THREE WAYS:

1. VERTICAL POSITION OF THE DOOR
This is controlled by adjusting the position of the inner part of the hinge.

Different models have different ways of controlling this. The simplest have oblong screw holes. To adjust these, loosen the A and B screws in the diagram on both the top and bottom hinges of a door, and move the door up or down before tightening the screws again.

Other models have solid, round holes for the A and B screws and a separate 'cam screw' (at position C in the diagram) that can be adjusted to move the inner part up or down a few millimetres.

2. DISTANCE OF THE DOOR FROM THE CUPBOARD
This is controlled by the D screw. On some models this may be a 'cam' adjusting screw that you turn one way or the other to move the door. On these models the outer and inner parts clip together and this screw simply controls their position.

On other models, this screw may actually fix the outer part of the hinge to the inner part. In this case, loosening the screw will enable you to slide the outer part in or out before tightening it again.

3. HORIZONTAL POSITION AND ALIGNMENT OF THE DOOR
If a door is wonky or if it is too close or too far from its neighbour, screw H on the diagram can be adjusted.

Tightening it will pull the door closer to the hinge and away from the neighbouring cupboard. For a door that is not parallel, you'll need to tighten only one of these screws, on the top or bottom hinge, to straighten it up.

4. A WOBBLY DOOR
If a door wobbles, this means that the screws holding one of the hinge parts is loose – most likely the A and B screws that fix the inner part of the hinge to the cupboard or the D screw that holds the outer part of the hinge in place.

Simply tightening these should fix this problem.

Simple Plumbing & Bathroom Repairs

The plumbing system runs through a home like arteries in a body – and we wouldn't last in comfort for long without a functioning water supply. I remember my mum's relief at finally being able to take a hot shower after more than two weeks without running water when floods in England put her local water treatment plant out of action.

Plumbers are usually easy to find in an emergency but come at a price, so it pays to be able to fix simple problems yourself. And, of course, with extreme droughts as well as extreme floods becoming more common as climate change takes hold, conserving water is important too. Fixing a tap could help save tens of thousands of litres of clean water in a year – all those drips really add up!

Having a better understanding of how water systems, radiators and taps work is also useful when creating a more beautiful, stylish home. If you know how to replace a tap, it can make those gorgeous retro fittings in the salvage yard a realistic purchase, not simply something to dream about.

And, on a more practical note, properly insulated pipes and tanks can save plenty of money in saved energy if we know how to keep our lagging in order.

This section will run through some plumbing and bathroom repairs and revamps that anyone can manage without specialist knowledge. From fixing a leaky tap to mending tiles and keeping mould and limescale at bay, it will help you conserve resources and keep your home looking great as well.

HOW TO TURN OFF THE WATER

If you don't know how to turn off the water supply to your home, you should set about finding your stopcocks (called stop valves in Australia) straight away. If a disaster happens and a pipe leaks, turning off the water quickly can make the difference between a damp carpet and major structural damage.

THE EXTERNAL SUPPLY

Depending on your home, there may be one or two stopcocks that turn off the water supply. For houses, one can usually be found on the property border near the street. This should be under a small iron cover, suitably labelled. You may have a water meter and, if so, you might find this under the same cover. (Most Australian and New Zealand houses have water meters, which are located above ground.)

The stopcock is simply a tap but, as in Britain it is normally a couple of feet underground, you'll need a simple tool called a 'stopcock key' to turn it. These are sold for very little money in DIY merchants. However, most homes come with one ready supplied by the previous occupants, so you may find one in your meter cupboard or garage.

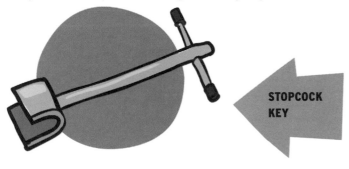

STOPCOCK KEY

CAUTION

In Australia and New Zealand, almost all plumbing work beyond simple tasks such as replacing taps or washers must be carried out by a licensed plumber. In particular, it is illegal for anyone other than a licensed plumber to perform work on any system connected to the main water supply or the sewer system. The purpose of these regulations is to prevent the contamination of the water supply and other serious problems. It is essential to check with your local authority before undertaking any plumbing work.

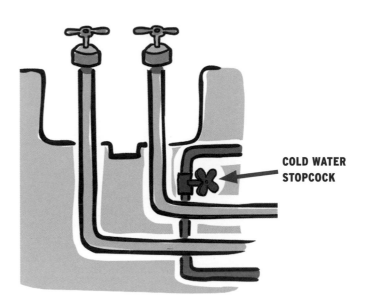

COLD WATER STOPCOCK

THE INTERNAL COLD WATER STOPCOCK

A second cold water stopcock is often found inside a property – commonly under the kitchen sink. This will be a large tap that you turn with your hand.

When you find your stopcocks, this is a good time to check that you can turn them on and off. They may become stuck if they haven't been turned for years, and you don't want to discover this when you are in the middle of an emergency. If you find a tap is stuck, spray it with some penetrating oil to loosen it and then close and open it to check it works.

THE HOT WATER STOPCOCK

Your home will also have a second internal stopcock for the hot water supply. This will usually be found at the outlet of your boiler or hot water tank. If you need to turn off the hot water, turn off the water heater at the same time.

OTHER SHUT-OFF TAPS

You may find taps that control individual parts of the water supply elsewhere in the home. For example, showers, baths and sinks may have valves in the pipes nearby that you can use to isolate these fittings without turning off the whole supply.

A constant drip from a tap should be fixed as quickly as possible, especially if you pay for your water via a meter. Even one drip per second can add up to more than 80 litres of water down the drain in just a day.

A DRIP FROM THE SPOUT

This is usually caused by a worn washer. Most of us know vaguely that 'replacing the washer' will solve this, but not where the washer in question can be found or, indeed, how to replace it. The diagrams on the next page aim to make everything clear. They show the two most common types of taps, and the washer that wears out most often at the base of the handle unit.

The washer forms a seal that prevents water from the pipe below from flowing out when the tap is closed. It is made of rubber and, when this gets damaged or perished, it no longer makes a proper seal and needs replacing.

TOOLS FOR REPLACING A WASHER
Depending on the type of tap you have, you will need an adjustable spanner or 'monkey wrench', a thin cloth or rag, pliers, a screwdriver, and possibly some petroleum jelly and penetrating spray oil to loosen any stuck screws and nuts.

BEFORE YOU START THIS REPAIR, YOU NEED TO DO TWO THINGS:

1. GET REPLACEMENT PARTS.
Washers for most taps above come in standard sizes. However, some modern taps do without washers altogether or may have different seals. See later for more on washerless taps.

2. TURN OFF THE WATER SUPPLY.
You may find an isolation valve on the pipe below the tap you need to work on. This needs to be turned with a screwdriver. If there isn't one, find the nearest stopcock and turn off the supply there instead. Turn on the tap to make sure no water is coming out before you start to dismantle it!

FIXING TAPS

THE STEPS

1. Remove the handle and cover from the tap (or the combined handle and cover) then unscrew the tap headgear nut to remove the body of the tap from the fitting. Cover the nut with a cloth if it will be visible while the tap is in use, to protect it from scratches.

It is important to secure the spout while you unscrew the headgear, in order to prevent the whole tap turning round. This can damage the pipework or crack the sink. Get a helper to hold the tap firmly by the spout or hold it with the hand not holding the spanner. Use penetrating oil to loosen the nut if it is stuck, rather than using too much force and breaking your bathroom suite.

2. Once the body of the tap comes away, you can remove the old washer from the pin at the bottom. It may just pull off with pliers, or you may need to remove a small nut or screw.

You should be able to see the damage to the washer that is causing the drip. If the washer appears to be in good condition, then the valve seat inside the fitting may have worn down instead. This can be repaired at home, but it's best to call a plumber as special tools are needed to regrind the surface of the valve.

3. Fit the new washer. It may be a tight fit to get the washer over the pin. If so, apply some petroleum jelly and use the side of your pliers or a spanner to push it down.

4. Now you can replace the tap headgear, taking care to hold the tap securely when tightening the nut. Turn the water supply back on and check the tap is working properly again.

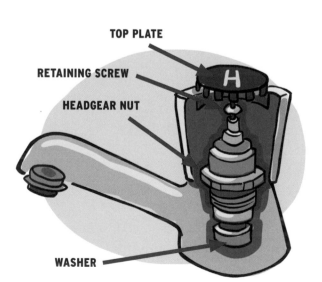

TOP PLATE

RETAINING SCREW

HEADGEAR NUT

WASHER

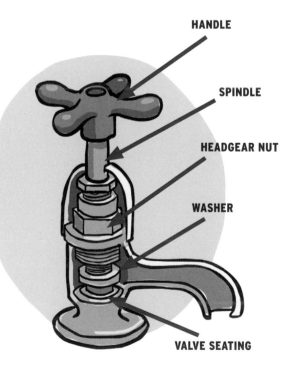

HANDLE

SPINDLE

HEADGEAR NUT

WASHER

VALVE SEATING

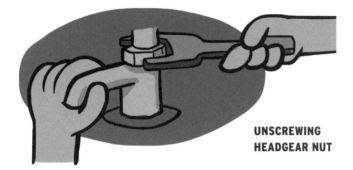

**UNSCREWING
HEADGEAR NUT**

WASHERLESS TAPS

Taps with ball valves or ceramic discs are two modern designs that don't have traditional washers to seal the pipe shut. These usually have a mixer function and pivoting handles that control water flow and temperature.

These taps are less likely to need maintenance than traditional models. However they do have various seals and moving parts that can go wrong. If you have had them fitted recently, you may find the user manual gives enough information on how to dismantle the tap head and replace a leaking 'o-ring' or another simple part.

If not, it's usually best to call in a plumber the first time something goes wrong and take note of how it's done. It's not strictly in their interest, but you could try asking them to leave a few spare seals for you to use next time!

MIXER TAPS

Mixer taps come in a range of different designs but most consist of two taps attached to a single, central spout. These taps can be mended in the same way as single taps. However, you will need to work out first which tap is causing a drip from the communal spout. The simplest way to do this is to turn off the supply to each tap in turn and check which stops the drip.

Mixer units may also have a separate 'o-ring' seal at the base of the spout. This can be replaced without turning off the water supply, but make sure you get the correct size replacement before starting work.

STEM SEALS ON A TAP (SEE OVERLEAF)

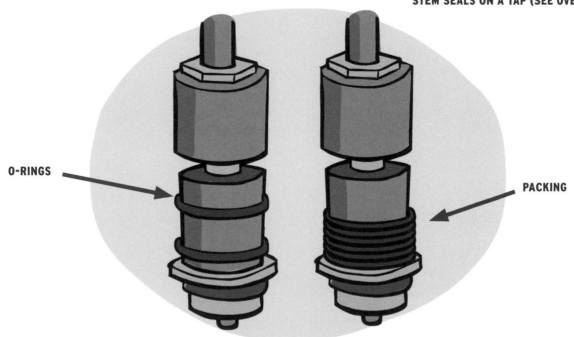

O-RINGS

PACKING

REPLACING TAPS

A DRIP FROM THE HANDLE OR STEM

If a leak is coming from the handle or stem of your tap, rather than the spout, your washer is not to blame. Instead, it's likely that the seal on the inside of the stem of the tap is at fault.

This seal can be made by either a washer-like rubber 'o-ring' (or several o-rings) or by string-like 'packing' wound around the stem of the tap.

Open up your tap in the same way as before to check which type and size of seal you need before buying a re-placement from a DIY shop.

REPLACING A TAP

Removing an old tap and putting in a new one isn't much more difficult than changing a washer. If you are replac-ing one standard-size tap with another, it's simply a case of switching off the water, removing the old parts and attach-ing the new taps to the pipes and fixings.

TOOLS YOU WILL NEED

For this repair, you'll need a screwdriver and monkey wrench, and a cloth to prevent scratches on visible nuts and bolts. Penetrating oil can help to unstick stiff fittings, and you may also need sealant or filler to seal any gaps around the new taps. Finally, a roll of plumber's PTFE tape is useful to wrap around the screw threads on your new fittings. It will help them to go on smoothly, and will also make the nuts easier to unscrew later, if necessary.

**MIXER TAP
WITH FLEXIBLE PIPES**

Remember to pay close attention to the order and function of the nuts and bolts you remove, and to replace the new parts in the same order.

If you are fitting a brand new tap, it will probably come with diagrams and instructions but, for a reclaimed fitting, you'll need to work out which parts correspond to your existing fittings. Remember to check and replace any worn seals and washers on second-hand taps.

When finished, turn the water supply on at a slow trickle via the stopcock or tap isolation valve. Check carefully for leaks before turning it up gradually to full pressure.

If you are switching from single taps to a mixer tap, the new system may need pipes to be moved or extra holes creating in your sink or bath, so you may need professional help. However, many mixer fittings come with flexible inlet pipes that will cope with a range of different hole sizes and locations.

Lots of nasty things can clump together in your waste pipes and drains and cause blockages. From food scraps and fat in the kitchen to twigs and leaves in the outdoor drains, via hair, tissue and some much less pleasant substances in the bathroom, most drains will clog up from time to time.

SINKS, BATHS AND SHOWERS

It's tempting to reach for strong chemical unblockers when a plughole starts to back up, but these are less than eco-friendly and unnecessary for most blockages. Try these greener methods first, and you can keep your drains clear without increasing pollution.

2. USE A PLUNGER TO FORCE IT OUT

If the hot water doesn't work, wait for it to cool (you don't want to be plunging in scalding water!) and then use a plunger to try to force the blockage down the pipe. Fill the sink with a few inches of water, then seal the overflow outlet with one hand to maintain the pressure in the pipe (placing a damp cloth in your hand can make a better seal) and plunge firmly to force water down the pipe.

Once the blockage clears, run some more hot water down the sink to really wash it out and clear any remaining fat deposits.

1. LOOSEN THE BLOCKAGE WITH BOILING WATER

In the kitchen, a large part of a blockage may be solidified fat from food products. Pouring a kettle full of boiling water down the sink can help melt and loosen the blockage. If the sink is draining slowly, wait until the water level has dropped before doing this, so that the hot water gets in close contact with the blockage.

UNBLOCKING DRAINS

3. USE AN AUGER TO BREAK UP THE BLOCKAGE

Plunging may still not create enough force to clear a really stubborn pipe blockage. In this case, a wire auger may do the trick by breaking up the blockage in the pipe. An auger is a long, flexible wire tool with a spiral end that can grip and pull a blockage apart. Some models have a handle that turns the end, while with others you simply twist the free end to rotate the whole wire. This tool is especially good at grabbing hold of a plug of hair that may be blocking a bathroom drain.

Remove the plug hole cover if necessary – normally this will come away if you push a pencil into one of the holes and lever it up, or it may be attached with a screw. Then, push the auger down the hole until you meet resistance where the drain curves into the U-bend below the sink.

Twist the auger and push firmly and it will work its way around the bend. Continue to push and twist the auger until it is far enough down the pipe to meet the blockage.

Then, break up the blockage by twisting, pushing and pulling the auger so that the end grabs and disrupts the blockage. Pull the auger slowly backwards if you can tell you have gripped a ball of hair. This can be dragged back up out of the plughole, which reduces the chance it will clog up again further down the pipe.

Run water down the pipe periodically to see how well you have unblocked it. Once you're confident it's running freely again, finish off with some hot water and washing soda to clean the pipes properly.

4. BREAK INTO THE TRAP

Dismantling the under-workings of your sink is the last thing to try if none of the methods above works. It may be that the blockage is something really tough, such as solidified plaster or glue, and bypassing the trap can also give you better access to the pipes with an auger if the blockage is further down.

You don't need to turn off the water to do this job, but remember to put a bucket underneath before starting to unscrew the U-bend or bottle trap, as the water from the sink will drain out as soon as you loosen the connections. The fitting should be designed with easy to turn plastic connectors, but you may need a large wrench if they have become stiff.

Once you have removed whatever is causing the blockage, add PTFE tape to the screw threads before reattaching to ensure a good seal and easier removal next time.

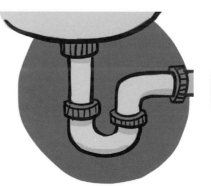

U-BEND

BOTTLE TRAP

TOILETS

Toilets usually block because a build-up of paper creates a plug in the S-trap or P-trap behind the bowl, and mechanical methods work best in this situation too.

A sink auger, while not strictly designed for the purpose, can be used to unblock a toilet as well. As the bottom of the bowl is quite wide, you may need to put your hand below the water line to guide the auger over the first bend and prevent it simply curling up in the bowl. Sorry about this – wear rubber gloves to make it less nasty, and wash the gloves and your hands thoroughly afterwards and you will survive!

As before, push and twist the auger through the pipes and attack the blockage to break it up.

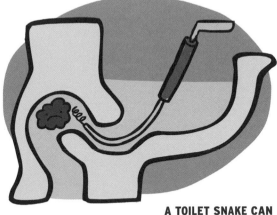

A TOILET SNAKE CAN CLEAR A TOUGH BLOCKAGE

**S-TRAP
DRAINS INTO FLOOR PIPE**

**P-TRAP
DRAINS INTO WALL PIPE**

If the blockage is too tough for the sink auger, more specialist tools can help. They can be hired from tool-hire shops if you don't want to have one permanently on standby in the house.

A TOILET SNAKE
This is shorter and thicker than a sink auger, and has a handle that will turn the end more firmly. The snake is easy to use, and can break up almost any kind of blockage in the bend.

A TOILET PLUNGER
This is larger than a sink plunger, and has a special cup designed to seal the exit of the toilet bowl and force out a blockage in the same way as a sink plunger. You can also try a large sink plunger for this job, and it will sometimes do the job well.

When the blockage shifts and the pipe clears, you will hear a very satisfying gurgle and the water level in the bowl will drop quickly. Flush the toilet several times to wash out the pipe completely, then clean the bowl and surrounding area very well to remove any splashes of dirty water.

UNBLOCKING DRAINS

OUTDOOR DRAINS

Clearing the drains that run under the ground outside your home is often a job for professionals with industrial-sized equipment. However, it is helpful to be able to check and fix simple problems that may occur at the entrances to this system in gullies and manholes.

UNBLOCKING A GULLY

Gullies leading to the sewage system are found around the walls of the house, where they collect water from gutters and pipes from sinks and appliances. They are normally covered with a metal grate or plastic grid.

Often, the first sign you will see of a blockage further down the drainage system will be an overflowing gully, but the gully itself may also become blocked due to items coming down the pipes or falling between the bars of the grate.

Sometimes, pipes will be positioned so that they discharge water above the level of the grate, and this means leaves or litter can get in the way of the flow of the water. Removing these blockages is simple, but you should also ask a plumber to extend the pipe below the level of the grate, or the problem is likely to recur (building regulations usually state that pipes in new homes should always be fitted this way).

If the problem is below the level of the grate, you'll need to remove it and check for blockages at the bottom of the gully.

TOOLS YOU WILL NEED
For this job, you'll need a tool to lever off the grate (any metal tool that will fit between the bars will do, such as a hand-held garden fork) and rubber gloves. You will also possibly need a sink plunger or a sink auger.

THE STEPS

1. Start by levering off the grate or grid. Clear off any debris or litter and, if necessary, scrub away moss with a brush.

2. Clear out the drain opening beneath the grate using your hand. Put on rubber gloves for this job and be careful in case glass, broken pottery or scrap metal has found its way into the gully.

3. Run water into the gully via one of the appliances that drain into it. If the gully is still blocked, try plunging or using the sink auger to loosen a blockage. If the blockage appears to be made from fat from a kitchen sink, boiling water can help to melt and loosen it (often fat that is liquid in warm water solidifies here as the water hits cold air outside and cools down).

If you can't identify and clear a blockage in the pipes near the gully, the problem is further down the system, and you should check the manhole covers that lead to the sewerage system under your street.

THE MAIN DRAINS

The gullies that collect waste water from baths, sinks and gutters meet up with the pipes carrying waste from toilets, and these pipes eventually join together to form a single drain leading to the main sewerage system in your street. (In Australia and New Zealand, rainwater is discharged into a separate stormwater drain).

There may be several manhole covers (circular inspection covers in New Zealand and Australia) on your property at the points where the pipes meet, and a final manhole will be located near the street. These covers can be opened to allow 'rodding' of the drains when the pipes become blocked.

If your gullies overflow and don't unblock when you clear them, or if one of the manhole covers starts to overflow or smell, it's worth checking the manholes to see if there is a problem you can fix, or if you need to call in a professional with a set of drain rods. If there is a simple blockage in the trap of a manhole, you can often clear this yourself.

SAFETY NOTE

If working on drains that carry sewage, make sure you clean all your tools and gloves (and yourself) thoroughly afterwards, as sewage can carry diseases and dangerous bacteria. (Australian and New Zealand should refer to the note on page 150.)

Also be careful not to trap your fingers when lifting and replacing heavy manhole covers. It helps to lift the cover slightly, using a lever such as a trowel or a spade, and then wedge a piece of wood under the rim before bending down and using both hands (wearing thick gloves) to lift up the cover. When replacing the cover, place another piece of wood diagonally across one corner of the hole and lay the cover on top of this to make lining things up easier.

When you have opened a manhole cover, make sure children are kept out of the way, and that adults are aware of the hazard and don't trip or fall in it. Leave a chair with a warning notice pinned to it in front of the hole if it lies on a common pathway around the home.

Open each manhole cover to see which are flooded and which are not. Locate the last flooded manhole before the street drain. The blockage will either be within that manhole or in the pipe leading to the next one.

It is possible that leaves, washed down the gutters, are causing the blockage, or that household waste or sewage has blocked the trap leading out of the manhole. After clearing any obvious objects, use a piece of wood or a sink or toilet auger to try to clear the trap. If this doesn't work, then call in a specialist.

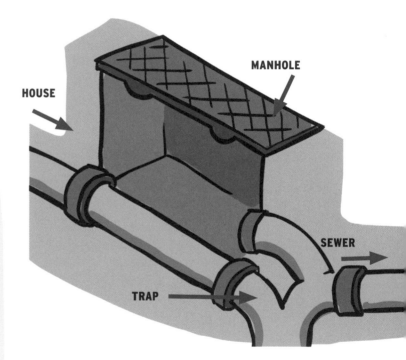

Even a couple of hours without a working toilet can be a very anxious time. Toilets are the cause of most emergency calls to plumbers, but the most common problems can be quite easily mended at home. You can even remove and replace the main working parts of your cistern without too much trouble.

HOW A TOILET WORKS

The basic principles behind all flush toilets are the same. A cistern holding several litres of water sits above a bowl that has a reversing 'trap' arrangement of pipes behind it.

To flush the contents of the bowl down and past the trap, the cistern empties its contents rapidly into the bowl when a handle or button is operated.

Cisterns can be separate from the bowl and joined with a pipe (two-piece cistern) or attached directly to the bowl (close-coupled cisterns).

Inside the cistern there may be a simple valve that empties it by gravity (common in high-level cisterns) or a siphon that pushes out the water.

The refilling of the cistern after flushing is controlled by a ball float that opens a valve when the water level falls, closing it again when it reaches the right level.

Also inside the cistern will be an overflow pipe, which may drain into the toilet bowl or through a pipe to the drains or outer wall of the house.

**SCREW ADJUSTS
HEIGHT OF BALL FLOAT**

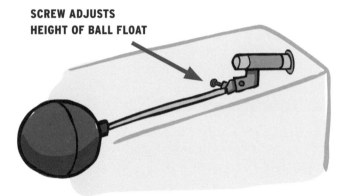

ADJUSTING THE FLOAT

If the cistern is overflowing or failing to refill, the position of the ballcock arm may need to be adjusted. Take the top off the cistern and check the position of the ball float. If it is sitting low in the water, it may have sprung a leak and need to be replaced. New floats cost very little money and are simple to change, usually being screwed directly on to the arm or held in place with a small nut or screw.

If the ball is floating, but the water level is too low, you will need to adjust the position of the arm. Depending on the age of your system, the arm may be made of metal or plastic. If it is made of metal, you simply need to bend the arm to raise the ball float. If it is plastic, you'll find a small screw near the base of the arm, which can be adjusted to angle it upwards. Always make sure the ball float does not scrape against the side of the cistern.

If the water level is too high, the ball float may be sitting too high, or the valve may be at fault. Test the ballcock valve by pulling up the ball float with your hand. If the water flow stops, then you just need to lower the ball float using the methods above.

A BALLCOCK VALVE PROBLEM

If the water continues to flow even with the ball float raised to its highest level, you have a fault in the valve itself. It may have become damaged or have grit inside it from the water supply and will probably need to be replaced. It is best to get a plumber to do this repair as the design of the valve varies widely, and special parts may be needed to fix it.

REPAIRING A HANDLE LINK

If the toilet won't flush at all, the metal link between the handle lever and the siphon may have snapped or bent and slipped off the siphon or handle. If the link is still in one piece, it may be possible to re-attach it and bend it back into shape with pliers, but this will weaken it and make it more likely to snap in future.

If the link is broken, you can rig up a temporary replacement with a wire coat hanger and pliers until you can buy a replacement from a hardware shop.

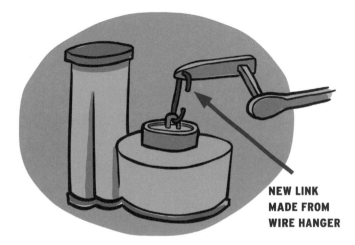

**NEW LINK
MADE FROM
WIRE HANGER**

TOILET REPAIRS

REPLACING A DAMAGED SIPHON

A toilet that flushes but only releases a small amount of water into the bowl is likely to have a damaged siphon. The most common fault is a broken siphon diaphragm – this part sits in the bottom of the siphon and is raised to push the water above it out into the flush pipe, which then pulls the rest of the water in the cistern through the siphon.

You can replace the diaphragm, or replace the whole siphon unit at once. Depending on the siphon design, it can be simpler to replace the whole siphon, as it comes in a self-contained unit, and means you get an entire set of new parts at the same time.

TOOLS YOU WILL NEED
As well as a replacement siphon, you'll need a large wrench, PTFE tape, and a sponge and bucket for clearing away water. If your toilet is a close-coupled model, you may also need a smaller adjustable wrench, a screwdriver and silicone sealant.

A QUICK-CHANGE SIPHON

Your toilet may be fitted with a quick-change siphon unit. This has an extra connection in the vertical flush pipe, which means it can be removed and replaced without emptying the cistern.

As the siphon is easy to remove, it can be better to replace only the diaphragm if the rest of the unit it in good condition.

For these siphons, you simply need to unscrew the connection to the vertical flush pipe, unhook the flush lever and replace the siphon or diaphragm. This takes just a few minutes.

ONE-PIECE SIPHON

CHANGING A ONE-PIECE SIPHON UNIT

If you have a one-piece siphon, this mending job means emptying the cistern, unscrewing and replacing the siphon unit and then putting everything back together again. It isn't a complicated job, but does need to be done carefully.

Siphon connections don't vary, but the units do come in different sizes. When buying a replacement, measure the length, width and height of your existing siphon and get one the same size to ensure it will fit into your cistern.

QUICK-CHANGE SIPHON

TIP!

Close the toilet seat when doing any toilet repairs to prevent any washers or parts falling into the bowl!

THE STEPS

1. You need to empty the cistern completely before you start. Turn off the water supply to the toilet, either via a local stop-valve or the main stopcock. Flush the toilet to clear the cistern, then sponge out any remaining water until the inside is almost completely dry.

2. If your toilet is a close-coupled model, you will need to remove the cistern from the wall and the toilet bowl in order to get to the siphon connections. The cistern will be mounted on brackets and bolts which you can undo with a wrench and screwdriver. If the cistern has also been sealed where it joins the wall, cut away the sealant with a knife (you'll need to reseal it after you have finished). In addition, you will need to disconnect the water inlet pipe from the ballcock valve and remove any external overflow pipes. Note the position of any washers of fixings you remove while you do this, and keep these safe.

3. If your toilet is in two pieces, you just need to release the flush pipe from the bottom of the cistern to get the siphon out (release this by undoing the bottom nut of the two nuts you'll see beneath the cistern). You don't need to remove the cistern from the wall, but place a bucket or bowl underneath the pipe to catch any water remaining in the siphon while you complete these steps.

4. Now disconnect the siphon from the cistern by undoing the nut holding it in place. Keep any washers used here, too (new ones may be provided with the siphon and, if so, you should use these instead).

5. Unhook the link from the button or handle lever and you will now be able to lift out and remove the old siphon.

6. Fit the new siphon in the same way as the old one, making sure any washers are in place. Use PTFE tape on the screw threads and tighten all the nuts firmly, but not so tightly to risk cracking the cistern.

7. Replace the flush pipe, or reattach the close-coupled cistern to the toilet bowl, wall and inlet and overflow pipes.

8. Turn on the water supply and the cistern will start to fill. Check for leaks during this process and then flush the toilet when the cistern is half full to check the new siphon is working and the flush pipe is not leaking. You may also need to readjust the ball float arm if this has been moved during the process of replacing the siphon.

REPLACING A TOILET SEAT

Toilet seats are usually fixed to the toilet bowl by a very simple system of bolts and wing nuts, which you can undo or tighten by hand. If a toilet seat starts to wobble, tighten these bolts and you will help prevent the wobble – and any sudden shifts that could lead to the toilet seat breaking completely.

To fit a new toilet seat, simply remove the bolts and replace the old seat. It is a good idea to get new nuts and bolts at the same time as the new seat as these rust over time and this can mean they work loose more often.

RADIATOR REPAIRS

Homes that are heated with a boiler and radiators have a second system of water pipes flowing through the walls and under the floors. Depending on how the boiler is heated, this can be a great, energy-efficient way to keep a home warm, as water holds heat for a long time, providing gentle, long-lasting warmth.

Only occasional maintenance is needed to keep a system of radiators running efficiently, but these jobs are often neglected, wasting energy as well as storing up potential problems for later.

HOW A CENTRAL HEATING SYSTEM WORKS

The diagram shows a very simple central heating system with just two radiators. Each radiator is attached independently to the system via two tap connectors that can be turned off to isolate it.

RADIATOR KEY

One of the radiator taps may be fitted with its own thermostat, which can increase or reduce the flow depending on the temperature in the room, or the system may be controlled centrally by a thermostat on the wall of a main room. In addition, the boiler may have a timing device to turn the system on and off at different times of day.

KEEPING RADIATORS WORKING EFFICIENTLY

Inefficient radiators, which leak heat through the walls or contain pockets of air, are the enemies of thrifty living. If your system is controlled by a thermostat, poorly functioning radiators will never heat the room to the required temperature and will mean your boiler has to work all the time, costing you money and wasting energy, too.

Here are some simple ways to make sure the heat in your radiators is used properly and not wasted.

HOME HEATING SYSTEM

BLEEDING

If a radiator feels hot at the bottom but cool at the top, it is likely to have air trapped inside it. To fill up the radiator properly again, you need to 'bleed' the air out of the top of the radiator. For this you'll need a simple tool known as a 'radiator key', available from hardware shops.

THE STEPS

1. Work while the heating system is off, so you don't risk scalding yourself.

2. Find the bleed valve (at the top of one end of the radiator) and insert the key, holding it in several layers of the cloth to protect your hands, and holding the rest of the cloth scrunched up below the valve in your other hand.

3. Turn the key no more than half a turn anticlockwise to release the valve. You should hear a hiss as the air starts to escape. Leave the key and cloth in place while this happens.

4. Eventually the hissing will stop and water will start to dribble out of the valve instead. As soon as this happens, tighten the key again to close the valve.

ENERGY-SAVING

Radiators give the most benefit when placed against inside walls of the home, so that heat radiated into the wall behind the radiator isn't lost. However, for some reason, house builders are very fond of placing radiators beneath windows, where heat can escape through gaps in the window and through the wall to the outside.

TWO WAYS TO MINIMISE THE HEAT LOST TO SAVE MONEY AND ENERGY, AND KEEP YOUR HOME SNUG:

1. Don't hang long curtains in front of radiators. This will channel the warm air towards the windows instead of into the room.

2. Place a reflective cover on the wall behind the radiator. This can be something as simple as pieces of kitchen foil, backed with card, although you can now buy special reflectors designed for this purpose.

REMOVING AND REPLACING RADIATORS

Since they can be isolated from the rest of the central heating system, radiators can be removed and replaced one at a time. The main problem to contend with is the fact that they are full of dirty and rusty water, so it's important to have appropriate containers to catch this, and to carry out the job of removing a radiator very methodically.

There are a number of reasons you may want to remove a radiator. An old radiator that gets full of rust may become blocked, or you may want to replace a single-layer radiator with a double radiator to improve the heating in a room.

HOW A RADIATOR IS ATTACHED TO THE SYSTEM

Each radiator is attached to the two tap valves by a nut fixed to the radiator called a 'union nut'. To tighten the nut (if it leaks, for example), turn in the clockwise direction, from the radiator's point of view. To loosen it, turn it anticlockwise.

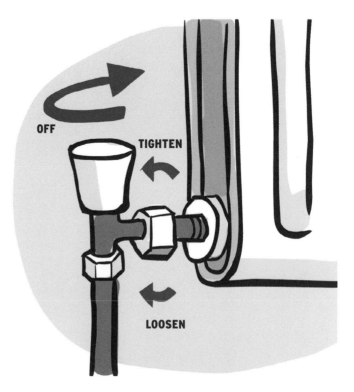

OFF

TIGHTEN

LOOSEN

RADIATOR REPAIRS

HOW TO REMOVE A RADIATOR

TOOLS YOU WILL NEED
You will need a large adjustable wrench, towels and a shallow bowl that will fit under the union nut to catch the water. You may also need penetrating oil to loosen the nuts if they are stiff.

THE STEPS
1. Start by switching off the taps at both sides of the radiator, turning them completely clockwise to cut the flow of water.

2. Then place a towel on the ground beneath one union nut, and place the bowl on top of this. Loosen the nut slightly, taking care not to shake the pipework leading into the floor. It is useful to have a helper who can hold the pipe steady while you work.

3. Water from the radiator will start to flow out of the union nut. Stop undoing the nut when this happens and allow the water from the radiator to flow slowly into the bowl. When the bowl is nearly full, tighten the nut to stop the flow and empty the bowl before continuing.

4. Keep emptying the bowl until the flow stops, then tighten the nut again and have an empty bowl in place for the next stage.

5. Tighten the first nut, then move the bowl to the other nut and loosen this until it nearly comes away from the tap valve. Then get your helper to keep the radiator level and undo both nuts completely.

6. There will still be a small amount of water in the radiator, so work with your helper to lift the radiator off the brackets that hold it on the wall and tip it up to drain the last of the water into the bowl.

7. Now you can take the radiator away and either flush it out to remove the corrosion (use a garden hose outside to do this) or take it away completely and bring in the new one. Hang the radiator on the wall brackets and then attach its union nuts to the two tap valves. Use PTFE tape on the screw threads to make them easier to tighten and to remove if necessary later.

8. Finally, open the two taps or control valves to fill the radiator. Open the bleed valve before you start, so the air in the radiator can escape, then close it as soon as water comes out.

After filling the new radiator, you may find the pressure in your system falls below the level recommended by the manufacturer. The pressure will normally need to be somewhere between 1 and 1.5 bars (recommended pressures may vary for different boilers, so check your manual). Low pressure is likely if you have a combination ('combi') boiler system that isn't topped up automatically from a tank.

To add more water into your system, you should be able to find a tap or valve below the boiler, but consult your user manual if it isn't labelled or very obvious.

TIP!

TOP TIP FOR LOST USER MANUALS

If you have lost your manual for any appliance, these are often available on the internet. Make a note of the make and model number and search for this with 'manual' added to the search query. If the manufacturer hasn't put it online, then some other helpful person probably has.

MOVING A RADIATOR AWAY FROM THE WALL TEMPORARILY

You can follow the process above if you need to remove a radiator temporarily, for example to paint or paper the wall behind it, or to repaint the radiator itself. However, it may be possible to avoid emptying the radiator completely by simply loosening the union nuts (being careful to catch any drips) and lying the radiator down while you work. Tighten the nuts again after lying it down, and you will lose very little water in this process.

The only question is whether you can free the radiator from its wall brackets while it is still attached to the pipes.

You may find that the pipes feeding into the floor have enough 'give' that you can simply lift the radiator off the brackets. However, this can cause damage so be careful you don't force the pipes to move further than they want to.

The alternative is to unscrew the brackets from the wall. This will be a fiddly job working in a very small space, but you can buy special angled, magnetic screwdrivers which can help. It may well be worth it to avoid all the fuss involved in removing the radiator completely.

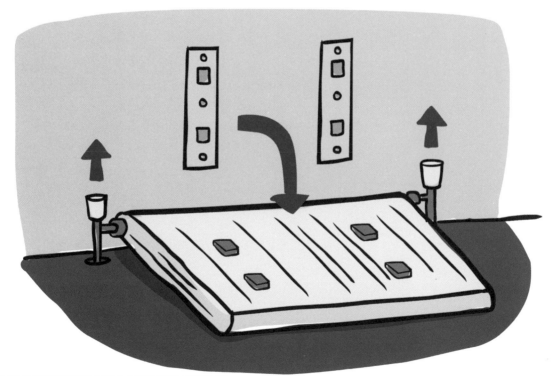

YOU CAN SOMETIMES LAY A RADIATOR DOWN TO WORK ON THE WALL BEHIND IT

LAGGING BEHIND

Pipes and tanks need effective insulation for two important reasons. The first is to save energy. Hot water tanks can lose most of their heat through their walls if they aren't protected, and re-lagging a tank can save the money spent on a new snug jacket in just a few months, making it one of the most cost-effective ways of saving energy.

The second reason to keep lagging in good condition, for cold water tanks and pipes, is to prevent freezing. If ice forms inside a pipe, it can lead to cracks and leaks that can cause a huge amount of damage.

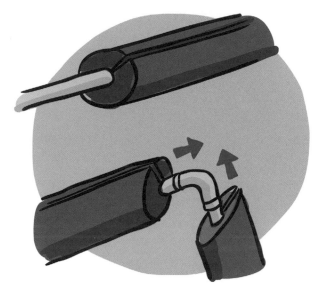

PLASTIC PIPE LAGGING

MAINTAINING AND REPAIRING LAGGING ON PIPES AND TANKS

HOT WATER TANK
Boilers that heat water 'on demand' don't need lagging but, if you have a hot water storage tank, it's very important to make sure it is properly insulated. Specially made 'jackets' are available for these tanks in a range of insulating materials, including wool and glass fibre wrapped in plastic. These are very simple to install. Normally you just wrap it around the tank and secure with tapes for a snug fit.

Buy a good one that is at least 75mm thick for the greatest savings.

COLD WATER TANK
Tailored 'jackets' are also available for cold water tanks, or if yours is very large or a strange shape, you can make your own from sheets of insulation board. Make a lid for the tank at the same time, but don't insulate below the tank as any heat reaching it from the house below will help to stop it freezing.

WATER PIPES
Pipes are simple to protect with snap-on plastic foam lagging – flexible tubes with a split along one side that can be pushed into place around narrow pipes. Lengths are available with different diameters for different sizes of pipes. Use strong household or 'gaffer' tape at the joins between lengths of lagging, and cut corners and bends at suitable angles to match closely at each joint, before taping these as well.

LOFT INSULATION

If you're not using the loft for living space, adding new layers of insulation in sheets (either glass wool or natural materials, such as wool or hemp) is a simple job that won't take more than an hour or two, but will save you energy and money very quickly.

New insulation can be added on top of any existing layers, so you don't need to dispose of these, and you can even get discounts on new materials under a range of government schemes.

TOOLS YOU WILL NEED
No particular tools are needed to install the insulation, as the basic process involves simply unwrapping it and laying it down. However, a sharp knife and a piece of board for cutting on, may be needed to cut sheets to length at the edges.

SAFETY NOTES

Wear old clothes or overalls and shoes that will grip the wooden joists that support the ceiling.

When working in the loft you should always make sure to step only on these joists and not in the spaces between them, or you will risk putting a foot through the ceiling below. If you need to kneel down, place a strong piece of wood or board across the joists to support you.

The fibres from glass wool can irritate the lungs and skin, so wear gloves and long sleeves and wear a face mask and eye protection when handling this material. Later on, after installation, ensure people entering the loft space are careful not to touch or disturb the insulation.

THE STEPS

1. The most efficient way to lay down sheets of insulation is with one layer between the joists in the loft space and another layer on top, laid in the other direction to cover the gaps. The minimum insulation depth should be 270mm, so two crossed layers of 150mm each is ideal.

2. Start by placing the rolls, still wrapped in plastic, around the loft space in approximately the places they will be needed. Then, starting in one corner, cut the plastic and lay down the rolls. Leave space at the eaves for ventilation, but push the ends of the rolls firmly together to reduce the size of any gaps.

3. Trim sheets if you need to using a sharp knife and a cutting board laid across the joists. Two or three firm strokes with the knife should cut right through them. Some insulation comes with perforations every 500mm or so along the rolls, which make this job much easier.

4. Now, begin the next layer, working from the farthest corner again. You'll be covering the joists as you work, so bring your toolkit with you as you move towards the exit or hatch, to reduce the need to step across the joists later.

CREATING A WALKWAY

You may need to create a walkway across the loft to reach the cold water tank or fusebox. If so, place boards in suitable places across the joists. It may be possible to avoid nailing these down, but if you want a more secure path, you'll need to put supports across the joists between the sheets of the second layer of insulation to support the walk-boards. It is important not to crush the insulation permanently or this will reduce its efficiency dramatically.

If you want to use the loft as living space, you should call in a builder to help with creating a firm, insulating floor.

EXTRA THINGS TO NOTE

• Keep an eye on ventilation when laying the insulation. Leave any air bricks clear, and leave a gap around the eaves.

• Don't insulate over wires, electrical cables or fuseboxes, as a precaution against overheating.

• Don't insulate without also checking or upgrading the lagging on your cold water tank and pipes.

• If your loft is unusual, consult a registered insulation installer or builder for advice – there may even be 'green' incentives.

• To avoid fire hazards, keep insulation at least 300m away from low voltage downlights and other electrical fittings.

REPLACING A BATH PANEL

Depending on how many walls it lies against, your bath may have a side panel or side and end panels to cover the ugly pipework beneath it.

These are often made of moulded plastic and designed to match the rest of your bathroom suite. In older homes, they are more likely to be made of plywood held in place with screws and covered in layers of paint or tiles.

All these components can become rotted or corroded in the damp conditions of a bathroom. Even a plastic panel can become scratched and warped with long use, and all types can start to look old and unattractive if you redecorate your bathroom in a new style.

Since these panels are made to be removable so you can get to the works of the bath, fitting a new bath panel is an excellent creative project that is well within anyone's abilities. Here's how to replace yours and make a huge difference to your bathroom with very little work.

OPTIONS FOR A NEW PANEL

New bath panels are available ready-made in a range of materials and designs, from plain plastic replacements to very stylish wooden products that come with built-in LED lighting to really bring a bit of bling into your bathroom. Ready-made panels can be bought off the shelf and fitted yourself, or you can pay for them to be fitted by the manufacturers.

You can save a lot of money by making your own panels. The choice of materials you can use is very wide, but remember always to choose materials that will withstand the damp and humidity in the bathroom.

Look for special damp-proof versions of standard materials, such as:
- 'marine' or 'exterior' plywood
- 'moisture resistant' medium density fibreboard
- 'yacht' or 'marine' varnish to protect a wood panel
- 'exterior' paint, along with special primers for humid conditions

The example below will run through creating a varnished veneer panel with a moulded skirting board along the bottom.

If you would rather have a coloured panel, follow the same process, but use plain water-resistant MDF and paint the panel after construction with primer and several coats of exterior gloss paint, using a foam roller for a finish without paintbrush marks.

TOOLS YOU WILL NEED
While you'll get the suppliers of your MDF and wood to do most of the cutting, you will need a saw and chisel to finish off any cut-outs for pipes, and to cut the moulding. You will also need waterproof wood glue, various grades of sandpaper and a sanding block, a spirit level, screws, and several sets of roller catches. If you need to repair or reconstruct the frame beneath the bath, you'll also need a drill and some long screws.

SAFETY NOTES
If you are using any power tools in the bathroom, such as an electric drill or screwdriver, always beware of the dangers of mixing water and electricity. Make sure the area around the bath is dry, and put the lid over the toilet if it is nearby.

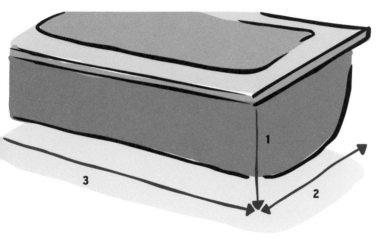

2. FIX THE SUPPORTING FRAME, IF NECESSARY

Once you have removed the old panel, you can check the condition of the frame that will support it under the bath. If the frame has rotted, this is a good time to build a new one.

For this, you'll need some very cheap lengths of 5cm x 5cm unplaned softwood, which are simply cut, screwed together and then secured to the floor. Make sure the frame is level vertically, as this will determine whether your panel looks good or wonky!

1. REMOVE THE OLD PANEL AND MEASURE UP

The old panels are likely to be attached to a wooden frame under the bath by a series of screws. These may only be found along the bottom on a plastic panel (which normally clips on to the lip of the bath at the top) or be distributed around all the edges of the panel in the case of plywood or MDF. Chipping off the tiles should reveal any hidden screws holding a tiled panel in place.

You can now measure up for the new panels. It is important to sketch out what you need to measure, and to allow for the thickness of the panel.

In this example, we want to have a simple mitred join at the corner, so we need to measure the whole length of the end and side panels and get our veneered MDF cut to this size, with the mitre cutting back from this measurement.

FIXING THE SUPPORTING FRAME

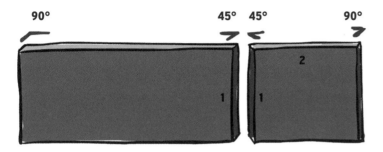

NEW PANELS

REPLACING A BATH PANEL

3. CONSTRUCT THE NEW PANEL

If you do reconstruct the frame, check your panel measurements once more afterwards, to make sure they are right, then order the MDF.

For this example, we'll need two pieces of oak-veneered water-resistant MDF, and we are going to ask the supplier to cut one end of each at a 45 degree angle, so we can get a neat end. Don't forget to specify which way the grain needs to run on each panel.

We're also ordering some narrow solid oak skirting boards, which we will cut to length ourselves.

Constructing the panels is relatively simple – measure the exact size of the newly cut panels that arrive, then cut the skirting to the same length plus the depth of the skirting Cut away a 45 degree mitre at the ends of the skirting that will meet at the corner with a fine saw (a mitre box helps to get this angle right).

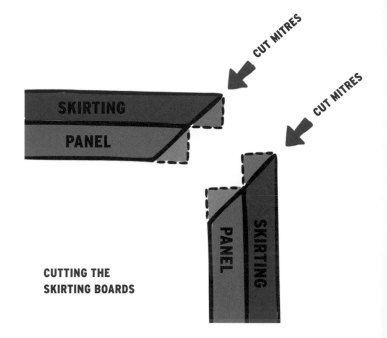

**CUTTING THE
SKIRTING BOARDS**

If any pipes run to the bath through the end panel, you will also need to cut out space for these. Measure the location and size of the pipes, then draw the required shape(s) on the panel. Cut down from the edge, using a fine handsaw or electric jigsaw, then use a chisel and hammer to cut the bottom edge of the recess away. Sand the edges lightly afterwards.

Finally, the skirting can be glued into place with wood glue. Spread the glue thinly on both surfaces then weight the skirting down overnight while the glue dries.

MITRE BOX

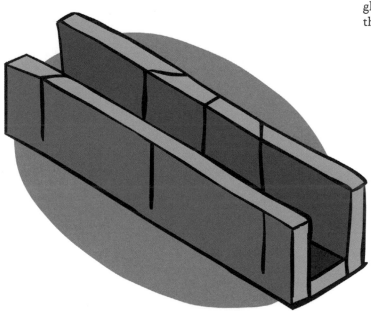

4. VARNISH THE PANEL

Now the panels are ready for finishing. Lightly sand any rough edges on the ends of the boards, then varnish with three coats of clear yacht varnish, leaving to dry overnight after each coat, and very lightly sanding between coats to keep the finish smooth.

Apply varnish to the exposed ends of the MDF as well, as this will help to seal it against any dampness in use.

5. FIT THE NEW PANEL

You can now fit the panel to the frame. The best way to do this is with hidden fixings such as the sprung roller catches shown. Start by attaching the rollers to the frame below the bath. Insert the catches and fix them to the sides of the vertical frame pieces in a position where the rollers will hold the panel firmly against the frame, flush with the rim of the bath.

For the end panel, this is fairly simple. Just put the catches into the rollers and place the panel up against them, marking the position of the screw holes by reaching through from the open side of the bath.

For the long panel, this process is much more fiddly – it can help to mark vertical lines where you know the rollers are, then attach the catches at approximately the right height with tape and see how well they match before screwing them on permanently.

After attaching the catches and pushing the finished panel into place, it is a good idea to place a narrow bead of sealant between the rim of the bath and the panel. This will need to be replaced if you remove the panel, but is a good way of protecting the panel from damp.

Once the rollers are fixed in position, you need to mark the correct places on the panel for the catches.

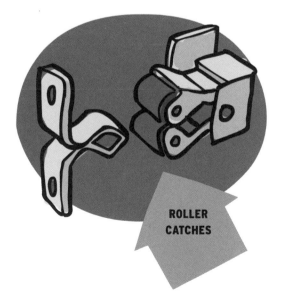

ROLLER CATCHES

TILING WITHOUT TRAUMA

Ceramic or stone tiles can provide an excellent water-resistant, easy to clean, hardwearing surface for walls and floors in the bathroom, and in other places around the home.

Tiles can last for decades with only minimal maintenance and are produced in an enormous range of styles and colours.

Keeping tiles looking great doesn't mean a lot of work and these easy repair jobs are well within the grasp of an amateur.

CHOOSING AND USING GROUT

Tiles are held on to the wall or floor with adhesive, while the gaps between are filled with a substance generally known as 'grout', which can be polymer-based or a kind of cement.

Grout comes in a small range of colours (always including white and beige) and can be bought in either powdered form or in ready-mixed tubs. The powdered grout is the best value, as you can mix up just what you need with water and keep the rest. Ready-mixed grout dries out and doesn't keep for long.

Waterproof grouts are made of plastic or silicone, similar to sealant. They are harder to work with but less porous than cement and therefore pick up less dirt and grease and are more resistant to mould and limescale build-up. Use these in very wet areas, but cement grouts are suitable for almost all other applications. Don't use grout at internal corner junctions between two surfaces, such as the internal corner of shower walls, where the wall meets the floor, or between the wall and the top of a surface.

If you are putting in new tiles, you can buy a combined adhesive and grout compound, which contains PVA adhesive to stick the tiles in place, as well as grout them afterwards.

On floors, applying a penetrating grout sealant is a good idea. You paint this water-based liquid on to the grout lines and it soaks into the pores in the grout, improving its water-resistance and durability.

Use dual-purpose tile and grout sealant for floors made of unglazed tiles, such as terracotta, and it will also help protect the tiles from staining. This sealant simply paints on to the floor leaving a low-sheen surface that isn't slippery but is much easier to keep clean.

CLEANING GROUT

Neat, clean grouting is the secret to good looking tiles.

If your grout has become stained or mouldy, clean it with bleach, which will kill the fungus as well as whitening the grout. You can buy labeled 'tile cleaners' for this purpose and they work very well, but any thick bleach will do the job, even eco-friendly options. Just make sure you choose one without any colour – not a bright blue toilet bleach – and wear rubber gloves while you apply it.

Leave the bleach on for about 30 minutes before rinsing away with a shower attachment or a wet sponge. Very stained areas may need a second application to get them really clean.

To remove limescale, lemon juice is an excelled choice as it also helps to whiten the grout and leaves things smelling fresh. See the chapter on kitchen repairs for more tips on natural cleaning with lemons.

TILING WITHOUT TRAUMA

REPLACING GROUT

If your grout has developed permanent stains or become damaged, your tiles can be made to look brand new again by replacing the grout. Getting the old grout off can be a bit fiddly, but reapplying the new grout is very simple.

You can do the whole area, or just replace the grout that has been damaged if you make sure you get the correct colour to match the existing grout.

TOOLS YOU WILL NEED

Getting old grout out from between the tiles without damaging them is much easier if you get a special grout remover tool from your local DIY shop. The kind where you can attach multiple blades alongside each other allows you to increase the thickness and makes the job even easier.

You'll also need a plastic spreader with a rubber edge and enough grout to cover the whole area in one go – check the packaging for coverage figures.

GROUT REMOVER

THE STEPS

1. Scrape away the old grout using the tool, being careful not to damage the tiles. Start with the vertical grout lines, scraping upwards to avoid slipping and damaging the tiles. This will give you an easier start on the trickier horizontal lines as well. You don't have to remove every scrap of grout, but aim to leave a good deep channel that will hold the new grout firmly. Don't worry if you dislodge any plastic spacers from the corner joints. These were used to space the tiles while they were stuck down, and aren't needed any more.

2. Clean the tiles and channels well to remove debris and dust. Dry off roughly with a towel. You want to avoid leaving water sitting in the channels, but the surfaces don't have to be perfectly dry.

3. Mix up your grout and spread it evenly and thickly over the area with your spreading tool. Push it firmly into the channels, and don't worry about leaving residue on the tiles themselves. The next step will clean the excess away. Spread in diagonal strokes to help prevent the tool from pulling the grout out of any of the spaces.

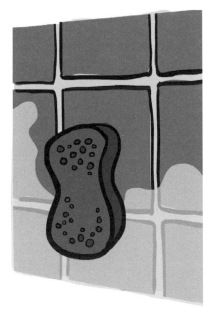

4. Now wipe the tiles lightly with a damp sponge. Don't scrape or dig in, as this could pull out the grout, and keep the sponge clean by rinsing in cold water as it gets covered in grout. Don't worry about getting the tiles perfectly clean at this point.

5. If necessary, you can now create a neat, rounded profile in your grout by scraping with the bottom of your grout remover or another tool, or even a plastic pen lid. Whatever you choose, keep it wet and clean and draw it along the lines at a very flat angle to avoid pulling out the wet grout.

6. Once the grout has dried, clean the tiles again with a soap solution to get off the dry film of grout. Polish with a soft cloth and admire what will now look like a brand new tiling job!

REPLACING A TILE

REPLACING A TILE

If a single tile becomes cracked, it can be removed and replaced without re-tiling the whole wall.

TOOLS YOU WILL NEED

Get a special ceramic tile bit for your power drill for this job. You'll also need a grout remover, hammer and chisel, and a scraper to remove the old adhesive. A replacement tile, plastic tile spacers, some tile adhesive and a notched adhesive spreading tool are also needed, as well as a length of wood to make sure the new tile lies flat with the others. Finally, you will need some grout for filling around the new tile afterwards.

THE STEPS

1. Start by removing the grout from around the tile. This will help prevent the vibrations from the drill and the impact of the chisel from being transmitted to the other tiles on the wall. Remove an extra couple of centimetres of grout at each corner, so you can remove and re-use the plastic cross-shaped tile spacers. If these are missing, you'll need to use new ones to make sure the tile sits straight.

2. Now drill several holes into the broken tile using the ceramic tile bit. This will weaken the tile and make it easier to remove with the chisel.

3. Using the hammer and chisel, carefully chip away at the tile and remove it in pieces. Start in the middle and work towards the edges.

4. Next use the scraper to remove all of the old tile adhesive. Clean the space and brush away any dust and pieces of tile before checking the new tile will fit into the space without protruding from the surface.

5. Now put spacers into the four corners (use the old ones if you have them) and apply tile adhesive to the tile with the notched tool, which will leave strips of adhesive on the back of the tile.

6. Push the tile into place, using the length of wood to push it flush with the surface of the surrounding tiles, and making sure it sits squarely in the hole. Leave the adhesive to dry before re-grouting, following the process described in the previous section.

TILING WITHOUT TRAUMA

WATERPROOF SEALS

Silicone rubber sealants are an excellent invention for the bathroom. Unlike traditional oil-based putty, they stay flexible pretty much forever, resist mould and are easy to clean.

However, they are very sticky when they come out of the tube and, when I first tried to use sealant to mend a leaky sink, I managed to make a terrible mess and get sticky plastic all over the place. I've since learned how to use it properly and neatly, so here are my tips for how to replace the seal around a bath or sink.

TOOLS YOU WILL NEED

For this job, you'll need a new tube of sealant (it doesn't keep fresh for very long) and a special 'sealant gun' which helps to produce an even flow and a neat result. You'll also need a sharp utility knife, a roll of masking tape and some washing up liquid and water.

THE STEPS

1. Remove any old sealant and grout and clean and dry the area to be sealed.

2. If you are sealing a bath, half-fill it with water. All baths will shift slightly when full and plastic baths will also flex, changing the shape of the rim. By half-filling the bath, you will put it at the mid-point of these extremes and ensure the sealant will withstand any movement.

3. Place strips of masking tape either side of the join, leaving a gap the size of the sealant strip you want to end up with.

4. Cut the nozzle of the sealant container so that it will produce the correct size of bead. Then, using the sealant gun, pipe a bead of sealant along the gap between the strips of tape. Make it large enough to slightly overlap the inner edges of the tape.

5. Smooth down the surface of the sealant with a wet, soapy finger. Mix up a strong solution with washing up liquid, and repeatedly dip your finger into this when smoothing. What you want to avoid is sticking your finger to the sealant and pulling it away from the edge of the bath – this is when you'll get into trouble and create a mess. Keep your finger soapy and it should slide slickly over the surface.

If you end up with a spare blob of sealant when you reach the end of the strip, don't put this down the sink or toilet or it may cause a blockage. Put it in the bin instead.

6. Peel off the tape while the sealant is still wet, then smooth down any ragged edges (using your soapy finger again) and leave the water in the bath until the sealant has set – check the packaging for setting times, as these will vary.

SAFETY NOTE

Remember not to use any electrical equipment near the bath while it contains water.

Letting mould grow in a bathroom doesn't just run the risk of unsightly stains on tile grout and paintwork, it can also be a health risk and cause breathing problems.

Regular cleaning, and the periodic use of mould-removing bleaches and fungicides will kill existing mould, but a much better long-term solution is to prevent mould by reducing the damp conditions that help it to flourish in the first place.

PREVENTING MOULD

VENTILATION
Good ventilation is by far the best way to help condensation disperse and encourage wet surfaces to dry quickly in the bathroom. If your bathroom has a window, try to make sure it is opened for an hour after every shower or bath.

You can also get ventilation channels fitted into the frame of a window so that, even when it is closed, air can circulate effectively.

A fan fitted to the window can also help, as can a ceiling fan that leads to the outside of the house.

You'll need professional help to have these appliances fitted, but you can help keep them working well if you already have these by regularly cleaning away cobwebs and dust to keep the air channels clear.

OTHER WAYS TO DISCOURAGE FUNGUS
The kinds of furniture, fittings and surfaces in the bathroom can also affect levels of damp and condensation.

Wherever possible, materials in the bathroom should have good water-resistant surface properties, so when you have to repair or replace items in the bathroom, bear these tips in mind:

• Use tiles, rubber or linoleum on the floor, rather than carpet, and have a good towel rail or radiator to dry rugs or mats efficiently when they get wet.

• On untiled areas of the walls, use special 'kitchen and bathroom' emulsion paint, which contains fungicidal ingredients and has a higher sheen surface with more water-resistance than matt paint.

• If you are putting up wallpaper, choose papers with water-resistant finishes, and use wallpaper paste with effective fungicides. Stick any paper that comes loose back down as quickly as possible, or the narrow gap between the paper and the wall will be an ideal breeding ground for mould.

• Replace your shower curtain with a solid 'shower screen' made of glass or strong plastic. This will dry much more quickly than a curtain with folds, and will make the bathroom look much neater, too.

REMOVING LIMESCALE FROM SHOWER HEADS

See the Kitchen repairs chapter on page 122 for lots of tips for removing limescale from taps, tiles and other fittings.

In the bathroom, the fitting that gets clogged up most rapidly with limescale is the shower head. Here's a lazy method and a thorough method for clearing it out.

LAZY METHOD
Cut the top off a plastic bottle and half fill with a suitable acid (vinegar is cheaper than lemon juice in these quantities). Stand the bottle in a bucket to prevent it falling over, and stand the bucket in the shower stall or bath.

Shake excess water out of the shower head, then lower it into the bottle and leave for a few hours.

After this, run cold water at high pressure through the shower head to force loose scale from the spray holes, and scrub any remaining limescale from the surrounding parts.

THOROUGH METHOD
Dismantle the shower head into its separate parts. Remove the main body of the shower head from the hose that leads to the shower unit or taps.

Place all the parts of the shower head in a bowl or bucket and cover with vinegar or juice for a few hours.

Rinse and scrub the parts clean, using an old toothbrush to get into tricky corners and grooves, such as the threads on screw-on parts. Wipe everything clean before reassembling the shower.

Simple Clothing Fixes

When it comes to saving money in the long term, very cheap clothes can be a very bad investment.

If we only spend a tiny amount on a garment, the temptation to throw it away and get an equally cheap replacement when something goes wrong is huge. But it pays to think more cleverly.

Investing in good, long-lasting pieces of clothing means that, in the end, you spend less – with the added bonus of wearing quality tailoring in the meantime.

However, even good clothes need a bit of maintenance now and again. Professionals, such as your local dry-cleaners, may offer a mending service at a price but it helps to be able to do simple repairs yourself.

Vintage clothes are also very desirable and, when you can't choose from a rack of different sizes, being able to make simple adjustments is a valuable skill.

Here I'll show how to make your clothes last longer with care tips, mending advice, and a few good ideas for adjusting clothes for a perfect fit.

I have tried to describe sewing repairs in plain terms wherever possible. Where I do introduce technical terms, such as 'seam allowance', I have explained these where they first appear.

THE RIGHT WAY TO SEW ON A BUTTON

Sewing on a button is probably the most common – and most basic – mending job there is. The steps may seem obvious, but there are plenty of pitfalls to avoid.

Doing the job properly is a wise move. It will keep the button in place for longer, reducing the risk it will fall off again and get lost permanently, and will ensure your clothes continue to hang properly, without pulling.

BUTTON TIPS

Buttons either have two or four holes for stitching. For a four-hole button, the best way to stitch is in two loops, rather than in a cross pattern. Crossed threads will form a pile in the centre of the button, which can wear through quickly.

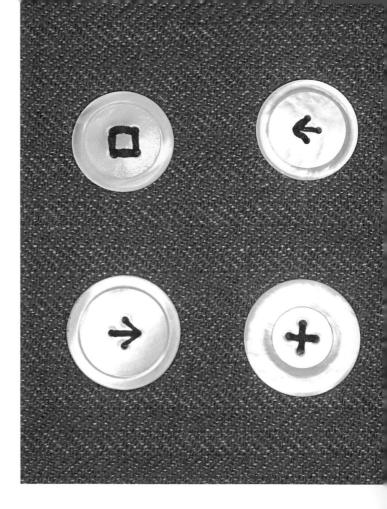

KEEPING SPARE BUTTONS

It is useful to build up a collection of replacement buttons. When I was a child, the 'big button jar' under the kitchen sink held a fascinating array of odd buttons, many of which seemed to be in the shape of flowers and animals (well, it was the 1970s!).

You should always keep the spare buttons that come with new clothes. If these aren't supplied, finding a close match can be a problem, so a great tip is to get into the habit of saving buttons from garments you have to throw away. That way, you will have full sets of replacements when you can't find a match for one button on a shirt, cardigan or coat.

However, unless you want to replace all your buttons when one falls off, it is best to follow the same pattern as the other buttons on the garment. Some button designs do have a depression in the centre that will allow the extra depth of crossed stitches to sit below their faces.

For a button to sit properly, it should not be sewn tightly on to the surface of the fabric. Instead, you should create a 'shank' behind the button by wrapping your thread several times around the stitches between the button and the front of your garment.

For thin materials, you can create a suitable shank simply by leaving threads relatively loose when stitching the button. For thicker fabrics, ensure the shank is long enough by stitching over a matchstick.

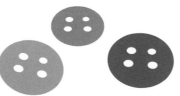

THE STEPS

At the start and end of sewing your button, don't tie off the thread with knots, which can easily come undone. Instead, add several tiny stitches into the fabric at either end for extra security.

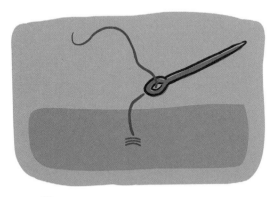

1 Start with a few tiny stitches to hold the thread securely.

2 Sew loosely in two loops across the holes in the button.

3 For thicker fabrics, ensure you leave a long enough shank by stitching across a matchstick.

4 Wind around the threads to create a shank (but don't make the shank too thick).

To finish off, take the thread to the rear side of the fabric and sew a few more tiny stitches to secure the end.

SEWING BASICS

If you want to make your own clothes or take up sewing as a hobby, then a sewing machine is probably essential. However, if you are only planning on the occasional fix or alteration, you can get by perfectly well knowing a few simple hand-sewing stitches and techniques.

Here I'll run through the most useful stitches you'll need to know, as well as some extra tips to help you get a neat, professional result.

TOOLS

For even the most basic sewing, you'll need a few good quality tools. These will save work, avoid damage to your clothes, and make your repairs last longer. None are very expensive, and all are well worth the investment.

NEEDLES
Get a range of needles. You'll need finer ones for very delicate fabrics, and round-ended or ball-point needles for knitted fabrics. For leather or suede, a special sharp needle with a faceted end is needed, as ordinary needles aren't able to cut through these tough materials.

SCISSORS
A good pair of scissors is vital. These need to be kept sharp, so reserve a pair of dressmaking shears purely for work on fabrics. Never use them to cut paper or (horror!) sandpaper, as the hard fibres and particles in these materials will blunt the blade and then they will chew up your fabrics.

Also useful is a small pair of scissors with pointed ends, for removing buttons and other fastenings.

A pair of pinking shears can be great timesavers. With these, you can cut a serrated, non-fraying edge on woven fabrics, saving a whole step when hemming.

PINS
You will need a stock of nice, longish pins for holding things together. As you will be ironing over pins occasionally, get some with metal ends as well as a stock of easier-to-see plastic-tipped pins.

THIMBLE
A metal thimble is very handy for protecting your fingers and helping to push needles through tough fabrics. You wear it on your middle finger.

SEAM RIPPER
This is a small tool for taking out stitches. It has a hook and a sharp blade on the inside, which means you can cut through individual threads without risking damage to the fabric.

MARKING TOOLS
Tailor's chalk is useful for marking seam lines and adjustments. It comes in a neat, sharp-edged triangular block and will brush or wash off fabrics without making permanent marks. You can also buy special fabric markers that are formulated to wash out of most materials.

IRONING KIT
Keep your iron and ironing board on hand when sewing. Pressing seams both before and after sewing can make the difference between neat needlework and a bumpy mess.

You should always press seams with a cloth between your iron and your fabric – use a linen tea towel or a folded cotton pillowcase.

CHOOSING THREAD

Good quality all-purpose sewing thread will be suitable for most jobs.

For decorative work (such as edging on appliqué) a huge variety of alternatives are available from craft and department stores. However, for repairs you will mainly want plain, sober colours to match your clothing.

Choose thread one shade darker than your fabric to keep your repairs as invisible as possible. Use pure white thread only on crisp white fabrics, or it will stand out.

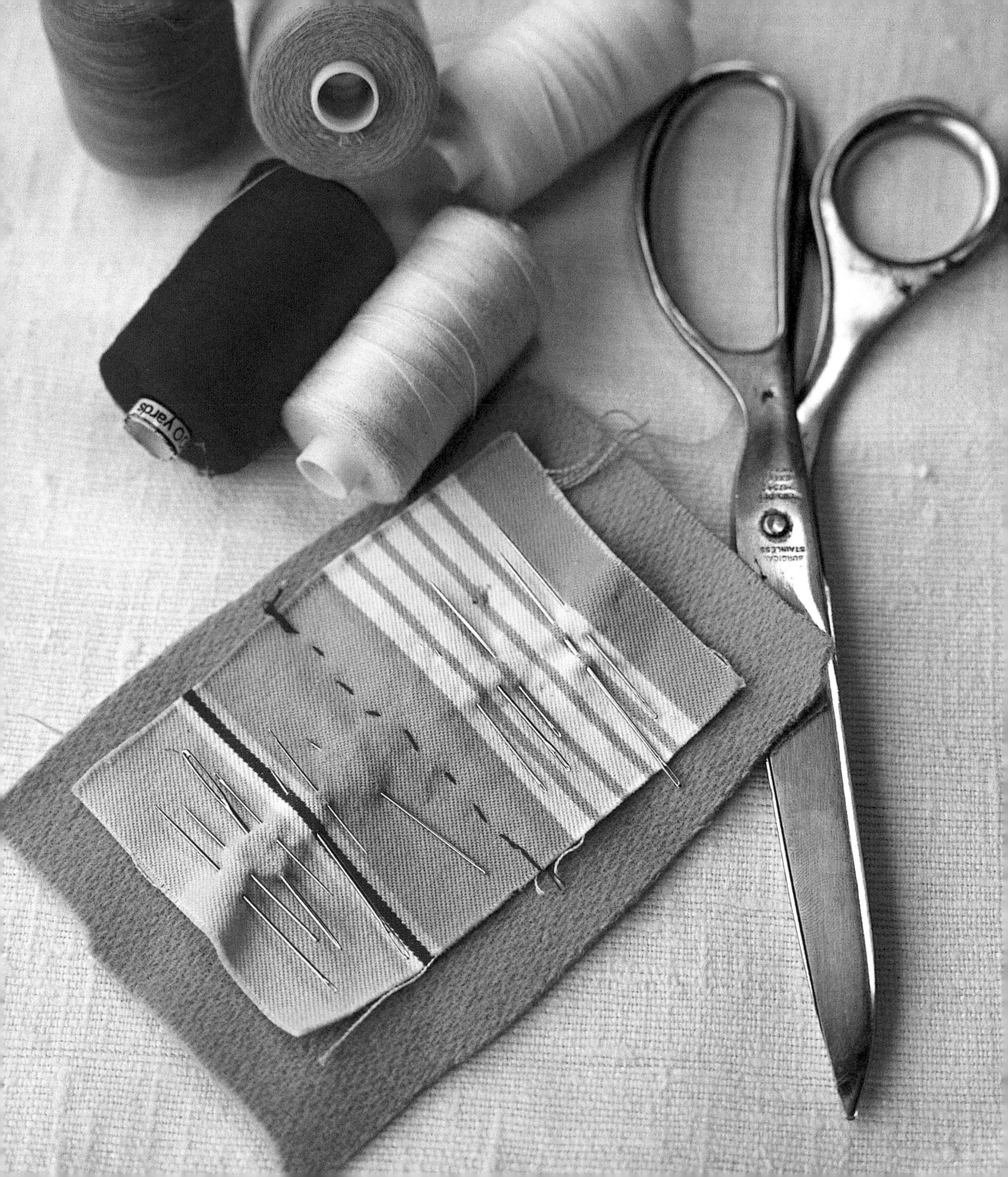

SEWING BASICS

HOW TO THREAD A NEEDLE

1. First, moisten the end of your thread with a tiny bit of spit.

2. Hold the needle and thread up to the light, with the needle between the middle joint of your thumb and the tip of your middle finger, leaving your first finger and the tip of your thumb free.

3. Move the thread to the needle, not the other way around.

4. Once the end of the thread pokes through, grab it with the thumb and first finger in the hand that is holding the needle, then take the needle in your other hand and pull the thread through.

And there is an even easier way if you have very poor eyesight, or are working with fluffy thread.

A needle threader has a stiff wire loop that is easier to get through the needle's eye. Push it through and it will open out again. Then simply put the thread through the loop and pull the tool back through the needle.

HOW MUCH THREAD?
For hand-sewing, about 50cm of thread is the maximum you can work with sensibly at any time. If you make your thread longer than this, it is likely to get tangled or knotted, causing lots of problems.

Don't tie the thread to your needle. The knot can get caught in your fabric and rip it. Just leave a long loose end, and re-thread if necessary while sewing.

I often use a double thread while making repairs, especially when sewing seams that are likely to come under pressure. However, you should always use a single thread when sewing hems and other 'invisible' repairs.

HAND-SEWING STITCHES

TACKING
Tacking stitches are temporary and are used to hold pieces of fabric together while you sew up seams with stronger stitches. They can be done in a contrasting colour, which makes them easier to remove. Tacking stitch is very widely spaced and can be done rapidly.

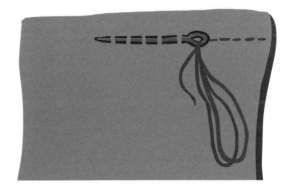

RUNNING STITCH
A narrow running stitch can be very strong and is suitable for lots of mending jobs.

If you need to gather material, such as for the top of a curtain, sew two rows of running stitches close together, then pull the threads to gather the fabric and tie them together.

When mending with running stitch, you can sew several stitches at a time, weaving the point of the needle above and below the fabric. Make the stitches about 1.5mm in length for a strong seam.

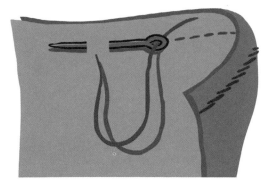

BACK STITCH

Back stitch is very strong so I use it for a lot of repairs, including sewing on zips and taking in seams. It is also a nice decorative stitch, as the good side has a line of very closely spaced, neat stitches.

You sew a backstitch seam in loops, so you end up with double-length, overlapping stitches on the reverse side.

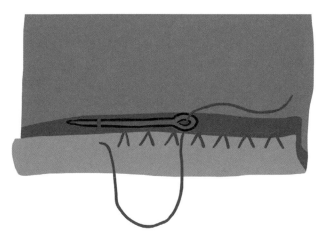

BLIND HEMMING STITCH

This is a secure stitch, used to hold up hems. Taking up only one thread from the main part of the fabric with each stitch along the seam, it is almost invisible on the good side.

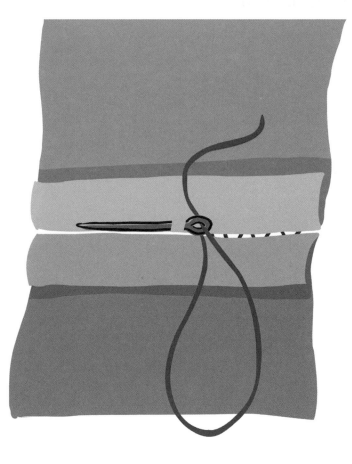

SLIP STITCH

Use this stitch to join two edges together. The stitches run along the line of the join between the two fabrics and can hardly be seen when the seam is finished.

This stitch can be worked from the good side, and is also useful in upholstery work.

SEWING BASICS

SLANT STITCH

Another hemming stitch that is invisible on the outside of the hem. It has much larger stitches than blind hemming stitch. As a result, it's quicker but less reliable.

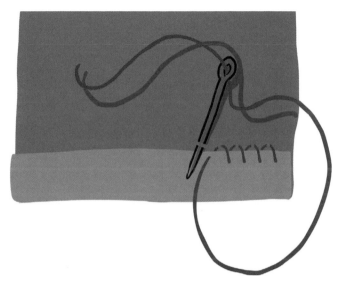

OVERSEWING

This simple, quick stitch can be used to finish off the raw edge inside a hem to prevent it from fraying.

Don't pull the stitches tight or the edge will fold over and form a ridge.

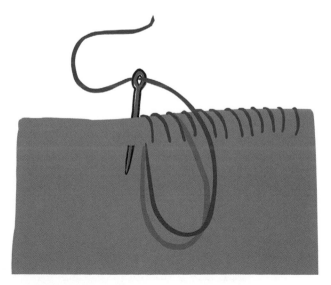

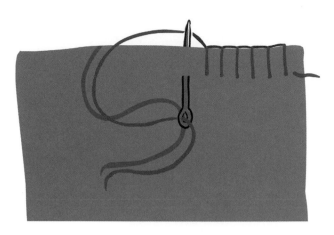

BLANKET STITCH

A decorative edging stitch, which can be used, as its name suggests, for finishing off the edge of a blanket or napkin. It is also a nice way to attach appliqué.

With each stitch, the needle is brought through the loop of thread to create a line of stitching along the edge of the fabric.

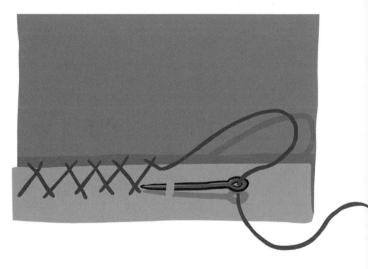

HERRINGBONE STITCH

This stitch can be used over an unfinished edge inside a hem. It is almost invisible on the good side, as it takes just a couple of threads from the main fabric with each stitch.

Unlike most stitches, this stitch is sewn from left to right (or vice versa if you are left-handed).

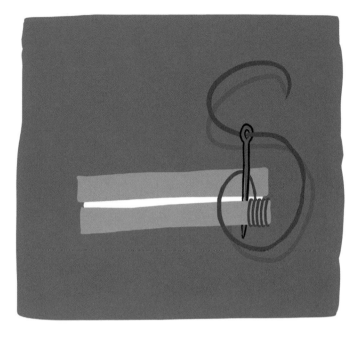

BUTTONHOLE STITCH

This stitch is used to reinforce a buttonhole, and creates a ridge along the edge of the hole.

It is similar to blanket stitch, as with each stitch the thread is looped around the point of the needle to create a protective ridge.

SECURING STITCHES

Tying a knot in your thread is not the best way to make sure your sewing doesn't unravel, as knots can easily come loose.

There are two more secure ways of anchoring your threads.

1. TYING OFF

At the start of your seam, tie your sewing thread into the fabric itself by sewing a knot or two through the fabric.

To tie a knot, make one small stitch, then loop back over it (as if you are sewing a back stitch) and push the needle through the fabric leaving the end poking out. Now loop the thread over your needle before finishing the stitch.

2. EXTRA STITCHES

At the end of your seam, you can sew another knot, or secure the end by sewing a few reverse stitches. Reverse direction at the end of your seam and a couple of small back stitches is all it should take to secure the threads indefinitely.

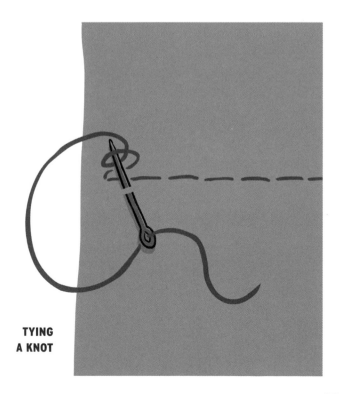

TYING A KNOT

SEWING BASICS

TAKING OUT STITCHES

Use your seam ripper to take stitches out or unpick a seam.

Pull the seam apart gently as you cut the stitches. Several will unravel at a time and then the seam will stick. Use the seam ripper to cut the next stitch and you will then be able to ease more of the seam apart.

Move down the seam in stages like this and use the seam ripper on individual stitches, pulling them upwards on to the blade inside the end of the ripper. Never run the ripper along a seam, or you will risk catching the blade on the fabric and cutting a hole.

NEVER RUN THE RIPPER ALONG A SEAM, OR YOU WILL RISK CATCHING THE BLADE ON THE FABRIC AND CUTTING A HOLE.

Permanent stains, small tears or obvious snags, can ruin the look of a piece of clothing, making it unsuitable for smart occasions.

However, with a bit of creative thinking, many of these problems can be covered up, while actually enhancing the look of your garments.

DECORATE IT

Food and drink stains, in particular, will tend to fall on the front of a smart dress or jacket, and this is an ideal location for covering up with decorations.

Simply adding a beautiful vintage brooch can sort out problems with weightier tailored clothes, but flimsier materials will need to have smaller, lighter decorations sewn on.

Haberdashery departments, sewing and embroidery shops, stock a range of decorative trimmings and motifs, from sequins in a range of sizes and shapes to elaborate fabric flowers.

You may need to add several decorations rather than just one to cover up the stain or tear. Try to achieve a balanced arrangement on a lapel, or create a trail of sequins across the front of a dress. Choose a complementary colour for impact, or match the colour closely to your garment for a more subtle, textured effect.

CLEVER COVER-UPS

CREATIVE PATCHES AND APPLIQUÉ

All kinds of clothing can look great with patches or appliqué in a contrasting material added to cover stains or tears. This creates an attractive homespun look, which is ideal for flowing skirts or summer dresses.

This doesn't mean these techniques can't be used for smart clothes too, if you think creatively. When the problem is along the hemline, a contrasting appliquéd band right around the bottom can look very stylish, as can the addition of a new, wider waistband.

APPLIQUÉ FOR BEGINNERS

The word 'appliqué' can sound a bit daunting, but it really means nothing more than placing one piece of material on top of another. And, whether you are adding a simple, square patch over a hole or a fancy appliqué design over a stain, the techniques are much the same.

For a neat result in both cases, the key factor is providing stability to the patch material so it keeps its shape while you sew. There are a number of different options for doing this, from special dissolvable paper that is sewn into the garment, to a stiff backing material (known as 'interfacing') that works well for thicker fabrics.

The easiest method for beginners is to use a paper template, which you sew in and then remove.

If you are using a patch to cover a hole, you should first neaten and prepare the hole by trimming it to a neat rectangle, then cutting diagonally into each corner to reduce the risk of tearing.

FIRST NEATEN AND PREPARE THE HOLE

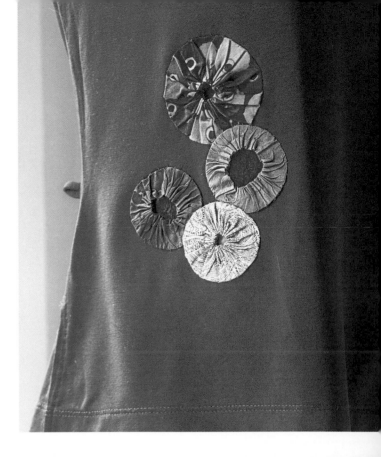

CLEVER COVER-UPS

2. PREPARE THE PATCH

Take the material you are using for the patch and arrange it so that it will match the grain of your garment when put in place. Use a few running stitches to attach the paper template to the patch material then cut around the design leaving another centimetre of extra fabric.

Cut a number of notches, then fold the material around the edges of the paper and press all around with an iron to create a neat edge. Repeat this process for all parts of the appliqué pattern.

THE STEPS
1. FIND OR DRAW A PATTERN

The internet is a great source of simple appliqué patterns, and has the advantage of making it easier to adjust the size of the design before printing. If you are covering a hole, make the design large enough to overlap the edges by at least 1cm. Then, print the pattern on to ordinary paper and cut out the design neatly.

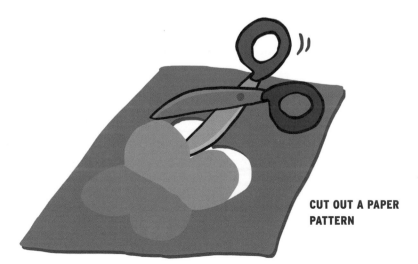

CUT OUT A PAPER
PATTERN

3. SEW IT ON

Now you are ready to sew the pieces of appliqué on to your garment. There is no right or wrong stitch to use, and your choice should depend on the final look you want. An easy option is a neat backstitch in a closely matching colour. However, a contrasting blanket stitch can also look very good.

For appliqué designs in multiple parts, sew the pieces into place one at a time, starting with those that sit at the bottom.

4. REMOVE THE PAPER TEMPLATE

Now you can remove the paper template. Unpick your tacking stitches, then cut away the paper from the reverse side, pulling it out in pieces. Tweezers may help with this job.

If there is no hole to work through, you have two choices: either cut a small hole behind the patch after stitching it on, or remove the paper when you have sewn about three-quarters of the way around the patch. If you have pressed a neat edge on to the patch before sewing, this should not affect the neatness of the finished result.

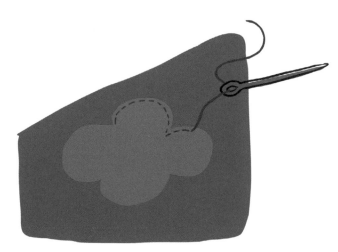

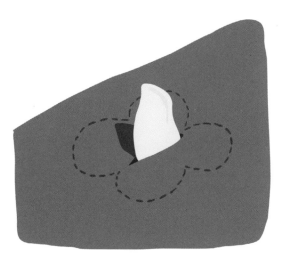

SOURCES OF FABRIC

Since you only need very small pieces of fabric, offcut bins are an ideal source of cheap, attractive and interesting fabric for patches. Alternatively, you can be really frugal by using pieces cut from old garments.

Keeping your own offcuts, left over from other mending projects, is another good way to build up a stock of scrap material for patches and appliqué.

APPLIQUÉ FOR CHEATS!

If you're not up to sewing, iron-on adhesive webbing is the cheater's way to create appliqué very quickly and simply. Be warned; the results may not last as long, but you'll save time and get a good result in the short term.

For this method, remove the paper after pressing the pattern into shape, then simply iron the patch on to the base fabric, following the instructions for timing and heat level that come with the adhesive webbing.

HEMMING

It's so easy to catch a heel in a pair of trousers or your toe in the hem of a skirt when you are putting on clothes.

Fixing a hem is therefore an excellent skill for everyone to learn – not just keen needleworkers.

It's also great to be able to adjust your clothes to just the right length. Particularly for trousers, if you wear them too short or too long, even the best style just won't look right.

Here I'll go through both emergency and long-term ways of sorting out a hemline. And don't forget, you also can hem shirts, tops and sleeves using the same techniques.

SMALL RIPS IN A HEM

If you don't need to change the length, you can fix a small amount of fallen hem very easily, just by sewing it up.

You'll find broken threads either side of the dropped hem, and you should unravel a few more stitches to give enough thread to tie these off without pulling on the fabric. Tie them off with knots, sewn in using a needle (see page 190).

Then, simply sew up the part of the hem that has fallen down, using a blind hemming stitch. This should not take more than a few minutes to do properly, but you can carry out this repair with longer stitches or a slant stitch, if you are in a real hurry.

When you have time, unpick and sew up the whole hem properly, as this part-repair won't be very durable.

TIP!

Don't use heat-activated sticky webbing for a quick hem repair. It is very hard to remove, and you will find it impossible to repair the hem properly later. Use a quick stitching method instead. Or, in a real emergency, hold up the hem for a few hours with a couple of tiny safety pins, or even double-sided tape.

CHANGING THE LENGTH OF A HEM

PREPARING THE FABRIC

To change the length of a hem, you will first need to unpick the old stitches and press the fabric flat to remove the old creases. This is particularly important if you wish to lengthen a hem.

Spray a small amount of water onto a hem before pressing, so that the steam can help soften the fibres in the crease to make it flatten more easily.

MEASURING UP

Now, you can measure and pin the garment accurately to the new length.

It's impossible to measure hems accurately on your own body, so two people are needed for this stage of the process: one model (the owner of the piece of clothing) and one measurer to pin up the hem.

IN AN EMERGENCY, TIE OFF THE THREADS EITHER SIDE OF A DROPPED HEM AND SEW A FEW STITCHES TO HOLD IT UP TEMPORARILY

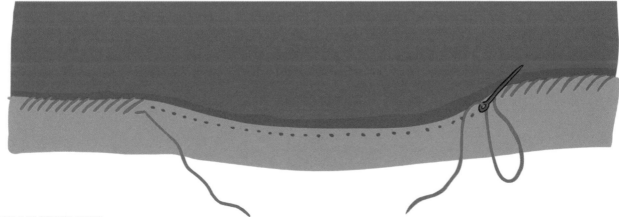

USE A MEASURING STICK TO PIN UP A HEM. WEAR YOUR SHOES!

PREPARING THE HEM

Now, press the pinned hem along the folded edge. Don't press over the pins – you just want to create a firm crease at the fold so you can remove the pins and work on the hem allowance.

The 'hem allowance' is a term that describes the length of the folded material that is turned over at the bottom of your garment.

The length you choose for your hem allowance depends on two factors:

1. How much fabric you have available.
2. How much weight you want your hem to have.

You will generally want some weight in your hem, as this helps garments to hang better. However, you don't want so much fabric that the hem becomes obvious or makes the fabric very stiff.

COMMON HEM ALLOWANCES

0.5–1cm, on shirts and tops
1–2cm, on full skirts and lightweight fabrics
3–4cm, on straight or heavy skirts and dresses
1.5–3cm, on trousers

Once you have chosen the length, remove the pins, flatten out the garment and cut the fabric to the correct hem allowance.

The model should put on the shoes they will normally wear with the garment and stand up straight in a position that allows the measurer to move around them. They should stay as still as possible during the measuring process – but without locking their knees or arching backwards like a soldier on parade!

When measuring trouser hems, it helps if the model can stand on a small table or stool. Make sure they can stand up naturally on it, and that it can take their weight safely.

The measurer should first roughly pin up the hem all around the garment to a good length. Make any adjustments so that the model is happy with the new position, and so that both legs of trousers are even.

For trousers, you can now add a more closely spaced row of pins around the garment, parallel to the line of the hem. Place these about 3cm above the hemline (or less, if not enough material is available) then move on to the next stage.

For skirts and dresses, where the circumference of the hem is much longer, getting an even length means using a measuring stick.

Take a garden cane or long ruler and mark the correct height at the front of the skirt. Wrap a rubber band around the stick at the hemline. Then, as with trousers, use the marker to pin up the hem around the skirt line, placing the pins parallel to the hem at close intervals about 3cm up from the fold.

TIP!

On non-stretchy fabrics, you can use sticky tape (masking tape or 'magic tape' are both ideal) to mark the hem allowance. This makes it especially easy to cut parallel to the hemline. In case it affects the finish, always put tape on the wrong side of the fabric.

HEMMING

USE TAPE AS A GUIDE TO CUT A PARALLEL HEM ALLOWANCE

FINISHING THE RAW EDGE

Jersey and finely knitted materials don't need finishing (they will curl up rather than unravel), but woven materials will fray if you simply hem the raw edge.

To finish the edge, you can either 'cheat' by cutting the edge with pinking shears, or use a simple oversewing stitch to protect the edge with a row of stitches instead.

LOOSENING THE HEM ALLOWANCE

With a long hem allowance (or even a short one on narrow trousers or A-line skirts) you may need to put more material into the circumference of the hem allowance before sewing up, so that the hem doesn't pull in the outer fabric when it is folded over and fixed.

You can do this by releasing the side seams in the folded over hem allowance to increase the amount of material available in the circumference. Alternatively, for a short hem, you can simply cut notches in the material before finishing the raw edge.

TIP!

It may not be obvious that you need to loosen the hem allowance. So, to save having to start again, it's usually best to unpick some stitches from the side seams of the hem allowance on every hem-shortening project.

SEWING UP THE HEM

Now you can sew up the hem using one of the hemming stitches described in the 'Sewing basics' section.

Work carefully and accurately, but without pulling on the fabric. It wants to hang naturally at the line of the ironed fold when you are finished.

FINAL PRESS

Finally, press the hem's edge once again to finish it off. Use a covering cloth, and focus your attention on the edge. Avoid pressing hard over the edge of the hem allowance or you may iron a mark on to the good side of your fabric.

HEMMING WITHOUT SEWING

You can also 'cheat' at this stage by using heat-activated webbing to hold up the hem. This is particularly suitable for heavier, woven fabrics, but isn't as good on stretchy or lightweight fabrics, as it can make these stiff.

Follow the instructions that come with the webbing strips for the timing and heat of the iron, and ensure you work accurately, as it is almost impossible to unstick the glue neatly if it goes wrong.

Place the webbing close to the edge of the hem allowance so you don't leave a fabric flap, but make sure it is clear of the notches in a pinked edge, or you will stick your iron or covering cloth to your garment.

LEARNING TO SEW A HEM IS A GREAT WAY TO GET TROUSERS EXACTLY THE RIGHT LENGTH

ZIPS

Since 1893, the zip fastening has revolutionised the way clothes, bags, shoes, coats, sleeping bags, cushions and many other everyday items are joined together at a seam.

Zips are quick, secure and last a long time. But a broken zip can force much-loved garments into early retirement, as it's easy to put off sorting it out. Repairing or replacing a zip can seem complicated but, in fact, it is a very approachable task.

Many zip problems can be mended without having to remove and replace them. And even replacing a zip entirely is not that daunting – providing you get the right replacement.

TYPES OF ZIPS

Zips come in a number of different types, and you use different methods for mending them. However, the process of removing and replacing a zip is the same for each type.

PLASTIC COIL

These zips are made from a continuous coil of plastic, with stitching holding the coil on to a fabric backing, and separating it into 'teeth' that lock together.

These zips are not as strong as the toothed type, but are suitable for side and back seams on clothing, and are often used on cushion covers.

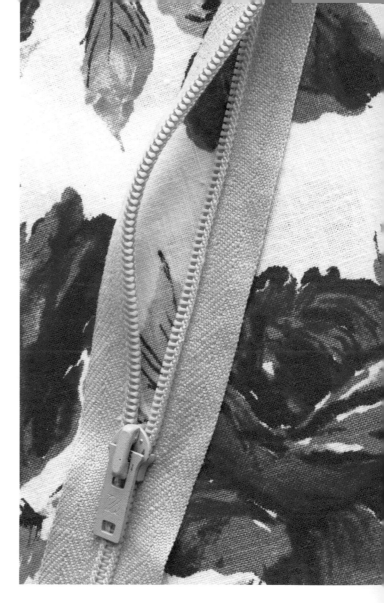

PLASTIC COIL ZIP

MENDING A COIL ZIP

These can pull apart under strong pressure. But they are self-healing and, in most cases, the zip will come back together again if you simply pull the slider back and forth over the break.

Sometimes, you'll end up with a kink, where a number of extra coils from one side have been pulled through the slider, preventing the two sets of coils from aligning properly. This kink will be a point of weakness and will make the seam very vulnerable to splitting again in the future.

Luckily, you can be quite rough with these zips so, to mend a kink, you just need to open the slider to the point where the kink sits, then pull firmly to force the extra coils through the slider and realign them.

Another common problem with plastic coil zips occurs when the metal slider becomes loose and stops pressing the coils together effectively. This can lead to the slider coming away from one side of the zip completely. To fix this, you'll need a small screwdriver and a pair of pliers.

THE STEPS

1. Start by opening up the slider even more. Push a narrow, flat-head screwdriver into the fitting, and twist to prise the two sides apart very slightly.

2. Run the slider to the centre of the zip. Then fold over the opposite row of coils, until you can see the stitching between two coils, then use brute force to push the gap between the teeth against the slider's edge, pushing the coils into the slider, where they will lock into the other row of coils.

3. Carefully run the slider along the two sets of coils towards the 'closed' position, making sure the coils remain between the plates. When you reach the end of the zip, check that the two sets of coils are aligned – pull any extra coils left on either side through the slider.

4. Now take the pliers and gently squeeze the slider so that it will grip the coils firmly again.

5. Finally, run the slider up and down the zip a few times to make sure everything works properly.

Sometimes, a few coils will become badly mangled and will no longer grip the other side. If this happens near the bottom of a zip, you can sew over the coils at this point to prevent the slider going beyond it.

This repair only works if your garment will still be usable with a shorter zip opening. If not, you'll need to replace the weakened zip.

ZIPS

TOOTHED ZIP

A zip made of solid, interlocking teeth is stronger and more durable than a plastic coil zip. These are used on coats and bags, and are also often found in the fly of trousers.

MENDING A TOOTHED ZIP
Occasionally, the sliders on these zips will also become detached from one row of teeth. It's not possible simply to force the teeth back into the slider so, to reattach the slider, you need to slide it off both sides and then slide it back on.

This will mean unpicking the bottom of the zip from your garment before re-attaching the slider. There may be a metal or plastic closure at the bottom of the zip and this will also need to be removed before the slider will come off. After re-attaching the slider, create a new closure by stitching over the teeth at the bottom of the zip. For a metal closure, you may be able to squeeze it back on to the zip with pliers.

Toothed zips may also break if they lose some of their teeth, which can cause the slider to slip off. Missing teeth will leave a gap, so the slider can usually be re-attached. However, the problem will recur, so you will need to sew up the zip at the point where the teeth are missing.

Again, if this is close to the bottom of the zip, your garment may still be usable. But, if not, you'll need to replace the zip.

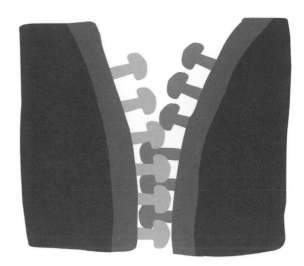

TOOTHED ZIP

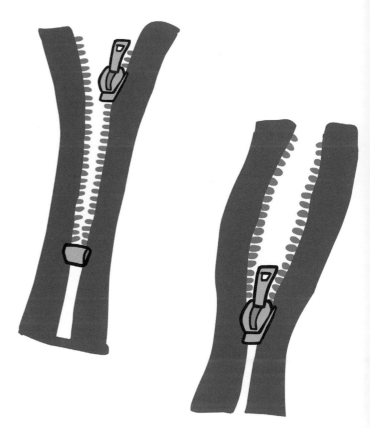

REMOVE THE BOTTOM CLOSURE TO RE-ATTACH THE SLIDER TO A BROKEN TOOTHED ZIP

INVISIBLE ZIP

An invisible zip is designed 'in reverse' with fabric coverings that come close together and conceal the plastic coil when the zip is closed. The zip has a special slider design that pokes through the narrow gap, and usually has an attractive 'dropper' style pull tab.

If the fabric of the zip closely matches your garment, these zips can be virtually invisible when closed, looking like a neat seam.

When letting out a skirt or dress, you may need to use some of the material overlapping a zip to create extra room. If so, consider replacing the zip with an invisible zip to make it less obvious.

INVISIBLE ZIP

ZIPS

REPLACING ZIPS

Replacing a zip isn't as difficult as it seems – it's normally just a case of noting how it is attached between the various layers of fabric while you remove the old one, and then sewing the new zip back into the same place.

Measure the whole length of the zip before you buy a replacement - get a new zip slightly longer than the old one, if you can't find an exact match.

REPLACING A STRAIGHT ZIP

Use a seam ripper to take out the broken zip. Note how the different flaps and seam allowances are arranged. For a zip at the waist of a skirt or pair of trousers, you will also need to unpick the seams that hold on the waistband.

If the garment was slightly too tight or loose, you can use this chance to let it out or take it in by moving the folds around the zip and increasing or decreasing the seam allowances, pressing the new seams before inserting the zip.

If working at a waistband, you will also need to remove or add material to the waistband length. Do the work on the waistband after replacing the zip within the main body of the garment.

For lightweight fabrics and long zips, tack the garment together along the length of the opening before sewing in the zip and you will ensure a really neat result. It is also a good idea to pre-shrink your zip's backing fabric by washing it.

Start with the zip closed and pin it into place. Ideally, you should complete the job with the zip closed but, on some areas of your garments, such as a zip on a narrow sleeve, you may need to open the zip to get at both sides.

Stitch the zip into place using a strong, narrow back stitch, working from the bottom of the zip to the top of the opening.

Sew close to the teeth or coil, but make sure you leave plenty of room for the slider to move up and down.

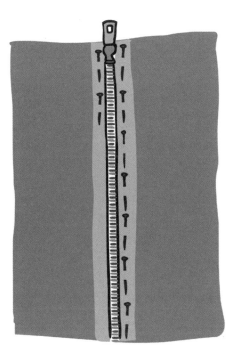

CLOSE THE ZIP AND PIN IT INTO PLACE

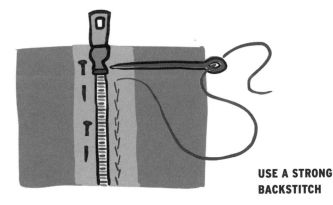

USE A STRONG BACKSTITCH

REPLACING A FLY ZIP

Fly zips usually have extra covering flaps, and are almost always attached to a waistband, so you need to take extra care when replacing these zips.

Note the position of all these pieces of fabric when you remove the zip, and put it back in exactly the same way. Otherwise, the general principles are the same as for a zip in a normal seam.

Unpick the waistband and all the seams holding the zip in place. The outer overlap may have 'top stitching' that shows on the outside of the garment. You may need to unpick these stitches to get to the reverse side of the flap where the zip is attached. If so, mark the line of the stitches with tailor's chalk or fabric marker to ensure you restitch them accurately.

Also note the appearance of this stitching, and get replacement thread to match. On a pair of jeans, this is often in a contrasting colour to the fabric.

Start by pinning and stitching one side of the zip to the lower 'underlap' flap, using a strong backstitch and sewing up from the bottom towards the waistband.

Then, open the zip and pin the other side to the outer 'overlap' flap. Close the zip to check you have pinned it in the correct place, then open it again and sew it into place.

You can now resew the 'top stitching', which will continue under the waistband.

Finally, re-attach the waistband. Use a closely matching thread. Since you are working from the good side of the fabric, a slip stitch can be useful to keep your work invisible, depending on the design of your trousers.

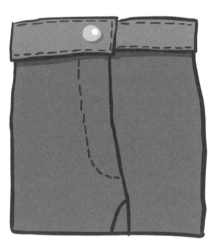

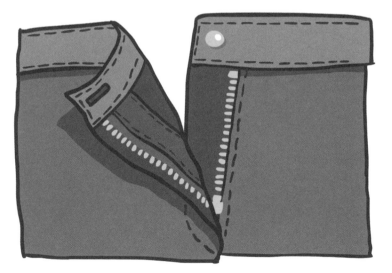

NOTE THE POSITION OF THE ZIP BETWEEN THE VARIOUS LAYERS OF FABRIC WHEN YOU REMOVE AND REPLACE A FLY ZIP

OTHER REPAIRS & TAILORING TIPS

From replacing fixings, to mending small tears, to making adjustments for a perfect fit, there are a whole range of minor repairs and tailoring jobs that you can complete at home without a sewing machine.

Here are some of the most valuable tips I have collected together, all of which will help to extend the useful life of your clothes.

THE RANGE OF FIXINGS

When a fixing breaks, you may want to replace it with something more attractive or more secure.

Most haberdashery departments, sewing and craft stores will stock these basic types in a range of colours and sizes.

HOOKS AND EYES
These fastenings are often used at the top of a zip to ensure it stays closed. They are sewn into place on the underside of an opening and are virtually invisible when closed.

PRESS FASTENINGS
These ball and socket fastenings aren't very strong, but can be used to hold together the front of a cardigan, or to hold a flap in place that covers a zip.

To sew on a press fastening, start with the 'ball' part, then press the fabric so that the ball makes an impression on the other side of the opening. This will show where to place the socket.

Both hooks and eyes and press fastenings are available ready-sewn on to tapes, making them easier to add to long seams.

VELCRO
Velcro is the trade name for a two-part tape fastening that is covered with tiny plastic hooks on one side and a fluffy looped surface on the other.

It is surprisingly strong as it can only be opened by a 'peeling' action, which is very unlikely to happen when a garment is in use. However, it isn't very long-lasting, especially as the hooked side is very adept at picking up fluff, which reduces its ability to grip.

Velcro can be bought in a range of colours and sizes and is easy to cut to size. You can sew it on or buy it with a heat-activated adhesive backing.

MENDING SMALL TEARS
Tears in the main body of a garment are very hard to fix securely and invisibly. On lightweight fabrics, the best solution is often to use a patch instead.

However, small tears in tougher and thicker fabrics can be darned using tiny diagonal stitches, as shown in the diagram.

The repair will be much stronger if you also attach a patch of iron-on interfacing to the back of the fabric to reinforce it. Interfacing is a loosely woven stiff fabric that is available in a range of colours and weights, and it should be applied carefully to the back of the tear before darning.

YOU CAN DARN SMALL TEARS IN STRONG FABRICS

TAKING IN A SHIRT OR DRESS

Taking in a shirt or dress at the side seam can be done without any special tailoring skills.

Get your model to put the item on inside out, then pin along the side seams to find a good fit. Remove the garment, then sew a new seam along the line of pins, removing them as you sew, and overlapping the old seam by several centimetres either side.

To make the new seam sit properly, you must press it in after sewing. If your seam has not created a large flap of spare material, this can be pressed to one side of the seam. However, you may want to cut away some of this excess material and then press the seam with the seam allowances opened at either side.

You may also need to tailor the armholes of the garment. For a shirt, lie it flat then mark a line from the new seam under the armpit and into the sleeve, tapering off smoothly to meet the seam of the sleeve.

Then unpick the sleeve seam and resewalong the line using running stitch. Finally, join the two seams together securely where they meet under the arm.

For a dress without sleeves, your seam adjustment may make the armholes smaller, so you may need to lower the bottom edge of the armhole to make more room.

ADJUSTING DARTS

Darts are small tucks sewn into garments to give them shape. You will usually find them at the tops of skirts and trousers, at the sides of bodices and under bust lines.

To improve the fit of your clothes, you can adjust these darts, taking in more material or letting some out. For darts that pass under a side seam or a waistband, you will also need to unpick and resew parts of the seam stitching.

Tie off the ends of threads used to sew darts, as this is less bulky than sewing extra stitches. A narrow running stitch is usually the best stitch to use.

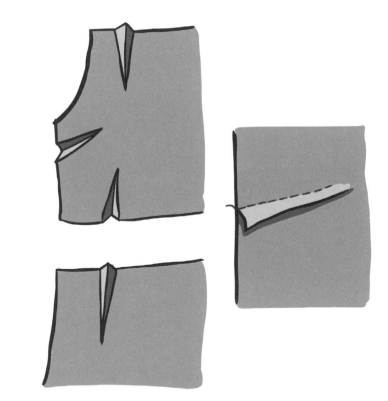

After adjusting the dart, press the new seam, folding the spare material down or to the centre of your garment (depending on the orientation of the dart).

OTHER REPAIRS & TAILORING TIPS

TAKING IN AND LETTING OUT SKIRTS AND TROUSERS

Making size adjustments at the seams of skirts and trousers is also a simple job.

REMEMBER THESE STEPS WHEN ADJUSTING A SEAM

1. Unpick and pin the seams to the right size, wearing the garment inside out.

2. Sew the new seams (backstitch is usually suitable and strong, although you may want to use slip stitch for small adjustments and work from the good side).

3. Press the new seam, first flat, then open.

ADJUSTING WAISTBANDS

TAKING IN

Taking in a waistband isn't a difficult repair.

It is best done along an existing seam at the back of a garment. If there is no seam at the back, take equal amounts from each side seam, so you don't make the garment uneven.

Unpick the waistband and seam, then fold in an extra seam allowance either side, press, pin and sew a new seam (use a strong narrow running stitch, backstitch or slip stitch). Press the new seam, first flat, then open.

You will now have too much material in the waistband. Depending on the thickness of the material, you can either fold this over and sew a neat edge using an invisible slip stitch (press afterwards to make it sit properly) or you may need to cut away some of the material and create a new seam in the waistband itself.

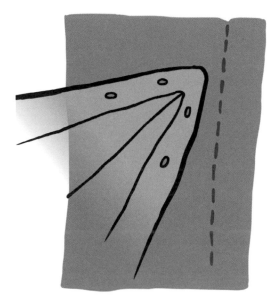

FOR A PROFESSIONAL LOOK, FIRST PRESS A NEW SEAM FLAT

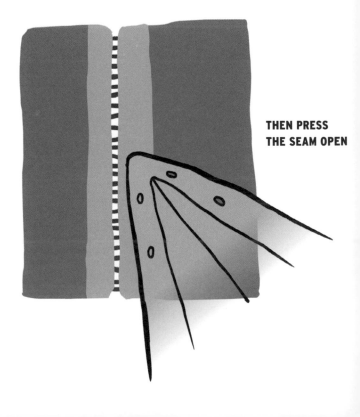

THEN PRESS THE SEAM OPEN

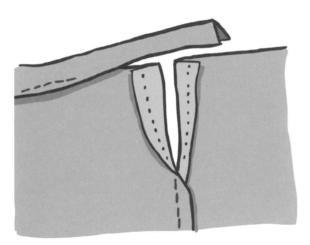

TAKE IN A SIDE OR BACK SEAM BY INCREASING THE HEM ALLOWANCE

Unpick then cut through the loose waistband, fold under the new seam allowances and press them, then use slip stitch to join the edges together.

Finally, re-attach the waistband, matching the thread to any existing stitching.

OTHER REPAIRS & TAILORING TIPS

LETTING OUT

If moving buttons and fastenings isn't enough to make a waistband fit, you will need to let out some of the seams and darts, and extend the waistband.

For this, you will need to find a small piece of closely matched material, and the best way to do this is to steal it from the garment itself. Measure how much the waistband needs to increase in length, then look in the hem allowance or inside pockets (where you can get away with patching the gap with non-matching material).

If you can't find enough material on the garment, then find the closest match you can and extend the waistband at the most inconspicuous point.

To add to a waistband, measure, fold and press the new piece of fabric. Then, open a seam in the waistband and use the new piece to bridge a gap of the right length, sewing on the new fabric with backstitch (or slip stitch for a more hidden result). Finish up by pressing and re-attaching the extended waistband to the garment.

If possible, try to gain the extra space you need from the seam allowance at a back seam and extend the waist there. If this is not possible, you will need to remove the entire waistband and let out seams and darts evenly around your garment, before extending and reattaching the waistband.

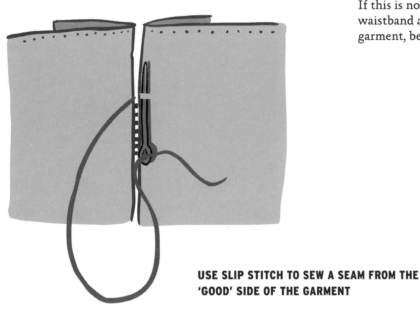

USE SLIP STITCH TO SEW A SEAM FROM THE 'GOOD' SIDE OF THE GARMENT

WAKE UP YOUR WOOLLENS

Knitwear often gets relegated to the bottom of the drawer as soon as it stops looking new and smart. But many of the defects that cause this premature abandonment can be easily removed.

Fluffy bobbles can be whipped away, snags can be hidden and holes can be darned to make your jumpers, scarves, gloves and cardigans good enough for meetings and smart occasions again.

CARE TIPS FOR LONGER-LIVED WOOLLENS

EASIER HAND WASHING

Hand-washed wool stays looking new for much longer, as you can use a milder detergent and only rub areas that are really dirty.

You should never wring or twist knitwear, so try to this great tip for taking the hassle out of drying your hand-washed woollies:

After a gentle squeeze, lie the garment flat on a towel that has lost its fluff. Then simply roll up the towel and walk up and down it a few times.

This will push out and absorb most of the moisture from the garment. Now you can dry it more quickly and easily, and with no drips!

KEEP MOTHS AT BAY

Moths will seek out your woollens as food for their larvae. If you aren't careful, they can cause terrible damage to your best clothes.

To deter moths, keep lavender bags or cedar wood blocks in your drawers or wardrobe (adult moths hate these smells).

Moths are particularly keen on patches of invisible dirt. As wool coats may only be cleaned once in a while, dislodge moth eggs acquired during wear by brushing regularly between washes.

When packing away woollies for a long period, place in sealed containers and add mothballs placed in a small cotton bag or old sock.

Mothballs contain toxic chemicals so use them only for long-term storage. Be careful not to touch them with your hands, and keep them away from children.

REMOVING SNAGS

Snagged threads and loops of wool decorating the outside of a garment can make it look old and worn before its time. These simple remedies help you deal with them in just a few minutes.

- Small, unbroken loops can be pulled back into place by stretching the fabric gently each side of the loop, in one direction after another.

- Large loops should be pushed through to the other side of the fabric instead. A small nail, needle, empty ball-point pen, or blunt pencil (for dark colours) are all good for this task, or you can buy small tools that are specifically designed for this purpose from craft stores. Don't use anything very sharp that might break the threads.

- Short broken threads should also be pushed gently back into the material. Never pull these threads or stretch the fabric around them, or you may cause even more stitches to fall out.

- Longer threads can be pushed through and threaded into the reverse side with a running stitch to keep them firmly in place.

WAKE UP YOUR WOOLLENS

BOBBLE BUSTING

'Bobbles' or 'pills' are those small balls of fluff that crop up on knitwear at points of friction, such as elbows and inside the arms.

Bobbles are the normal result of wear. They are made from loose fibres shed by the yarn, and the friction is what causes them to join together in little balls, which then cling to the surface of your woollens.

They can be removed safely, using a range of methods, without causing any harm to the underlying fabric.

CASHMERE
These fibres are very soft and bobbles form on garments made from cashmere very easily. They should be removed regularly to keep your luxurious knits in good order.

Since the wool is so soft, bobbles on cashmere come away very easily without pulling out more fibres. A gentle fabric comb is all that's needed to pull them off.
Find a good comb in a department store or pick one up from your local pharmacy.

OTHER WOOLLENS
Thicker woollens also gain bobbles over time. As these are tougher, removing bobbles by pulling can loosen other fibres and make future bobbling more likely.

The best method is to cut or slice the bobbles off cleanly with a sharp blade. If you don't have time to snip them off one by one with scissors (who does?), run a disposable razor lightly over the surface to slice them off.

The razor will clog up rapidly so, for even quicker results, use a special 'bobble busting' gadget. There are a range of inexpensive models on the market, from catalogues and household stores.

Most of these work very effectively. It is important, however, not to press them into the fabric – a light skimming action across the surface is all that's needed.

DARN IT!

This isn't just for socks. Hand darning, carefully done, can mend a woollen garment almost invisibly. I have successfully darned small holes on even my fine knits.

The main key to success is to match your darning thread closely to the garment. Luckily, department stores and craft shops usually stock a range of woollen embroidery yarns, which come in a huge number of colours and weights.

It's a good idea to wash this new wool before using it for a darn (put it in a sock to prevent tangling). This will ensure any shrinkage occurs before it becomes part of your clothing, rather than risking a darned area pulling tight later on.

You now know how to repair your clothes when they suffer damage, and how to adjust clothing for a better fit.

1 Place the hole over a smooth, rounded object. Special 'darning mushrooms' are available, but a plastic ball, paperweight or even a lightbulb will do. Work with the 'good' side upwards for neatness.

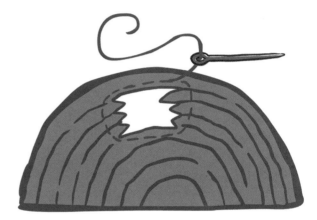

2 Run a stitch around the edge of the hole first. This will help the hole keep its shape as you darn it. Be careful not to stretch the fabric throughout the darning process, and don't tie off any threads. Use only three long threads (one for each stage) and the darn will keep them in place.

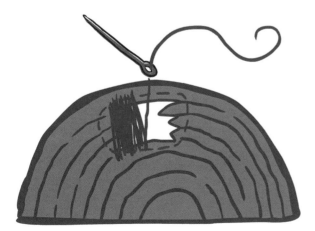

3 By darning you are, in essence, creating an integrated woven patch. So now create a 'warp' with your second thread, adding extra stitches each side. Set the spaces between the threads at about same density as the surrounding fabric.

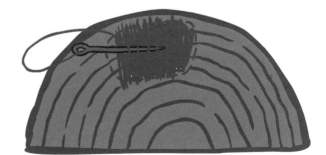

4 Now add the 'weft' threads at right angles to the first set. Again, sew a couple of stitches before and after the hole. Across the darn, weave the needle above and below alternate threads, reversing the order each time you change direction.

CLEANING & FRESHENING

But an even more common reason for clothes being left on the shelf is when they get marked by spills from food, drink and other substances in the home, street or workplace.

Here are some tips for preventing stains from becoming permanent, and for freshening up clothes with lingering smells.

STOP THE SPILL BECOMING A STAIN

Rule number one in stain prevention is to act quickly. Normal laundry detergent will clean off most substances that might cause a stain, as long as they have not been allowed to dry.

The first thing to do is blot off any spilled liquid, then act according to the stain and fabric type below.

FOOD AND DRINK STAINS ON WASHABLE FABRICS

Food, drink, blood and other biological stains on washable fabrics should be soaked as quickly as possible in cold water – not hot, as this may fix the stain instead.

First, soak for about half an hour in plain water, then prepare a cleaning solution by dissolving detergent in cold water (biological detergent works best for these stains) and leaving the garment to soak overnight before washing.

Adding a small amount of borax to the soaking solution can also work well.

Don't soak coloured fabrics with lighter fabrics, as the colour may run during soaking.

OTHER STAINS ON WASHABLE FABRICS

Some stains, including ink and paint, will be removed more easily if you dab on an appropriate solvent before soaking. For example, with ink stains, blotting with a cloth dampened with methylated spirits will help loosen the stain, and make it much easier for the detergent to soak it out.

Check the list of solvents in the 'Common home repairs' section of this book (see page 63) for which solvent to use on different stains.

GLYCERINE

Glycerine (available from pharmacies) is a gentle solvent for softening all kinds of dried-on stains before washing. Dab it on to a stain and leave for 30 minutes before washing, and it will give even old stains a fighting chance of coming out in the wash.

PRE-WASH STAIN REMOVERS

There are a number of proprietary brands of pre-wash treatments available, most of which are based on oxygen bleach. Unlike chlorine bleach, this is safe for use on most clothes, including colours. For very delicate fabrics, a mild solution of borax, used for pre-soaking and then to boost the detergent, is even safer.

BLEACHING WITH LEMONS AND THE SUN

A good home-made solution for stains on white fabrics is to use the mild bleaching powers of lemon juice. When

combined with sunlight, this is surprisingly effective at bleaching out stubborn marks.

Soak your garment, then dab lemon juice, diluted in equal parts with water, on to the stained area. Squeeze and hang out your garment to dry in the sun, and your stain will gently disappear, while the lemon juice will freshen your garment at the same time.

DRY-CLEAN ONLY
Spills on non-washable clothes should be taken straight to the dry-cleaners whenever possible.

If you can't do this immediately, try to keep the stain from setting by dabbing on an appropriate solvent.

Follow the same process as for carpets and upholstery in the 'Common home repairs' section of this book (see page 63), and also place an absorbent pad under the stain to prevent the solvent spreading too far.

Always test your solvent on an inconspicuous part of the material first.

As with upholstery, use only the minimum amount of solvent and avoid wetting the fabric.

KEEPING CLOTHES FRESH
A build-up of deodorant under the arms of your clothes can prevent them ever getting really fresh when they are washed. And some nasty spills and stains can leave a lingering smell behind, preventing clothes being worn even after the visible stains have gone.

Mild acid solutions will dissolve deodorant deposits and also cut through smells. Apply diluted lemon juice or vinegar (two tablespoons in half a litre of water) to the area with a sponge and leave for an hour before washing to freshen your clothes.

To freshen a whole batch of clothes at once (for example, seasonal clothes that have been packed away and developed a 'musty' smell), try pouring a cup of vinegar into the conditioner compartment of your washing machine when it begins its final rinse cycle.

Drying the clothes outside in the sun will also help to reduce discoloration and boost the freshness even more.

Personal & Household Accessories

Favourite items we use every day, such as shoes and handbags, can get damaged, broken, lost and worn out much more quickly than we would like. But, with some regular maintenance and these repair tips, they can last a lot longer, putting off the day when they need to be replaced with something new.

Smaller items in your home also have a big influence on how it looks and works. Along with picture frames, rugs and curtains, items such as lamps, plant pots, and waste-paper bins are essentials that can add to the overall style of a room if you get them right.

Repairs to ceramics and glass are covered in 'Common Home Repairs' and there is a wealth of upholstery tips and ideas for picture frames in the 'Furniture' chapter. 'Simple Clothing Fixes' also covers repairs to garments, but this chapter shows the main techniques you will need in order to repair a range of smaller personal items, including spectacles and jewellery.

Although many of these jobs are just simple repairs for when things go wrong, there's also plenty of scope to use your imagination when working on the items in this chapter. Use these ideas creatively to co-ordinate your home better, or to revamp old items that have gone out of style.

SHOES

Shoes are needed every day, and it's easy to put off repairs until it's too late. But, with the right care, shoes can be tougher and last longer, and many simple repairs can be carried out at home.

WEATHER AND EVERYDAY DIRT

Like your skin, shoe leather looks nicer, and resists wrinkles better, if it is kept moisturised and protected. Polish leather shoes regularly and keep outdoor boots protected with wax before going out in the mud, and your footwear will stay looking younger for longer.

Water and extremes of heat will make leather brittle. Wet shoes should be dried gently, not placed in front of the fire or on top of a radiator.

You can speed up drying, and help wet shoes and boots keep their shape by stuffing them with newspaper. Remove the newspaper after a day, and replace with dry paper if the stuffing becomes too damp. Don't forget to remove the paper when the shoes are dry, or it may encourage mould.

Damp mud can dry out the surface of leather. After removing major clods, don't rub mud in or clean it off immediately. Leave it to dry before simply brushing off the mud and adding shoe cream or polish to restore moisture and shine.

Suede shoes need to be looked after carefully. Brush them after use with a soft brush to keep the nap smooth. Suede is more absorbent than leather, so mud and stains should be cleaned off when wet to prevent them soaking in. Scrape off as much dirt as possible with cardboard or a butter knife, then dab off the remaining stain with a damp sponge.

If you want to use a stain removing solvent to remove a stain on leather or suede (see page 63), be careful it doesn't remove the dye and leave an ugly tide mark. Test the effect of the solvent on a hidden part of the shoe, such as the tongue under the laces, and use only a tiny amount on a dry cloth.

SCRATCHES AND SCUFFS

Hide minor scratches with coloured polish, or use a liquid scuff cover.

Very badly scratched, scuffed or faded shoes can be made to look new again if you dye them back to their original colour using a kit from a shoe shop or heel bar. The shoes should be cleaned thoroughly before brushing on the dye. Remove greasy marks and old layers of polish by sponging with methylated spirits before dyeing.

Deep scratches, burns or scrapes on both suede and leather can be removed by sanding gently with very fine sandpaper. This will remove the polish and reduce the nap, so you should add several layers of new polish to leather shoes after removing the mark. Brush suede all over with a stiff brush to bring back the texture and hide the area that has been sanded.

**LIGHTLY SAND DEEP SCUFFS
TO REMOVE THEM**

SHOES

SMELLY SHOES

Each day, your feet can produce several hundred millilitres of perspiration just from walking around, and this vapour passes into your shoes to be absorbed by the materials and lining. You can help prevent smells by airing shoes to let them dry out thoroughly before you wear them again.

Wearing the same pair of shoes several days in a row never lets them dry out properly, and is asking for trouble.

If you notice the beginnings of a smell in a pair of shoes, spray them with antifungal, antibacterial shoe spray and leave them for several days to dry out properly and prevent the problem developing further.

Canvas or fabric sports shoes have to deal with even more perspiration and also get covered in grass and mud stains. Most fabric shoes can be put in the washing machine once in a while for a short, cool wash. Any dye is likely to run, so be careful with white canvas shoes that have bright trimmings, and don't wash shoes with any clothing that may become discoloured.

Afterwards, dry your shoes in a warm place, away from direct heat, stuffing with regular changes of newspaper or tissue to help them keep their shape. Check seams and glued parts are still intact before wearing, and repair any problems with rubber cement or new stitching.

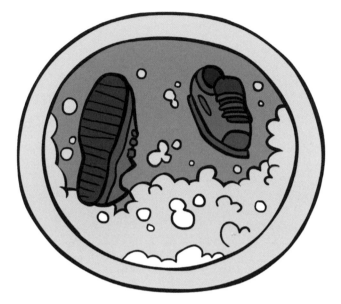

BROKEN SHOES

Prevention is better than cure, and a timely repair to a heel can prevent a more dramatic failure later. I ignored a worn heel on a favourite pair of work shoes for so long that it became weak and snapped down the centre - even a cobbler couldn't fix it after that.

Learn from my mistake and keep your shoes in good condition by checking soles, heels and lace holes regularly, and repairing problems before they get worse.

Soles will wear down more quickly in some areas than others, and you should replace these long before any parts wear down to the leather above. As well as soles, stitched seams and nailed-on heel bases can also be repaired at home.

SHOES

A LOOSE HEEL BASE

The rubber or plastic tip of a heel is usually held in place with small nails or pins, which may fall out or twist, causing the base to wobble.

To repair the heel, hammer in a narrow panel pin to anchor the base more firmly. If the heel is made of hollow plastic, it can be hard to find something to push the nail into without splitting the heel. Tap your heel to see if it is hollow and, if so, remove the base completely and fill some of the channels with epoxy resin. When this is nearly set, replace the base and hammer in new nails to anchor it.

Tap the nail heads beneath the surface using a nail punch, unless you enjoy making a loud clicking sound when you walk on hard surfaces!

REPLACING A SOLE

Home repairs to rubber soles can achieve a neater, less 'mended looking' result than you get in while-you-wait heel bars. Re-sole both shoes from a pair at once, to ensure they remain at equal heights.

Buy a sole replacement kit from a cobbler's or hardware shop, which will include two shaped soles and a tube of the correct glue.

Place the shoes on the rubber soles and draw around them in pencil, then cut the new soles slightly inside the pencil lines using a craft knife or scissors.

You can sand a thinner, bevelled edge around the new sole, so that it will stick down neatly all around your shoe. How thin you need the edge to be depends on the design of your shoe. With smart high heels you will want the sole to be virtually invisible, but a loafer may suit a flatter profile.

Remove the old rubber sole from your shoe (pulling it off with pliers if necessary) then clean and sand the surface beneath. If your shoe has a leather sole, don't remove it but sand the thicker parts to even out the wear, and to create a surface for the glue to grip on to.

Apply glue all over the rubber and press it on to the shoe. Place your hand inside the shoe and use a small hammer to tap the sole firmly on to the surface, focusing attention on the edges.

After the glue has dried, you can use sandpaper to neaten up any rough edges.

PUT EPOXY RESIN INTO A HOLLOW HEEL TO HELP WITH NAILING ON A NEW HEEL TIP

REPAIRING STITCHES

Split seams can be restitched using a sharp leather needle and strong twine. Match the colour of the twine as closely as you can to the leather, and rub polish over the seam afterwards to hide the repair.

If the leather around the stitches has split, you will need to stitch the new seam further into the leather, which will make the shoes tighter. If the shoes are old and stretched, they may still fit your feet, but you may need to stretch them if they are too tight (see below).

REPAIR EYELETS AND LACE HOLES

If an eyelet for a shoelace falls out, try to avoid lacing through bare leather or fabric, which may split. You can buy replacement eyelets in packs with a tool that is used to hammer the eyelets flat after pushing them through a hole.

If a lace hole without an eyelet splits or stretches, restitch it to its original size with a couple of stitches of strong thread – avoid putting too many new holes in the leather when you do this.

Lace holes in leather shoes can be reinforced by gluing a strip of leather or thick fabric behind the holes and piercing holes through the new patch with a hot skewer (see page 224).

STRETCHING TIGHT SHOES

New shoes are often very slightly tight and 'wearing them in' can be a painful process. You can speed this up by using heat to soften the leather.

Put on a very thick pair of socks (or several pairs) and squeeze your feet into the shoes. Then, take a hairdryer and blast the tight areas with hot air while flexing and stretching your feet.

Keep the shoes on while they cool down and then check the results while wearing your normal socks or stockings.

You can repeat this process several times until you get a good fit. But be aware that too much heat will dry out the leather, so give your shoes a soothing treatment of shoe cream or polish afterwards.

ADD A REINFORCING STRIP TO REPAIR BROKEN LACE HOLES

MENDING & ADJUSTING BELTS

Belts can be made of any stiff material, and are joined to the buckle in a number of different ways. All methods apart from riveted joints are simple to unpick or prise apart to replace a buckle. If a belt needs shortening, it is neater to do this by cutting away material at the end fitted to the buckle, especially if the other end is shaped or has decorative stitching.

To replace a belt buckle with a grip fitting, a screwdriver is needed to wedge into the fitting and loosen it, and you will need pliers to squeeze it back together again. If the buckle has a shiny finish, protect it from the grips of the pliers with a cloth.

Some belts have a screw or bolt fixing, for which you will need a small adjustable spanner, a pair of pliers or a small screwdriver.

Quick-release belts are even easier – simply use a flat screwdriver to flip up the serrated plate and remove the belt.

Riveted belts are hard to fix without special tools. It is easier in these cases to cut through the belt below the rivets and attach a new buckle by sewing it into place.

If the buckle is held on with a stitched loop of fabric or leather, you will need to unpick the stitches and then use strong thread and a needle to sew a new loop.

You should buy a special, very sharp, three-faced leather needle for these repairs, which will pierce the material easily, without tearing it.

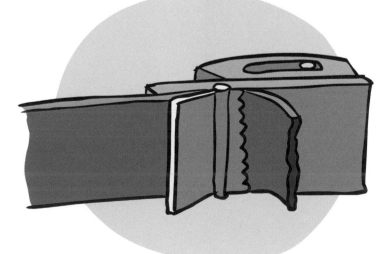

A QUICK-RELEASE BUCKLE IS EASY TO REMOVE IF YOU NEED TO REPLACE THE FABRIC

MENDING & ADJUSTING BELTS

MAKING A NEW HOLE IN A LEATHER BELT

To make a new hole in a leather belt, you can puncture the material and seal its edges in one step by using a hot metal bradawl or skewer.

Start by marking the position for the new hole on the 'good' side of the belt. Then, secure the belt by wrapping it around something solid, such as a table leg, so you can hold it tight with one hand and push the skewer through with your other hand.

If you need to make a new hole that will make the belt tighter than the existing holes, you can wrap the belt around a frame, such as the back of a chair, attaching the loosest hole to the buckle, so the location of the new hole lies across the frame.

Now, heat the skewer or bradawl by holding one end in the flame of a gas burner or against a very hot electric stove top. Wrap the other end in a cloth, and hold it with thick gloves or an oven mitt, to protect your hand from the heat. When the metal starts to glow, take it to the belt and push it through the leather. It will probably smoke slightly as it burns through the leather.

After making the new hole, put the skewer or bradawl into an empty metal or ceramic sink to cool down – it will stay hot for some time.

SAFETY NOTE

Wear thick protective gloves for this job, as the metal needs to be very hot in order to burn through the leather.

TO BURN A NEW HOLE IN A BELT, SECURE IT SO YOU CAN HOLD IT FIRMLY WITH ONE HAND

MENDING & ADJUSTING BELTS

MAKING A NEW HOLE IN A FABRIC BELT

You can cut a new hole in a fabric belt with scissors. Tiny, curved nail scissors are the best tool for this, rather than large dressmaking scissors.

You will need to seal the edges to protect them from fraying. You should do this to match the other holes in your belt, if possible. On very thick, stiff fabric, nail varnish can do the trick, or you may prefer to sew around the hole with a neat, strong buttonhole stitch.

If the belt has eyelets, you can often find matching eyelets in craft shops.

Do-it-yourself metal eyelets come in inexpensive packs in a range of metal and enamelled finishes, with a special tool that allows you to flatten and secure them using a hammer.

NOTE
These eyelets are also useful for repairing lace holes in shoes and trainers (see page 221).

REINFORCE A FABRIC HOLE WITH STITCHING

OR HAMMER ON A METAL EYELET

HANDBAGS

Handbag care and repair uses a combination of the techniques described elsewhere in this book to repair shoes and to do upholstery work.

CARE AND CLEANING

Like shoes, leather handbags need regular moisture to keep the leather supple. But coloured polish would rub off on your hands and clothes, so use clear 'hide food' or leather cream and rub it in with a soft cloth every few weeks.

Scuffs and stains must be treated with something coloured, such as shoe polish or scuff cover. To remove excess colour, wait for the stain or polish to dry then rub in leather cream and buff with light coloured rags until you can no longer see the colour rubbing off on the fabric.

Be careful if you decide to use sandpaper to remove a bad stain or scratch, as handbag leather is thinner and more delicate than shoe leather. Specialist shoe cleaning blocks or a 'magic eraser' sponge are gentler abrasives more suitable for delicate bags and suitcases.

Ink and other stains can be removed by dabbing with the correct solvent (see page 63), but always test a hidden part of the leather to check its effect and avoid creating patches and tide marks.

HANDBAG REPAIRS

Bags commonly fail at the handles or straps, due to age and overloading. If a stitched handle tears or comes loose, you can unpick and restitch it using a leather needle and thick twine.

If you can't find twine that exactly matches the existing seams or the leather colour, you can colour the stitches afterwards using a permanent marker, such as those used to label CDs, but be very careful not to mark the leather.

A metal handle link that snaps or bends can be replaced, and the exact repair will depend on the design of your handbag. The handle may be attached to the fitting with stitched loops or with riveted joints and you can change this method of fixing if needed, which may mean making the straps shorter.

With handle repairs, symmetry is important, so it may be best to find new parts and replace all the handle fittings at once. Old handbags in charity shops can be a good source of parts, as well as craft and even hardware shops – brass rings intended for curtains or furniture may prove to be an ideal replacement for your handle links.

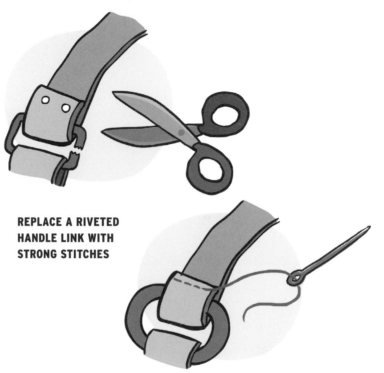

REPLACE A RIVETED HANDLE LINK WITH STRONG STITCHES

Replace riveted handle fittings with brass rings, stitched into place.

Side seams, flaps, pockets and other stitched parts can be repaired by stitching with strong thread and a sharp leather needle, following the existing seams and using existing holes where possible.

As with upholstery, you are stitching thick material around corners and other three-dimensional shapes, and the neatness of the final result depends on working slowly and carefully.

In addition, handbags often have stitching as part of their design, so it's even more important to work methodically, one stitch at a time, ensuring the leather or fabric sits neatly, and that the spacing and length of the stitches follow the original pattern.

REPLACE THE LINING OF A BAG

Most of my handbags fall out of use when they develop holes in the lining, or when a leaky pen creates a flood of ink that stains the lining.

In these situations, a treasured bag with other parts in good condition can be made as good as new by fitting a new insides.

TOOLS YOU WILL NEED

This repair needs no special tools, just new lining material, scissors, pins, a straight needle, a half-circular upholstery needle, plenty of thread and perhaps a zip.

THE STEPS

1. Start by removing the old lining. This will be stitched into the leather, and these seams are unlikely to be broken. Therefore, a good way to make this repair easier is to stitch the new lining on to the remains of the old one, rather than unpicking and restitching the leather seams. To do this, cut the old lining out leaving at least 2cm of spare material all around the edges where it joins the leather.

REMOVE THE OLD LINING AND USE IT AS A TEMPLATE

2. Now use the old lining as a model for creating the new one, adding extra material all around the top edge. Stitch the seams using a strong backstitch (see page xx), remembering that the 'right' side of the finished lining will be the inside.

3. Take the opportunity to think about adding useful extra pockets and accessories to the lining, such a loop for a key-ring or a vertical storage area for potentially leaky pens.

4. Now take the new lining and pin it inside the handbag, folding over the old lining and the hem of the new lining to create a hemmed seam around the top. Make sure the base of the lining rests on the base of the bag, so that the lining does not have to bear the weight of the things you put in the bag.

FOLD HEMS THEN PIN AND SEW THE NEW LINING TO THE EDGE OF THE OLD LINING

5. Finally, sew the lining into place using the upholstery needle, which makes sewing much easier when you can only work from one side of a seam.

Use backstitch for strength and place the stitches as close to the edge of the leather as possible. If you use thread that matches the background colour of your lining material, this seam will be virtually invisible from outside the bag.

Umbrellas can be repaired after most kinds of damage, so don't simply abandon yours in frustration if it fails to open in a downpour or blows inside out in a storm. Fold it up as neatly as you can, then take it home and see if you can fix the problem.

MENDING THE FRAME

The mechanism of an umbrella looks complicated, but is actually just a simple system of levers that pull the fabric tight when the central knob is pushed up the stem and locked into place.

If the arms seem to be tangled or bent in the wrong direction, you can often simply ease them back into the correct shape and alignment one by one to solve the problem.

If any of the ribs are bent or broken, you can straighten them with pliers, then strengthen them with a 'splint' of stiff coat hanger wire and some strong household tape.

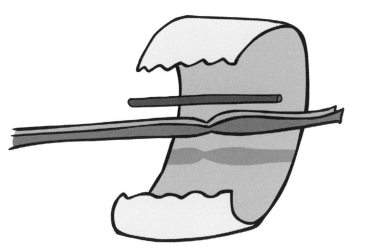

CREATE A SPLINT FOR A BENT UMBRELLA ARM

The hinged joints between ribs are fixed with small hollow rivets, which also sometimes break. These joints can be mended by wrapping thin wire several times through the holes in the two ribs, and around the 'outside' of the joint (the side that is exposed when the joint is folded). This repair is not infallible, but will last for several months if done carefully and not too tightly.

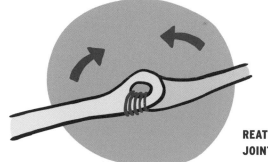

REATTACH A BROKEN JOINT WITH WIRE

Sometimes, the plate in the metal catch that holds the umbrella open will become trapped inside the stem.

Repair this problem by using the blade of a craft knife to prod the plate inside the stem back into a position where it will pop out again. If you find the plate is bent, straighten it with pliers to help it stay free in future.

USE A CRAFT KNIFE TO EASE OUT A STUCK CATCH

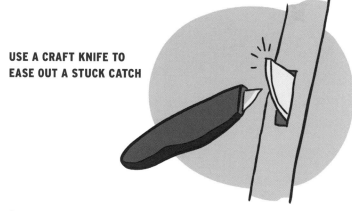

The same problem can occur at the bottom of the stem of a button-operated umbrella, where a catch holds the umbrella closed. The same method can be used to repair this catch, too.

UMBRELLAS

MENDING THE FABRIC COVER

The fabric cover of an umbrella is attached to the frame with thread. Re-attach a loose cover using sewing thread and a needle that is fine enough to fit through the holes in the frame.

A hole in the cover can be patched with household tape, but this isn't very attractive! More acceptable results can be achieved by gluing on a patch of similar thin nylon material, using clear adhesive. Put a thick layer of adhesive all around the edge of the patch material, then press it down firmly until the glue dries.

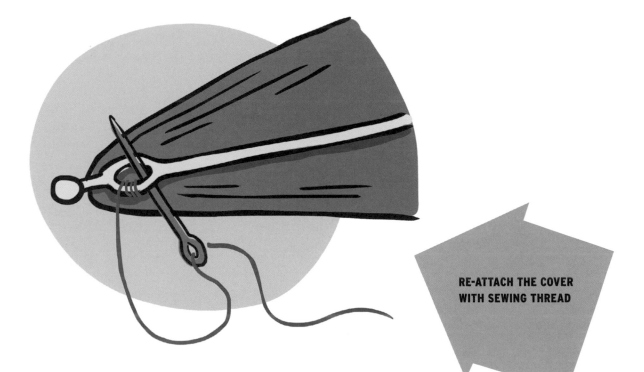

RE-ATTACH THE COVER
WITH SEWING THREAD

TAKING CARE OF HATS

The way you handle and care for your hats can make a big difference to how long they last.

Avoid grabbing your hat by its crown, especially if it has an inviting peak your fingers can fit around, such as on a trilby or panama hat. This constant pinching will cause a straw hat to split and cause wear marks to build up on felt. Handle your hat by the brim instead. This is more resilient and easier to clean.

When putting a stiff hat down on a surface, avoid resting it on its brim, especially if it has an angled, turned down shape. This will make the brim turn up, ruining the shape. If you have to put your hat down, leave it upside down, resting lightly on its crown, and it will maintain its shape better.

Letting hats dry out properly when they get wet is particularly important. Never use a hairdryer or direct heat to dry out a straw or felt hat, or the material can shrink. Instead, turn out the inner sweat band and rest the hat in a warm place on this band. This will allow air to circulate and ensure the hat dries evenly and completely.

RESHAPING HATS

Dents and creases in both straw and felt hats can be reshaped using steam.

A stove-top kettle is ideal for creating the jet of steam needed, but a saucepan can be used as a substitute. Place a lid on the pan until it boils, then shift the lid slightly to one side, leaving a narrow opening through which the steam will pour.

Hold the hat over the steam for a few seconds at a time, gently working out the dent or unfolding the crease. It only takes a small amount of steam to loosen the fibres of the felt or straw.

Avoid over-handling the material, and work with clean hands or you may leave grime behind on the surface.

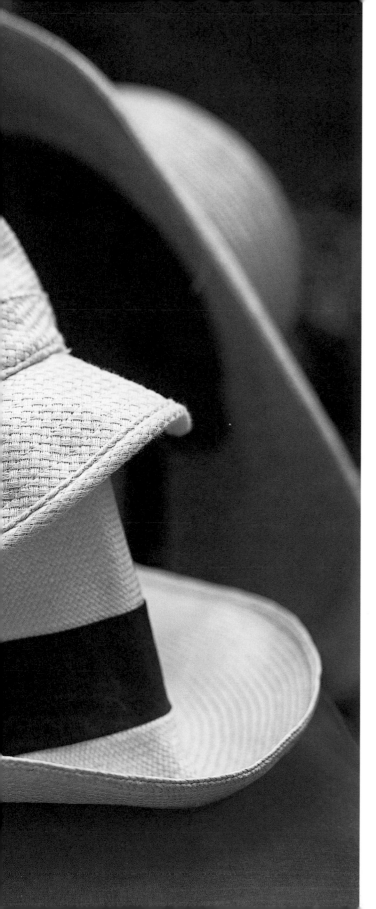

TAKING CARE OF HATS

A crease in the brim of a straw hat can be ironed out, using a steam iron. Place a linen cloth or tea towel between the hat and your iron, and use a low heat.

After reshaping, dry your hat thoroughly, resting it on its inner band, as before.

HAT TIPS - STRAW

Straw hats should be looked after by regular brushing with a soft brush to remove dust, and they should be stored in a box or bag over the winter to avoid a build-up of dust.

Depending on the cause, dirt and stains can be brushed off when dry, or cleaned off with a very slightly damp flannel. Alternatively, draw out a deeper stain using a fine-pored make-up sponge that is squeezed out and nearly dry.

A microporous 'magic eraser' can be useful to remove very difficult stains on light-coloured straw. This should be used with care as it may damage the sheen, but this result may be preferable to a dark, grubby stain.

If a straw hat splits, or if the stitching holding it together comes undone, you can restitch it using a blunt needle.

A straw hat that has become slightly loose can be tightened either by stitching a tuck into the inner band, or by replacing the outer band with a new, tighter one. A wide range of ribbons can be used to make a replacement band – almost anything non-stretchy will do the job.

REPLACE A HAT BAND

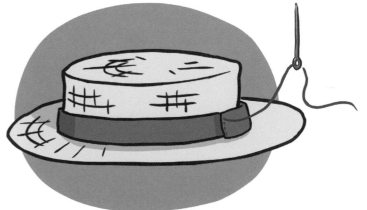

TAKING CARE OF HATS

Measure carefully (or ask a friend to pin it in place while you wear the hat) to get the right length to make the hat fit perfectly. Then, sew it onto the hat using small stitches in matching thread at the back of the crown.

Note that this method can only be used to make very small adjustments in fit. A large change in tension in a hat band will cause the crown to pinch in and look dreadful!

Although a sun-faded coloured hat can't be made bright and new again, you can make the fading more even by dabbing the darker areas gently with a sponge soaked in a mild solution of oxygen bleach (not chlorine bleach or toilet bleach). Leave the hat balanced on its inner band to dry out completely afterwards.

HAT TIPS - FELT

Felt has a delicate surface, and only very soft brushes should be used on it. Brush a felt hat to remove dust and surface grime, and to keep the nap of the felt bright.

When storing a felt hat for the summer, bear in mind the threat of moths, which will love the tight woollen fibres and seek them out. Place mothballs in a small bag or an old sock inside your hat before storage, then air it well before wearing it again.

Brushing will also remove most surface stains – use a towel or sponge, very slightly damp, to rub off stickier substances.

Commercial 'dry cleaning' stain removers can help to dab off a coloured stain, such as ink, but this may also affect the dye in the felt, so always test these solvents on a hidden area first.

Burns and other marks that have damaged the felt are trickier to deal with. The best method of removing damaged fibres is to use the finest grade of 'wet and dry' sandpaper to rub them off. Afterwards, brush the whole hat with a soft brush, to restore the nap of the felt and hide the damaged area.

USE FINE SANDPAPER TO REMOVE DAMAGED FELT FIBRES

Valuable jewellery should always be repaired by a professional jeweller. Confine your DIY mending efforts to plated and costume jewellery items, and restrict yourself to simple cleaning for anything made of solid gold, silver, platinum and precious stones.

CARING FOR YOUR JEWELS

You can wash both gold and silver and cheaper pieces of jewellery in mild washing up liquid. Use a plastic bowl to bathe these items, and never run jewellery under a tap or wash it in a sink with a plug hole – it's just too risky for valuable items.

Brush very gently with a toothbrush to remove dirt from crevices, and use cool water. Heat would expand the metal and risk stones falling out of loosened settings.

NEVER CLEAN JEWELLERY UNDER A TAP

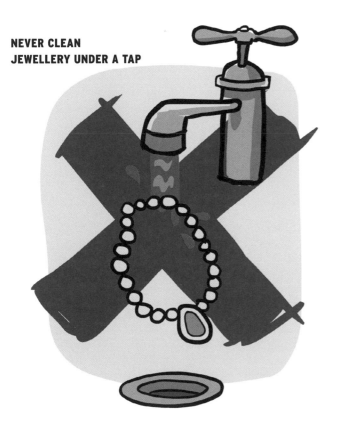

Always check the pieces when you remove them from the bowl, and don't pour away the water until you are sure all the stones and pieces are accounted for.

Dry jewellery with a chamois leather rather than a towel or tissue to avoid causing scratches on soft gold and silver.

Washing strings of beads or pearls can weaken the thread, so clean these by polishing with a dry brush or chamois leather instead.

MENDING JEWELLERY

Costume and fashion jewellery can be mended at home if links, strings and settings break.

TOOLS YOU WILL NEED
The most useful tools for mending jewellery are two sets of small, pointed-nose pliers.

Two pairs are needed to bend jewellery wire into shape because everything is so tiny it can't be held in your fingers. Use one pair to hold the pieces and use the other to bend and shape them.

It is also helpful to have a soldering iron at hand for securing joints and rings of wire. These are cheap and also useful for electronics. See page 55 for the principles and process of soldering a joint in an electrical appliance.

REPLACEMENT PARTS
Your supply of household wire can be used for jewellery emergencies but, being made of steel, it will corrode, may cause allergies if left next to the skin, and is also not a very attractive colour.

You can buy a wide range of replacement costume jewellery parts from online and high street craft suppliers. These can be complex, such as new earring hooks and brooch fittings, or simple lengths of gold or silver plated wire.

A set of spare 'jump rings' is a useful item to keep in your jewellery box. These are circular links that hook on to two parts that need to be joined and are then closed up using pliers.

JEWELLERY CARE

SOLDERING A JUMP RING

You can make a jump ring repair more secure by soldering it with a tiny piece of lead-free solder (the same solder used in electrical repairs).

TOOLS YOU WILL NEED
As well as your soldering iron and coil of lead-free solder, you will also need a craft knife and tweezers, and a bathroom tile or another heat-proof surface to work on.

THE STEPS
1. After mending your item by squeezing the jump ring into shape, clean off any grease by dipping the jump ring into methylated spirits.

2. Then, arrange the jewellery piece with the tiny gap in the jump ring facing you and lying as flat as possible on the ceramic tile.

3. Cut a tiny chip off the coil of lead-free solder, using the craft knife, then use the tweezers to balance this on top of the gap in the jump ring. If necessary, squash the solder on the tile using the back of your tweezers to give it a flatter shape and help it balance.

4. Heat the soldering iron, then bring it very slowly across the surface of the tile until it touches the jump ring about a quarter of a circle away from the solder. Be very careful not to dislodge the solder. If it does fall off, remove the heat immediately so it doesn't melt and get stuck to the side of the ring. Then, replace it and try again.

5. As soon as the solder melts and runs into the gap in the ring, remove the soldering iron (the whole melting process should take no more than a couple of seconds).

NOTE
Pure gold and silver jewellery is soldered with a special solder made of an alloy of precious metals with a lower melting point than pure gold and silver. This melting point is still much higher than that of traditional solder, and it has to be melted using a blow torch. This is a more dangerous and specialised process and requires lots of other equipment.

Although this is something that can be done in a home workshop, this kind of soldering is only to be tackled by a serious jewellery-making hobbyist.

SOLDER A JUMP RING BY PLACING EVERYTHING CAREFULLY ON A CERAMIC TILE

JEWELLERY CARE

MENDING CUFFLINKS

Some cufflinks have chains that can be mended using pliers and new jump rings, as above. Others have a solid post attached to a decorative face and a common problem occurs when the joint between the face and the post snaps.

This joint can be soldered back together using a similar technique to that used for an electronic repair on page xx.

Hold the cufflink together with masking tape while you apply the solder. Lie the piece on its side on a heat-proof surface and work through the gap in the tape.

Apply the heat to the post rather than to the rear of the face of the cufflink, to avoid damaging any enamel or decorative finish.

Add plenty of solder to make this joint secure, and don't worry too much about how it looks – it won't be visible when the repaired link is being worn on a shirt cuff.

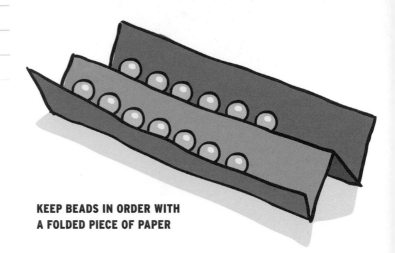

KEEP BEADS IN ORDER WITH A FOLDED PIECE OF PAPER

RE-STRINGING A SET OF BEADS

You should replace the thread on a beaded necklace or bracelet with specialist silk thread, man-made necklace twine or wire wherever possible. Choose a colour that closely matches your beads to ensure it doesn't show while the piece is being worn.

To help speed up this job, use a fine needle to thread the beads, and line them up in the correct order beforehand, folding a piece of paper into a 'w' shape and resting them in the grooves. For heavy beads, turn the 'w' upside down and rest just one row in the middle groove of the resulting 'm'.

Your necklace will be more secure if you tie a knot in the thread between each bead. These knots will sit mainly inside the holes in the beads either side and won't be obvious, but will help prevent the whole set of beads hitting the floor if the thread breaks.

Tie the knot using the needle then push the knot tightly against the bead as you tighten it, using the side of the needle to ensure the knot ends up close to the bead.

At the clasp, tie the beads on to the jump rings or clasp hooks using a secure figure of eight knot (see page 33) and tuck the stray ends of the thread into the final beads at each end.

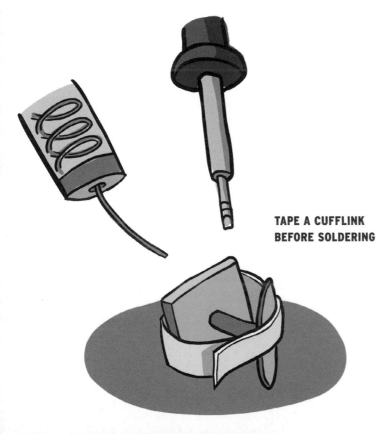

TAPE A CUFFLINK BEFORE SOLDERING

SPECTACLES & SUNGLASSESS

Expensive and essential prescription spectacles should have permanent repairs carried out by a qualified optician. However, it helps to know how to hold your glasses together temporarily in an emergency, and to be able to repair your 'reserve' spectacles and cheaper pairs of sunglasses.

IF A SCREW COMES OUT

The folding arms and nose supports on spectacles and sunglasses are often held together with tiny screws, which may work loose and fall out.

To fix these, you will need tiny screwdrivers. Sometimes these turn up as prizes in Christmas crackers, but both electronics shops and opticians will also sell them. They are normally much cheaper from electronics suppliers.

If you have lost the missing screw and don't have a replacement, you can obtain the correct replacement and have the repair done by an optician. As an emergency measure, use thin wire and pliers to fashion a temporary repair.

Push the wire through the hole and wrap it around the inside of the frame several times before twisting the ends together with pliers. Work with the arm in the 'open' position and pull the wire as tight as you can and this repair can last for up to a week if you don't try to close the frames.

For a better temporary repair to spectacles (and permanent repairs to cheaper sunglasses) keep some spare tiny screws in your toolbox. I remove the screws from broken and scratched pairs of old sunglasses and keep them in a matchbox for emergencies.

IF THE FRAME BECOMES LOOSE

Frequently removing and fidgeting with your frames, or pushing them on top of your head when they aren't in use, can bend the arms out of shape and make the frames loose.

Both metal and plastic frames (including plastic frames with a metal core) are designed to be reshaped while warm. Heating them gently will soften the material slightly and allow you to bend the arms back to the correct shape.

The best heating method, which doesn't risk melting your frames, is to place them in water the temperature of a hot bath for a minute or two. Remove the frames from the water and bend the arms very gently back into shape, replacing them in the water to reheat if the frame cools and stiffens.

Don't force the arms or you will risk snapping them or bending a sharp corner into the frame, which will weaken it. Instead, hold each arm lengthwise between the thumbs and forefingers of both your hands and squeeze gently, using a 'bouncing' motion and moving your fingers up and down the arm to reshape it gradually.

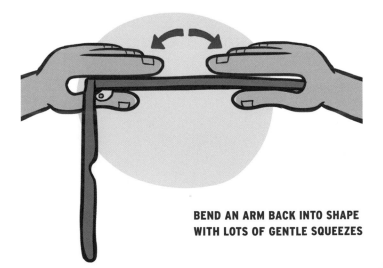

BEND AN ARM BACK INTO SHAPE WITH LOTS OF GENTLE SQUEEZES

IF A LENS FALLS OUT

Lenses may be held in a solid plastic frame, in a metal frame held together with a small screw, or secured in a 'rimless' frame using a strong nylon wire that sits in a groove along the edge of the lens.

Metal frames can be mended with a screw or, temporarily, with wire. If a plastic frame has not broken, you can snap the lens back into place by pushing it firmly into the frame, usually from the reverse side.

Putting a lens back into a rimless frame is trickier. A good tip is to pull the nylon wire around the edge of the lens using a strip of thin, non-stretchy fabric, such as a piece of thin binding tape or a cut strip of calico or polyester.

Put the lens into the top half of the frame then use the fabric to pull the wire around the lens and into the groove. At the end of this process, the fabric will be trapped between the wire and the lens. Bring it back round to the bottom edge of the lens and, holding the wire down with one hand, carefully pull out the tape with the other hand.

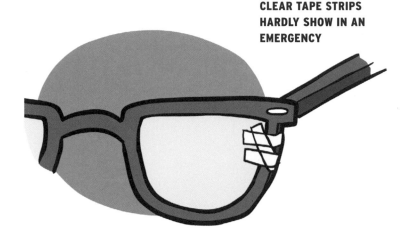

CLEAR TAPE STRIPS HARDLY SHOW IN AN EMERGENCY

IF THE FRAME SNAPS

Repairs to expensive spectacles will need to be done by a professional, so hold these together temporarily with tape.

Cut clear sticky tape into strips then patch and bandage the break, using paperclip wire as a splint if needed.

If necessary, you can even place tape strips over parts of the lenses. These are invisible from a short distance, as long as you make sure not to touch the sticky side of the tape and leave finger prints.

Prepare your mending strips from a piece of tape stuck to a surface and handle them only with tweezers and scissors until they are on the lens. You can safely touch the shiny side once the pieces are in place, smoothing out any air bubbles.

These tape repairs won't last long (especially if you go out in the rain!) but should help ensure you can see properly until you can take your frames in for mending.

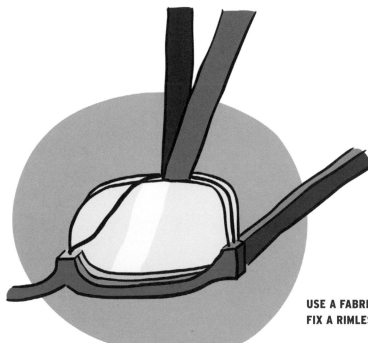

USE A FABRIC STRIP TO HELP FIX A RIMLESS LENS

SPECTACLES & SUNGLASSESS

For cheap sunglasses, you can be braver and make more permanent repairs. For breaks in plastic frames, use epoxy resin glue for a permanent, strong, waterproof repair. Be careful not to use too much, and wipe away any excess glue that oozes from the break using a cloth dampened with white spirit.

For metal frames, you can also make minor repairs with solder.

A very neat result is difficult, especially if the frames are very thin, but you can sand down the solder afterwards and paint over the join with gilt or silver paint to hide the repair. Or be creative and give your frames a new coat of paint by removing the lenses and covering in spray enamel, which is also available in metallic shades.

A useful tip when soldering, or when fixing frames with wire, is to support the parts in the correct position using pieces of modelling clay.

HOLD METAL FRAMES IN MODELLING CLAY FOR SOLDERING

LAMPSHADES

Because they are such a matter of individual taste, it can be hard to find the perfect lampshade, and ready-made lamps are expensive, too. So, it pays dividends to be able to fix and re-cover lampshades yourself.

Lampshades have a huge influence on the style of your home, especially in the evening. Light changes colour and texture as it passes through fabric or glass shades, and opaque shades can cast distinct pools of light into a room, creating a very different atmosphere. The flexibility of lampshade design means that many any other effects can be achieved with a wide range of materials.

THE MAIN STYLES AND SHAPES

Lampshades are sometimes made of single pieces of moulded glass or plastic. Breaks in these materials can be fixed with glue, but they are hard to restyle.

To replace a glass lampshade that is part of a set, try to find matching replacements in salvage yards and second-hand shops.

Most traditional lampshades are based on a metal or wire frame, covered in paper, fabric or other material, and are held on a lamp base or pendant fitting by a supporting ring.

Frames come in range of shapes, and may be straight-sided, cone shaped or made of separate panels. All these styles can be re-covered successfully at home.

MENDING THE FRAME

The frame of a lampshade is normally held together with wire or with simple bolted, soldered or riveted joints.

These can be mended with new wire or by soldering. A good tactic can be to wrap thin wire around the joint, like a bandage, and then use solder to hold it in place permanently. Don't be afraid to improvise to mend a broken frame securely. When the frame is covered, your bodges won't be visible.

If thin metal parts or wires are bent, heat them gently before bending them back into shape (for example, by placing the frame on a radiator). This will reduce the 'work-hardening' effect, which can make metal brittle and easy to snap if it is bent back and forth too many times.

TOOLS AND MATERIALS FOR COVERING LAMPSHADES

BINDING TAPE

Where the metal frame comes into contact with fabric or paper, it should be wrapped in this thin fabric tape. This is bound diagonally around the frame, and then sewn around the joints to protect the fabric from corrosion and marks.

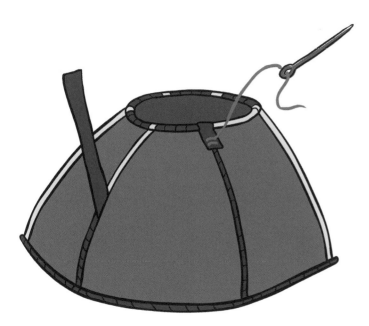

BINDING TAPE HELPS PROTECT LAMPSHADE FABRICS FROM THE METAL FRAME

SPRAY GLUE

Lampshades made from fabric bonded to cardboard are great. However, since light shines through the resulting material, brush or spatula marks created by thick glue would show up. Repositionable spray glue is easy to use and gives a very neat result. It takes up to a day to set properly, and the fabric can be peeled off and stuck down again during this period to get it perfectly flat.

LAMPSHADE CARD

Special card intended for lampshades can be bought from craft shops and online suppliers. It has a waxed surface, comes ready fireproofed, and is great to work with, though is not strictly necessary. Ordinary cardboard can be used instead, as long as it is properly fireproofed afterwards.

TRIMMINGS AND BIAS TAPE

Joints between panels and the oversewn edges of top and bottom rings need to be covered with a trimming to finish off your lampshades. This can be a simple, neat strip of 'bias tape' which is glued on with clear adhesive. Or you can choose from a massive variety of decorative trimmings and fringes for a range of modern and traditional looks.

FIREPROOFING

Old-style light bulbs are very hot and, even if you use cooler low-energy bulbs, it's important that your lampshade materials are resistant to fire. You should avoid using man-made fabrics that might melt in the heat, and your finished lampshades should be sprayed with fireproofing before use.

You can buy fireproofing spray (which is also suitable for upholstery and other household items) in small 'tester' bottles which cost very little. Most fireproofing will not stain, but make sure you test it on your chosen fabric or paper covering before you make the lampshade, to check its effect on the finish and colour. Choose a different material if your selection is marked by the spray – it's important not to leave out this safety measure.

LAMPSHADES

COVERING A STRAIGHT-SIDED OR CONE-SHAPED SHADE

These frames don't normally have side struts, so the strength of the shade depends on the stiffness of the covering material. These are therefore ideal for re-covering with fabric bonded to card.

TOOLS AND MATERIALS YOU WILL NEED
Medium weight card or lampshade card, repositionable spray adhesive, masking tape, a suitable thin fabric, scissors, clear glue, needle and thread, and bias tape or other trim. You may also need binding tape to repair the binding on the frame.

THE STEPS
1. Measure the card using the old shade before dismantling it. Place it on the card and roll it along (or around a curve if the shade is cone-shaped) drawing a line with a pencil along both edges. Cut the card half a centimetre outside the pencil line all around, allowing an extra 2cm at one end for an overlap.

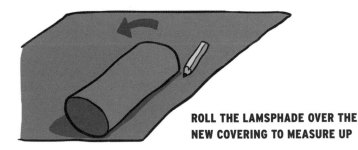

ROLL THE LAMSPHADE OVER THE NEW COVERING TO MEASURE UP

Put a strip of masking tape over one edge. This will be left free of fabric to allow the shade to be glued together by sticking card on to card, rather than on to fabric.

2. Press the fabric to remove creases, if needed. Then spray the whole piece of card with adhesive and lay down the fabric on top of it, pressing with a clean cloth or towel to stick it down without creases, folds or finger marks. Trim the fabric all around the edges of the card up to the pencil lines, and along the edge of the masking tape, before peeling off the tape.

3. Now, prepare the frame by removing the old covering from the two rings, and repair any binding on the outer parts of the rings, if necessary.

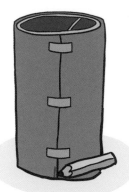

USE MASKING TAPE TO HOLD THE CARD WHILE YOU MARK THE CORRECT POSITION

4. Roll up the new shade cover and ensure it is the correct diameter to fit around the top ring (if the shade is cylindrical, ensure it is parallel as well) and tape it with masking tape. Make tiny pencil marks to show where it needs to be stuck together.

5. Then remove the masking tape and apply clear glue to the fabric-free strip at the end of the covered side. Roll up the shade and stick the two edges together. Put it on a flat surface and place a flexible paperback book inside the shade, adding heavy objects to hold the join together while the glue dries.

6. Now you can stitch the shade to the rings. Start with the top ring, taping the card on to the ring with masking tape, then sewing it into place with a narrow overstitch (see page 186). Repeat this process with the bottom ring, ensuring the rings are parallel.

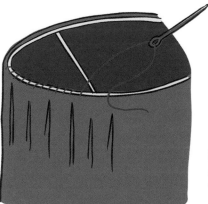

USE OVERSEWING TO ATTACH THE CARD AT THE TOP AND BOTTOM

7. Finish off your shade by covering the top and bottom seams with bias tape, folded over the edge and glued on with clear adhesive. Alternatively, you can glue or stitch on a decorative trim.

8. Finally, don't forget to spray the shade with fireproofing before fitting it to a lamp.

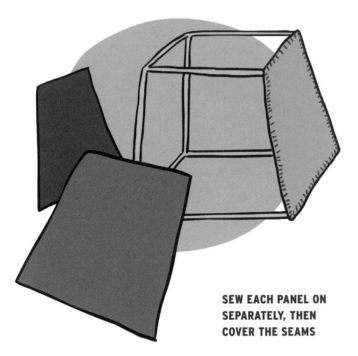

SEW EACH PANEL ON SEPARATELY, THEN COVER THE SEAMS

COVERING FLAT-PANELLED SHADES

Lampshade frames with flat panels can be wrapped in fabric or covered with separate panels of bonded card.

The process of covering these shades with bonded card is the same as for a cone or cylinder shade, but each panel needs to be cut carefully so the edges meet along the lines of the frame. The cards are then stitched into place individually, and each seam then needs to be covered with bias tape or trim to finish.

To cover this type of frame with fabric, choose a material with a slight stretch, or use woven fabrics cut 'on the bias' (at 45 degrees to the weave) so that they will give slightly around the circumference of the shade.

Measure the total length around the frame with a measuring tape, then sew a fabric sleeve slightly smaller than this so that it will be pulled tight. Cut the hem allowance on the seam very neatly, as this overlap will be visible when the lamp is switched on, then press the seam open.

Slip the cover over the frame and line up the seam with one of the struts.

Pin the fabric over the top and bottom rings and check the tension and neatness of the shade before sewing the fabric into place using a running stitch. Use small scissors to trim a neat hem allowance around the inside of the rings after pinning, and before folding the hem, for a really neat result.

Finally, line up the side seam along the strut again, and stitch this in place with overstitching. You should not need to sew the fabric to the other ribs.

The shade may look neat without a trim, but you may want to cover the seams around the top and bottom rings with a suitable ribbon or tape.

FOR A FABRIC COVER, HEM THE TOP AND BOTTOM THEN OVERSEW THE MAIN SEAM TO SECURE IT

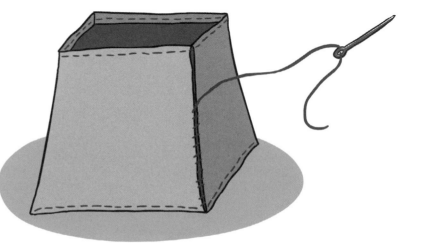

LAMPSHADES

Small shades can also be covered in paper, and a great idea for lamps in a library or study is to cover them with pages torn from an old book.

Use wallpaper paste and start with large pieces of your chosen paper to build an initial framework. Wrap the ends of the pieces around the frame to anchor it in place. Further pieces of paper can then be pasted in place over these to build up an attractive pattern of overlapping plain paper or printed words.

Don't forget to fireproof paper shades before installing them.

Make a sleeve for this shade in a similar way to the project to cover a flat panelled frame, making sure it is smaller than the dimensions of the shade at each point, with a seam that follows the same profile.

Then, use the same steps to slip the cover over the shade and pin it into place on the rings and the two struts.

Pulling in the fabric along just two struts should ensure it hugs the frame all the way around the shade and looks neat. If any creases appear around the sides, pull the fabric tighter over the top and bottom rings until it lies flat.

Once you are happy with the fit and the tension, sew the seams, starting with the top and bottom rings, then finish with the struts, making sure the seam in the fabric lines up with the strut beneath it.

Finish off with your choice of trimming along the top and bottom seams, placing a strip of plain bias tape along the main fabric seams if you also want to hide these stitches.

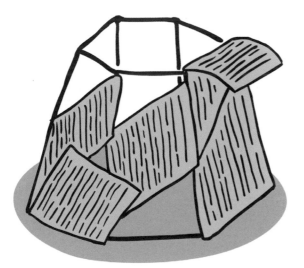

COVERING CURVED PANELLED SHADES

These traditional lampshade designs need to be covered in fabric that will fit closely around their curved shapes, and this should have significant 'give' in order to achieve a neat result without creases.

Check the frame and ensure that the rings and two of the struts (one either side of the shade) are properly covered in binding tape, repairing this if needed.

FOR A CURVED FRAME, CUT FABRIC 'ON THE BIAS' SO IT WILL STRETCH AROUND THE SHADE

CO-ORDINATING OTHER ACCESSORIES

You can co-ordinate other home accessories using the decorative techniques described in this book. Here are some ideas for revamping existing items in your home to match a new colour scheme or co-ordinate with new fabrics.

REPAINTING CERAMIC POTS

Ceramic pots for houseplants can be painted and varnished to look as if they are glazed and create a new finish that is very durable.

Paint several coats of new base coat to cover the existing glaze, then add accents or patterns and, once dry, several coats of polyurethane varnish.

Unlike when painting wood, don't sand or scrub the paint or varnish between coats. Before the final coat of varnish, you can gently smooth the surface with wire wool.

REVAMPING A WASTE-PAPER BIN

Bins for waste paper can be made of almost any material, from wood to metal, plastic or even cardboard.

Wooden bins can be treated, stained and varnished using the methods described for picture frames on page xx

Solid plastic or metal bins are particularly suited to being covered in fabric to match your lampshades. Simply prepare the fabric and glue it into place using spray adhesive.

LAMP BASES AND OTHER ORNAMENTS

Again, depending on the materials, lamp bases and other non-valuable ornaments such as bowls, dishes, pen holders and small vases, can also be repainted and decorated to match your new decorations.

Grouping a previously mismatched group of items together, once they have been given a matching finish, can be a very effective way to bring style and harmony to your home at very little cost, especially if they have interesting or contrasting shapes.

INDEX

WEBSITES & USEFUL INFORMATION

SUPPLIERS OF TOOLS AND MATERIALS

UK

For timber and wood products that you need to have cut to size, local suppliers often have the best value and the most personal service. For tools, specialist supplies and hardware, these online suppliers will deliver to your home and have a very wide range of products that cover all the different types of repairs in *Mend It!*.

Tools, hardware and materials for home delivery.
www.screwfix.com
www.toolsonline.co.uk
www.diy.com

Locks, handles, hinges and more.
www.ironmongerydirect.co.uk
www.franchi.co.uk

DIY and building materials.
www.wickes.co.uk
www.buildbase.co.uk
www.timbersupplies.co.uk

Specialist plumbing suppliers.
www.plumbworld.co.uk
www.plumbcenter.co.uk
www.uk-plumbing.com

Find local architectural merchants across the UK at this site.
www.salvo.co.uk

Advice and toolkits for DIY repairs to your sash windows.
www.diysashwindow.co.uk
www.heritagesashwindow.co.uk

Wood veneer sold by the sheet.
www.originalmarquetry.co.uk
www.selectveneers.com

A wide range of melamine laminate products, including wood grain effects and natural timber.
www.formica.co.uk

Equipment, fittings and components for electrical and electronics repairs.
www.maplin.co.uk

Sewing and fabrics.
www.sewessential.co.uk
www.habbyworld.co.uk
www.calicolaine.co.uk

Suppliers of upholstery tools and materials.
www.jamiltonupholstery.co.uk
www.upholsteryshop.co.uk
www.upholsterywarehouse.co.uk
www.brownandcook.co.uk

Foam fillings cut to size.
www.cutfoam.co.uk
www.foamcut2size.co.uk
www.efoam.co.uk
www.bandmlatexupholstery.co.uk
www.smfoam.co.uk

Replacement hides for leather desks, and other leather supplies.
www.antiqueleathers.com
www.antiqueleathers.co.uk
www.designerleathercraft.co.uk

Beads, jewellery and other art and craft suppliers.
www.bfnt.co.uk
www.the-beadshop.co.uk
www.fredaldous.co.uk
www.craft-supplies.co.uk
www.regalcrafts.com

AUSTRALIA

Hardware centres.
www.bunnings.com.au
www.redboxhardware.com.au
www.truelocal.com.au/HardwareStore

Suppliers of alternative and after market spare parts and equipment for air-conditioning, refrigeration, washing machines, dryers, dishwashers, stoves, ovens, hot water systems.
www.stareast.com.au

Fabric & sewing
www.spotlight.com.au
www.craftonline.com.au

ADVICE AND INFORMATION

UK

www.hse.gov.uk/electricity
Electrical safety advice from the Health and Safety Executive (intended for workplaces, but very useful for DIY repairs too).

www.energysavingtrust.org.uk
Government advice on saving energy in the home, with links to suppliers and information about help, loans and grants available.

www.biggreenswitch.co.uk
www.energysavingwales.org.uk

www.actonco2.org.uk
More sites with energy-saving tips for householders.

www.waterwise.org.uk
www.savewatersavemoney.co.uk
Advice on saving water in the UK.

www.diydoctor.org.uk
Reference and training videos, and an advice forum for DIY jobs of all kinds.

www.sash-style.co.uk
Information about repairing sash windows, including tips on dealing with planning regulations.

USA/AUSTRALIA

www.diynetwork.com
www.doityourself.com
DIY advice, videos and information from the USA.

www.buildeazy.com
A wealth of woodwork and DIY projects and ideas from New Zealand.

www.renovateaustralia.com
Home renovation advice and contacts from an Australian homeowner.

www.thisoldhouse.com
This US site covers all aspects of remodelling and refurbishing period homes.

www.etsy.com
www.internationalcraft.com
Craft supplies, including jewellery parts and leather hide.

www.savewater.com.au
Saving water in Australia.

www.energyaustralia.com.au
www.eeca.govt.nz
www.nrcan-rncan.gc.ca
www.energystar.gov
Government and NGO energy-saving advice from Australia, New Zealand, Canada and the USA.

www.threadbanger.com
Popular, quirky and original videos covering a wide range of sewing projects and repairs.

www.wardroberefashion.net
Clothing repairs and renovations blog and advice site.